What The Father Seeks

In Two Combined Books,
Touching The Light
And
Lectio Divina

BY BOHN PHILLIPS

The Revised Standard Version of the Bible (RSV) is an authorized revision of the American Standard Version, published in 1901, which was a revision of the King James Version, published in 1611.

For copyright statement concerning most Popular Translations, see StudyLight.org, which states of the Revised Standard Version as follows:

Revised Standard Version

The Revised Standard Version (RSV) is a translation published in several parts during the mid-20th century and is a revision of the American Standard Version (ASV) authorized by the copyright holder. The RSV posed the first serious challenge to the popularity of the King James Version (KJV). It was intended to be a readable and literally accurate modern English translation. Translation type: - Borderline of formal equivalence and dynamic equivalence.

This version is also endorsed by the Roman Catholic Church under an egis as follows, "The Catholic Edition of the Revised Standard Version of the Bible, copyright © 1965, 1966 National Council of the Churches of Christ in the United States of America. Used by permission. All rights reserved worldwide."

Both the Protestant and Catholic versions say the same things. Only, some of the books, called "apocrypha" by the Protestants, and considered "deuterocanonical" by the Catholics, are in different places or sections.

To my wife, Jennifer, for her constant and unfailing love, assistance and support.

To John Heim for loyal editing and proof reading.

John 4:23-25

"But the hour is coming, and now is, when the true worshipers will worship the Father in spirit and truth, for such the Father seeks to worship him. God is spirit, and those who worship him must worship in spirit and truth."

RSV

TOUCHING THE LIGHT

Table of Contents

Chapter 1. A Mystical Happening.

Touching the light has involved me in several adventures. While "in the spirit," I was taken through the vast universe and experienced a third party's "agape love" for everything in it. In the Holy Land, I was frightened by demons and wielded the power to heal. Most importantly, I have been transformed over the years, brought to the threshold of loving as Jesus loved. There is a self-sacrificial element of service in it. These things have not been by my choosing or intent. But, they are real and unspeakably fulfilling. Now, late in life, I continue to press on toward the light through meditation and contemplation. This capacity remains in me, but at 82, I am no longer able to do much physically.

This whole story is conceptually unwieldy, difficult to "get your arms around." So, in struggling to present it in a coherent way, I begin with the first <u>mystical</u> happening. It preceded the first of the <u>religious</u> experiences, which have dominated my life since they first began. Then, I will back-track to my childhood, so the reader will better understand the warp and woof of the author. From the back-track, I race directly down the ribbon of time to the current date.

As we begin, I am reminded of a very expensive and powerful sports car I saw at a stop light one night, in Miami, Florida. I noticed on the passenger side window, the following in small white vinyl letters: "Get in; sit down; shut up; hang on":

~~~~~

I was divorced from a 20-year marriage, in Houston, in 1979. It left me feeling uncomfortable, restless and desperate for a change in both scenery and people. As fortune would have it, I secured a position as a senior trial attorney with the Fraud Section of the Department of Justice in Washington D.C. After being there for a while, I purchased a 41' Morgan Out-Island sailing vessel, which I named "Justice", joined the Capital Yacht Club on the Potomac River, moored the yacht "Justice" there and began to live aboard. It was located in walking distance of my work on Pennsylvania Avenue.

Less than two years later, an opportunity opened up for a Public Corruption specialist in St. Thomas, VI. I was still restless and the opportunity to live in paradise and sail the Caribbean seemed ideal. I applied for and was accepted in the office of the United States Attorney at St. Thomas. I then set sail down the Potomac to the Atlantic, then due East beyond Bermuda, then South to St. Thomas.

I navigated the voyage by dead reckoning, with a cheap plastic sextant and a $4.00 hand-held AM radio with a loop antenna. Believe it or not, I made land-fall at St. Thomas after 13 days at sea. I had been taught dead reckoning navigation during pilot training by the U.S. Air Force several years before. (more on that later)

There were many sights for a restless adventurer on that trip, whales, flying fish, the Sargasso Sea, a severe, almost capsizing, bump from something at night (a whale?), lonely nights and nothing to see but the sea during the day. When I arrived at St. Thomas, I moored the Justice at Red Hook lagoon on the Eastern end of the Island. I lived there all during my stay and sailed around the Lesser Antilles Islands in my spare time. After three years, I had had enough of paradise and took a job as an Organized Crime and Racketeering prosecutor for the Justice Department, in Miami, Florida. I had wanted to live in Florida since I attended pilot training at Bartow, thirty years before, in 1954. In Miami, I leased an apartment on shore, moored the Justice, and bought a Chevy Corvette, determined to settle in.

One Sunday, I was exploring the area in my new car and happened into a pine forest in Coral Gables. In the midst of the

10

trees was a church called the Church of St. Teresa, the Little Flower. I noticed on a sign in front that confessions were scheduled during the week. From the life I had been leading since my divorce, I knew I needed a confession and decided to come back during the week to get right with the Lord.

When I returned, I entered the quiet, cool atmosphere in church, found the confessional booth and saw the little light that indicates that a priest is inside, waiting for customers. I entered the booth for an anonymous confession. I did not confess anything prior to my divorce and did not even say that I had ever been married; however, as I was leaving, the priest called out to me to come back for a moment. I returned to the little kneeler to hear what he wanted. He told me his name and asked me to call the rectory for an appointment next Saturday. He said he wanted to talk to me about my marriage. I was sufficiently shocked and surprised that he knew I had ever been married or that he wanted to talk to me about it, that I did as he requested.

The next Saturday, I came to the rectory as scheduled, met the priest and we sat down for an interview. We sat in a small office with only a desk, a side table and two chairs. He began by asking me to tell him about my divorce. This shocked me anew, but I began to tell him anyway. After I had talked for about half an hour, he waved his hand, indicating he had heard enough. Then, he said with a bit of an accusatory tone, that I had told him what I wanted him to hear. He said he wanted to know what I really felt about it. I told him that I was a trial lawyer, trained in embellishing and emphasizing just one side of a story and that I had been trying to be fair to both my former wife and myself with a "middle of the road" approach. He answered by advising me that he was a trained psychologist and that I could not mislead him, even if I tried. He wanted to know how I really felt.

With this, I pulled out all of the stops. I told him my side of what had happened, how I had been betrayed over and over again, how I felt about that and why. In an abundance of caution, I also advised him that I had been an attorney for the Catholic tribunal in the Houston-Galveston Archdiocese, implying that I knew what makes a binding marriage. I had carefully married in accordance with the laws and traditions of the Catholic Church, solemnizing a civil marriage from some 5 years earlier. I advised him that, in my opinion, there was no way I was entitled to an annulment.

When I finished, I was greatly relieved. I had never told anyone what I really thought about the divorce, including the down and dirty truth. But, I still had no hope of any annulment. To my surprise, when I finished, the priest turned around and took up from behind him an application for annulment and began to fill it out. Surprised, I furnished him with all of the needed information. He filed the application on my behalf. I only did the things required of me and had no ulterior motives for an annulment. In those days, annulment proceedings were not normally entertained by the Church unless there was some reason to request it, like wanting to marry again. The idea was that it was presumed that a marriage was valid and not subject to being tested without a compelling reason.

Despite my personal convictions, the annulment was granted before the process was technically complete and earlier than scheduled. For several years, I had a problem with this. I didn't know whether or not I should rely on an annulment I did not personally feel entitled to. Eventually, I realized that Church authority was entitled to declare a marriage valid and it was equally entitled to declare it void. I had absolutely no right to contest their determination that I had been invalidly married in the Church. Once I realized this, I accepted the annulment and have had great peace about it ever since. Thus, I proved the old legal axiom that a lawyer who represents himself has a fool for a client.

I feel to this day that the Holy Spirit had a hand in all of this and that the confession and annulment were mystical occurrences. That annulment opened the way to the religious experiences which followed. In turn, the religious experiences encouraged me to energetically pursue the kingdom of heaven. Eventually, I found it and, like a pearl of great value, I examine it in my hands each day.

This pearl has been known through the years as the Holy Bible. The tool which exposes the pearl within has been known through the years as *Lectio Divina.* (Divine Reading) *Lectio Divina* allows one to glimpse heaven indistinctly, as through a mirror of compromised quality. Even so, it transports the spirit into the very presence of God. There, He loves and speaks with the spirit without words and in silence.

The experience is indescribable in human words, but it is so fulfilling that the Lord must expand the soul to receive it. He makes this pearl available to all who seriously and humbly take it in their hands and examine it with *Lectio Divina.* You, too, can discover the pearl of great value and examine it with *Lectio Divina.* That is why I have written about it.

Chapter 2. The First Religious Experience.

I remember a little room at my parish church, not St. Teresa's where I had gone to confession. There were about 24 chairs in the room, with an altar in front and a kneeler that is about 8 feet long. It is called the "perpetual adoration room." The holy Eucharist is on display behind the kneeler. It can be visited at any time, day or night.

One Sunday, just a few weeks after I returned to the Church, I received holy communion during services. I thought I felt an unaccustomed and pleasant warmth in my stomach. Then, as services were coming to an end, I had a powerful urge (I don't know how else to describe it) to go to the perpetual adoration room and pray. I had never had that urge before and thought it curious. But, it would not go away and I decided to respond. I had to abandon a group of friends with whom I attended mass and had planned to lunch, but I proceeded to the perpetual adoration room.

Almost immediately when I knelt in front of the Holy Eucharist, I felt as though I was leaving my body and being borne into the vast expanses of the universe. I was carried at indescribable speed, much faster than the speed of light. I had no idea what was happening and I did not know what was carrying me. It didn't say. I took it to be a spirit, or an angel of some sort.

The spirit, or angel, was not visible to my eyes, but I could somehow sense its vast, ethereal substance. There were no arms or legs or other body parts to it. I was being borne along as a part of its total person. I had no idea how it picked me up or whisked me away. No words were spoken to me. We were passing through the universe at a tremendous rate and I could feel the love the angel had for each material thing as we passed by and through them, whether stars, planets, suns, galaxies, gases, or whatever. We seemed to be covering distances almost at the speed of thought.

15

The angel somehow gave each celestial object a loving regard and embrace as we passed, almost like hugging them to its breast. I have no idea how I sensed these things, but the sensation of love was extremely powerful. Everywhere, I could see Celestial activity, such as supernovae, black holes, pulsars, gaseous clouds and other things as we whizzed by. I had a distinct impression of wonder that I had never seen or dreamed of them before. Even so, the overwhelming impact of my voyage was the experience of love expressed by the angel. It encompassed everything I saw. We traveled tremendous distances. Then, I realized I was being brought back.

As I was returning to my body, I concluded that what carried me had an unfamiliar, massive love for all that there is in the universe, whether living or not. I was perplexed by this. I could not understand how it could have such affection for all of those desert, desolate and barren heavenly constellations. I could sense no life in them for it to love. They were merely dust. I had awe, but no personal loving reaction to them and did not understand such outpouring from the angel. It seemed to express its love with its entire ethereal being.

Years later, I came to realize that, but for the life force that is breathed into the dust of this earth, all of the heavenly constellations are composed of the same raw material as earth. God can choose to breathe life into any of it. Since he created all of the dust, he loves it all. It is no wonder if he loves what he created, because he saw that everything he created is very good.[1] What was I missing? I did not know.

Life is referred to in Biblical literature as "living water". Except for living water, the stuff of our earth and all that is in it is no different from, no better and no worse, than any of the other barren heavenly constellations. We have discovered no evidence of life on any other constellation. Yet, everything is apparently composed of the same basic "matter." The one incidence of life, so

---

[1] Gen 1:31

16

far as we currently know, is apparently unique to the earth. Of course, I have no idea of my own about this. Indeed, I do not know what I am talking about. But, that is what I speculated during my trip with the angel through all of creation, and afterward. I saw no indication that there was life elsewhere. Everything I saw was barren.

I know for myself that I was shown, and experienced from the angel, a love that was completely different from, and far above, any love I had ever experienced before. I suspect that it is the "*agape* love" attributed to Jesus and his Father, described in the Bible. It exceeds the self-protective desire to live. The angel's embrace transmitted its all, its very essence, even its life, to all of the barren constellations that we encountered. At the same time, it was transmitted to my inmost being with an intensity which I cannot describe. I experienced the love as though I were a sentient and equal part of the angel.

After seeing things that simply defy description, including every sort of explosion and color I had ever seen on earth, the angel (Lord?) began to gently place me back in my physical body in the perpetual adoration room. I did not want to leave His presence. I tried to stay with him, but it was no use. Then, having been returned to my body, I continued to try to go back to him with all my strength, but that was of no use either. I was back in my body, and that was that. As I knelt there, knowing I was back in my body, I could still see the white light of what I now thought of as God, in the upper part of a tunnel. It was devastating to see him and not being able to reach out to him.

The light was in the upper-right part of the tunnel through which I had first been taken into the universe and through which I was returned. I did not know whether it was the angel of God or God himself that had me, but I believed at the time that it was the Lord. Then, I tried my best to reach out to him with my spirit, instead of trying to reach out. I struggled to leave my body again, but without success. As I became convinced it was no use, a beam of light, slightly bluish and vaguely liquid, came down from him and into me. I was attached to him by the light but still intensely desired to go nearer to him.

This seemed to be the most wonderful thing that had ever happened to me, but that I could not move out of my body toward him frustrated me greatly. The light connecting us was about 3 inches in diameter and did not seem either hot or cold. It did seem to bend, somewhat like the gradual bend in a rainbow, but more gradual. It entered me just at the bottom of my rib cage, about where I supposed my stomach to be.

I did not know what to do with this thing sticking into me. It seemed vaguely luminescent and I felt it could be seen by anyone. It was like a transparent hose, or beam, of slightly glowing water, but, I did not discern any movement, or flow, in the water.

There were other people in the perpetual adoration room and I did not know whether or not they saw it, whatever it was. I wondered if it was going to stay attached to me like that forever, if I would have to walk among people with that light sticking out of me.

Finally, I got up and moved to the back of the room just to see if the light stayed with me. It did. At the same time, I was sobbing freely and uncontrollably. My entire world was changing and I did not know what to do. Then, without my knowing it, the light dissipated. No one saw. Nevertheless, I still felt very much like I had been in the presence of the Lord and felt embarrassed at how different I had become. Only one little boy seemed to notice that I was sobbing.

The last thought in my mind was that my religious experience was normal, usual or ordinary in the history of man, but it is. Every book of the Bible recites examples that could be similarly classified. Many more contemporary examples are set out in a book, *The Varieties of Religious Experiences* by William James, published in 1902. These are examples of life changing experiences which "convert" or permanently change the person.

18

They are not "near death" experiences. I have attached two examples in Exhibit A for review by the reader.

Reports of near death experiences continue to be recorded daily. Conversion experiences receive much less attention. Mine was actually common, even if extraordinary in certain details. The Varieties of Religious Experiences documents many other conversion experiences fully as extraordinary as mine. None are identical.

When I was returned to my body, I was changed although I did not know it for sure, until later. I knelt there in the perpetual adoration room for at least an hour more, tears flowing profusely. I was unashamedly overwhelmed by the intensity and the wonder of it all. I thought that perhaps I had suffered a nervous breakdown, but I had not.

That I was permanently changed dawned upon me slowly. I gradually learned that I was no longer comfortable earning my livelihood as a federal prosecutor for the Department of Justice. I did not want to hurt anyone, even criminals.

Even so, I could still function in my job. I had not become a misfit of some kind. My goals had simply changed. I had been made into a more deeply loving person. My work made me feel unproductive, even though successful. My entire perspective had changed. I was much happier than before and had an unfamiliar inner peace. I was being wrenched from a worldly to a more spiritual focus. When I felt most uncomfortable from the wrenching emotions of the change, I experienced powerful waves of soothing and calming peace, almost like being stroked by a loving and protective mother. Otherwise, I think I might have gone back to my old ways.

As I adjusted, I knew I had been permanently changed. I could provide many, many, examples to demonstrate how I came to know this, but mostly, I know it because the change has not gone away in over 30 years.

Here is an example. The first out of body experience occurred on Sunday, March 31, 1985. Recently, on Sunday, May 7, 2017, my car was rear ended in the parking lot of a local supermarket. The crash was jarring to my body, but not sufficient to cause great damage to the automobiles, even though it caused my head to hurt severely. This is possibly because my head was turned sideways on my neck at the time of impact.

Afterward, as I got out of the car, holding my head, I saw that the lady who hit me was getting out also. She looked like a young mother in her early 30's. She was very solicitous of my condition and admitted that she had backed into me. She wanted to make certain that I was not badly hurt. I guess I look fragile, being I am at age 82.

Actually, I was in pain and she could see it, but neither of us said so. I could see that her concern for me was genuine, and suspected she was also afraid of a law suit. This moved me to have both love and pity for her. Immediately, I stepped over, kissed her on the cheek, and told her not to worry, that she will never hear from me again.

Whereupon, we got back in our cars and drove away. I do not know her name and did not record the number of her license plate. This is how I was moved to act, not how I chose to act. I did not think about it at all. I recognize that this is not natural. It wells up from within me. It reminds me of the love I felt from the angel who took me through the universe. That is how I have been for the last 32 years, since the first experience in 1985.

I have always thought of the light as living water, or the Holy Spirit, and that it is still in me. Some years later, in 1990, I was driving along the highway at night, on a long trip from Texas to Florida and I was listening to a tape recording of the King James version of the Bible. I was listening to the book of John and heard: "He that believes on me, as the scripture has said, out of his belly shall flow rivers of living water."[2] When I heard this scripture, I knew what the bluish light protruding from my belly was and felt overwhelmed once again. Did this mean I was "saved?" I did not know. I felt unworthy. But, I have gotten ahead of myself.

I eventually left the perpetual adoration room and joined a friend for a delayed lunch. I was still overwhelmed. I wanted normal again, but did not calm down for several days. Something was different inside and I did not know what. I felt helplessly limber and limp, as though I had been kneaded like dough. The consolations began during this time of feeling helpless.

---

[2] John 7:38 (ASV)

Chapter 3. Continuing Experiences.

A little more than a month went by from the time of the first experience until the week end of May 5, 1985. During that time, I was casting about for ways to better worship and serve the Lord. On, May 5th, I began a week-end retreat at a monastery in Central Florida. It was guided by the Passionist Fathers. I was a little intimidated by the strangeness of it all, but thought the religious atmosphere was less intense than I was accustomed to at church. This surprised me. It was not what I expected. The manly camaraderie from the others attending the retreat was something I had not experienced in years. I began to relax and tried to go with the flow.

On the second day, one of the priests was lecturing about contemplative prayer. He read a beautiful Scripture about God's perfect love and how we receive it through Jesus Christ. This interested me greatly. The idea was that God loves us perfectly and totally, and the only worthwhile love we could return in worship was the same love we were receiving from him. Living water? He said this was only possible because Jesus had been crucified for us and thereby atoned for our sins. He said that Jesus is the only channel through which we can return God's love or gain entry into heaven. Then he read a scripture passage supporting his lecture. (I do not recall what it was, or make a note of it.) I recognized that it aligned perfectly with my out of body experience the month before, including the light of living water that had attached itself to me. I supposed it to be the love which he and the scripture described, flowing both ways.

In demonstrating contemplative prayer, the priest told us to keep this scripture in mind. He started a tape recorder which softly played a slow, rhythmic tune and then he began to speak. He told us to close our eyes and sit in a relaxed position. He said to picture in our minds the room we were in, the ceiling, the walls, the floor, the pictures and windows. He then told us to envision the people in the room, all the chairs and ourselves as we were sitting there. Then he said to imagine ourselves alone in the room with only two chairs in it; to imagine ourselves sitting in one of the chairs and to imagine Jesus coming into the room and sitting down with us, talking to us, telling us how much he loves us.

I was thinking to myself that this was not contemplative prayer, it was self-hypnosis. Regardless of what it was, it worked for me! I did not envision him walking in, but was astounded that my mind's eye suddenly saw Jesus beside me in that empty room. He came next to me with a smile and talked with me, but I did not hear any words.

He did not sit down. He stood somewhat to my right. He was beautiful. Love, health and happiness exuded from him. I could feel it. It was equal to the love I felt when I was out in the universe. He told me loving things, without words, for about 30 seconds. I thought it was the same still small voice heard by Elijah at the entrance to a cave.[3] Then, he was gone.

The experience was extremely moving. Tears flowed freely down my face. I wanted to go somewhere to adore the Lord in private. I was overwhelmed with an experience that was unique for me. I wondered, "how did this happen?" Then, I knew I really did not care. I did not even care if it was real, or if I was insane. I knew that this was the Lord that I love so much, regardless of anything else. Even if I was manufacturing the image in my own head, like viewing a motion picture, it was an image of the Lord whom I worship. I then knew clearly that he was real, regardless of the vision.

I went outside to be alone, to a place in back of the retreat house, where stations of the cross were standing. I walked the stations, looking at each one, still sobbing, and prayerfully

---

[3] 1 Kings 19:12

24

contemplating God's love for me as well as mine for him. Even though the experience was very moving, I refused to take it as a serious, or actual, visit by Christ. After all, I had simply done what I had been told to do. The priest had set a psychological stage and psychological things happened. However, I later talked to several of the other men who were there and found no others that had similar experiences. I continued to say to myself that if this was mere self-hypnosis, why was I the only one? Was I the only one that was subject to hypnosis, or did I have a genuine vision?

At this stage, I still did not know the "genuineness" of either this or my earlier experience. I only knew that they seemed very important to me and the gentle, loving feelings which began with them were continuing to console me.

The following afternoon, Sunday, the retreat ended. I went from there to a Bible study class in a private home. I was new to the group, but the others all knew each other. They had been meeting there for quite some time. During the evening, despite my attempts to pay attention, my mind kept drifting back to that beautiful experience with Jesus. I suppose I spent much of the evening with a vacant, contented look on my face. Eventually, the leader commented on it, asking what was happening. I simply said that I had a beautiful experience this weekend and it was still on my mind.

After the class, some of us were talking in the kitchen. I told them of my experience of the prior day and how beautiful it had been. I commented that it had surely been some sort of self-hypnosis, but it was extraordinary anyway. As the conversation progressed, the leader expressed her opinion that self-hypnosis like I had apparently had is not a good idea. She said that she suspects the soul leaves the body and that if it goes too far away, it may not be able to return, causing the person to die.

She explained that the reason for her feeling was that she had been clinically dead while on the operating table one time and had an out-of-body experience. While out of her body, she had seen

God. He looked like a white light. He was down a corridor or a tunnel of some sort. This sounded similar to the last part of my own experience on March 31st. So, I asked her to explain further. She did not want to come back either. It is a place she would still like to be. This was why she cautioned us about self-hypnosis, we might not come back. I was glad to hear someone else had a similar experience.

Soon, I learned that it was not over for me. On Wednesday, May 8, 1985, I had a second vision in the perpetual adoration room. Almost immediately upon kneeling, I felt myself going out of my body, the same way as on March 31st. The tunnel was the same, but the light was different. At the upper right end of the tunnel was an orange glow. I thought it was quite like the reflected glow of burning pine logs. I have no idea why, but I specifically thought of the light of the fire was like pine logs. I had seen many pine log fires as a child.

Then, as I was extending down the tunnel toward the orange glow, I could see what was making the light. I did not feel any heat from it, but it did seem to be an actual flame. I was extremely attracted to it. In great anticipation, I strained to extend through the tunnel toward the light. I say extend for lack of a better term. I did not know then, and do not know now, whether my spirit was stretching or actually separated from my body. At first, I thought I was not going to be able to reach it, but I stretched out as far as I could and finally touched the source of the light.

The source looked like a cylinder, or a small log. It was bright orange, streaked with red blazes and flecked with yellow. It was beautiful. The whole thing was blazing. I do not know why it seemed important, but I could not tell if it was pine or not. It was not shiny or smooth, was slightly indistinct, or blurred in appearance, and yet felt firm to my touch. The instant I made contact, I was "given" the knowledge that this was the Holy Spirit. I was not spoken to in words.

26

As soon as I touched him, I was physically and totally under his control. He began giving me information while at the same time, moving me back through the tunnel toward my physical body with inexorable force and at what seemed like a great speed. While receiving the information, I resisted the return movement. In the same way that I had strained to extend myself before, I now strained to avoid returning to my body. I wanted to stay there. That seemed to be the most important thing, just to stay there, with him.

My efforts to resist were without any effect whatever. I kept going back as though I offered no resistance at all. As I re-entered my physical body, I was distinctly surprised as I realized the Holy Spirit was entering it with me. I remember thinking to him that he would not fit, to which he made no response. When we were both in my body, it felt very full. I thought I perceived an orangish aura surrounding me. My entire body seemed to have increased in size by about one inch, all around. Once inside, the Holy Spirit told me to be patient, to mature and to take life more seriously. Then, after a slight pause, he said that I would heal with my hands.

Since then I have been able to turn my mind's eye inward and simply pay attention to the inside of myself and feel him there, even now. But, I have never since been brought to the entrance of the tunnel or seen the wall where it had been. The peace and comfort I feel remains with me. I wish I was capable of telling how great a gift this has been to me. The peace and comfort alone would have been sufficient to change my life, but I know more than that happened to me. I am to heal with my hands.

Upon arriving home that night, I was not able to sit still. I had to tell someone what had been happening. So, I called my original facilitator from a program called the Beginning Experience. We went to the same church and she seemed to understand quite a lot about spirituality. I respected her. At the Beginning Experience, she had tried to assist and guide me to recover from the trauma of my divorce. As a facilitator, she had already heard me tell the story of the visit by Jesus during the retreat. She did not reject me because of it, but was excited and thrilled when she heard it. I felt better and less like a nut because of her acceptance.

During the course of our conversation she told me that she was going to a house the following Friday evening to show some pictures of the holy Land. They hoped to make a trip there in late May of that year. She asked if I would like to see the pictures also. I said that I would and she suggested that I pick her up Friday evening at eight. After that, I was able to go to sleep. I had been excited, puzzled, thrilled, and hopeful. But, I had no idea what was happening in a general way, only specific experiences.

The next evening, on Thursday, May 9, 1985, I returned to the perpetual adoration room late in the evening. To my astonishment, the Holy Spirit filled me again, the same as the evening before. Almost as soon as I began to pray, I had the out of body experience, made contact and was returned to my body, the same as before. I was again told to be patient, to mature and to take life seriously. After a pause, I was told that I was endowed with the gift of healing. I remember thinking suspiciously, "Wait a minute, we did this last night." Surprisingly, there was an immediate reply of "No, last night I announced that you would heal with your hands. Tonight, I am endowing you with the gift."

I believe that since that occasion, the Holy Spirit has never left me. The overfull feeling went away quickly that evening and the seeming orange glow to my skin soon dissipated. Even though I tried on several occasions, I could not leave my body again or find the tunnel with my mind's eye. Its entrance had seemed to be in a dark, roiling substance, which now appeared to be like a solid wall. The entrance had become sealed and it could no longer be seen.

After the Holy Spirit entered me this last time, I had no idea how I should feel. I wanted to feel the way one should feel when something extraordinary happens to him. How does one do that? To ignore a gift is to belittle it. To be proud is to misconstrue it. I had certainly not earned anything. Perhaps this was why I had been told to be patient, to mature and to take life seriously. It was on this occasion that I actually began to believe the visions, but I did not know what to do with myself or with the gift. I decided it was distinctly possible that something important was happening to me and started making notes that evening. This story was drawn from those notes.

Chapter 4. About Charisms.

I must admit that the experiences which I had did not give me answers. Instead, they left me with questions. I knew I was changed, but what was I to do? How does one be patient, except to serenely allow time to pass, without intervening or otherwise hurrying events? How does one mature, but to simply allow maturity to occur? Would maturity occur from study, worship and love of neighbor? How does one take life seriously, but to simply be sober in word, thought, and deed? Surely, I was to do things that would not derail God's plan for me, things that would help me learn patience and become mature?

How does one heal with his hands, but by the grace of a merciful God? Am I to gradually grow into a sober agent of the healing power of God and have nothing to do about it, but let it happen? On the other hand, I could not believe that I was to placidly let time pass. Else, why the messages in the first place? Was everything up to the Holy Spirit, which had filled me? If I am to do nothing, why give me instructions? How do I not mess this up?

The next morning, my head was filled with all sorts of new thoughts. But, I continued to feel uneasy and in need of worldly guidance. Shamefully, I also felt an uncontrollable pride and joy as I thrilled at the prospect of becoming a healer. I suspected the Lord wanted me to be a famous agent of his healing love and power. I remember looking in the mirror and telling the Lord what had to be corrected about my image, if I was to make a proper presentation as his agent. As it turned out, that is not the case. I know I possess the gift, but it is not often noticed by others, even when they are healed. They tend to think it would have happened anyway.

That evening, I picked up my Beginning Experience facilitator, as agreed. When I arrived, she gave me three books about charismatics. At that time, I did not even know what the word "charismatic" meant and asked her about it.

She began by telling me not to expect anything further from the Lord in the way of revelation. She explained that these things happen regularly to people, but things usually calm down quickly with just an occasional future boost from the spirit, when needed. She was afraid I would demand too much of the Lord or of myself. I told her I had already experienced a further visitation the prior evening and one earlier than that which I had not mentioned to her.

With that, she indicated that she did not know how to guide me any further. Instead of giving me advice, she specially recommended one of the books, *A Key To Charismatic Renewal In The Catholic Church*, by Rev. Vincent M. Walsh. I began reading it right away.

A Key To Charismatic Renewal In The Catholic Church opened an entirely new spiritual vocabulary to me. In my childhood, I had been a Baptist, but they were not "Holy Rollers." Indeed, they seemed to look down on Holy Rollers. So far as I was aware, I had never even seen a "charismatic."

I converted to Catholicism after reading some of the works of St. Thomas Aquinas and being taught the catechism of the Catholic Church by a US Air Force chaplain. This was in 1955. I was 20 years old and stationed at an air base in France.

At any rate, *A Key To Charismatic Renewal In The Catholic Church* was granted the *nihil obstat* (that the Church has no objection to its publication) and the imprimatur (a declaration by Church authority that a book may be printed) The *nihil obstat* and *imprimatur* of the Catholic Church are official declarations that a book is free of doctrinal or moral error, but it is not an endorsement or rejection of doctrine or morals taught therein.

Because of the imprimatur, I felt relatively safe that the book would not mislead me about charismatic renewal. Its preface states, at p. xi: "Throughout the writing, I have tried to keep in mind the many who have never even participated in a charismatic prayer meeting and are yet to know what this movement is all about; and the many who pray regularly with a group and need a clear and simple explanation of what the Lord is doing among them."

I certainly identified with that passage. As I read, I learned that charisms are spiritual gifts from the Lord described in the books of Acts and Corinthians in the Holy Bible. In his book, Rev. Walsh devotes a chapter to each of the spiritual gifts set out in Acts and Corinthians, how they are acquired, how they are manifested and how they are used. From the first chapters of his book, I saw that it described exactly what had been happening to me! I had been experiencing charisms!

The book teaches that the charisms are granted by the Holy Spirit to individuals in the community when the <u>community</u> prays that the gifts be granted. Some people are granted some gifts, while others are granted other gifts. People can, and usually do, have more than one gift.

I could already see one major exception from what I read in the book. Personal prayer is sufficient to release the charisms. No one had prayed for me to have any spiritual gifts. I soon found that there were others in the church community that had gifts who had not been prayed over for them.

The most obvious example of spontaneous gifts of charisms is in the book of Acts. The gifts were spontaneously bestowed on disciples of Jesus in the upper room, at Pentecost.[4] They all received the Holy Spirit and began praying in tongues. For all I know, there are millions of others out there, receiving gifts the same as I.

---

[4] Acts 2:1 *et seq*

33

I read on, late into the night.

Although it is a bit out of the story line at this point, I should take this opportunity to disclose my current knowledge concerning the charisms. So far as I have discerned, the charisms are available to all Christians. The Holy Spirit determines which charisms to bestow, and on whom. After we are baptized with the Holy Spirit, he resides in us and especially activates and releases in us the charisms he has chosen. Of course, all of the charisms reside within the Holy Spirit who resides in us and his releasing them is axiomatic if he chooses to do so.

When we pray for additional charisms in good faith, the Holy Spirit within us releases them like a loving father, even those he did not originally bestow upon us.

St. Paul advises us to affirmatively seek the spiritual gifts. He explains that the gift of tongues can be understood by men of spiritual maturity and that all charisms have a special purpose for Christian communities in both worship and evangelism. According to St. Paul, every church should be overtly charismatic.

Here are 40 verses of St. Paul's teaching to the Corinthians about tongues. He begins by describing two sorts. One is prayerfully speaking in tongues. The other is prophesying in tongues I have supplied underlining and italics. The material in brackets is supplied to help the reader clearly understand what Paul is saying. He often alludes to other letters he had written or to other Gospels. The Gospel of Luke and the book of Acts were being written when Paul wrote the scriptures below. The Gospel of Mark was probably being written about the same time as the letter. But, the Gospel of Matthew was already written, in Aramaic, and was well circulated among Jewish Christians. Paul was writing the below verses to the faithful of the church he had established in Corinth, a large and busy, morally corrupt and pagan seaport on the lower Southwest corner of Greece. Paul established the Christian community at Corinth about 51 A.D., on his second missionary journey and wrote his first letter to them about 5 years

34

later. The community had many problems resisting the immoral and pagan influences in their locale. As with all Christian communities at that time, the Holy Spirit was palpably present among them and they had all been baptized in the Spirit when originally prayed for by the evangelist. Paul, in this case. Among other things, Christians began to speak in tongues when so baptized. In the verses quoted below, Paul explains the variety and importance of the spiritual gifts, especially the gifts of tongues, how the gifts should be employed to benefit them. He explains that today, we see indistinctly and the gifts build us up for when we see the Lord clearly, face to face and converse with him:

"Make love your aim, and earnestly desire the spiritual gifts, especially that you may prophesy. For one who speaks in a tongue speaks not to men but to God; for no one understands him, but he utters mysteries in the Spirit. [These initial sentences say that praying in tongues is speaking directly to God in the language of God, not of men.]

"On the other hand, he who prophesies speaks to men for their upbuilding and encouragement and consolation. He who speaks in a tongue edifies [teaches] himself, but he who prophesies edifies [teaches] the church. Now I want you all to speak in tongues, but even more to prophesy. He who prophesies is greater than he who speaks in tongues, unless someone interprets, [What was spoken in tongues] so that the church may be edified. [Paul encourages the community to prophesy because they knew how to speak in tongues from the time of their baptism in the spirit.]

"Now, brethren, if I come to you speaking in tongues, how shall I benefit you unless I bring you some revelation or knowledge or prophecy or teaching? [Tongues only benefit he who speaks in them, unless there is an interpreter. Then, Paul gives examples:]

"If even lifeless instruments, such as the flute or the harp, do not give distinct notes, how will anyone know what is played? And if the bugle gives an indistinct sound, who will get ready for battle? So, with yourselves; if you in a tongue utter speech that is not intelligible, how will anyone know what is said? For you will be speaking into the air. There are doubtless many different languages in the world, and none is without meaning; but if I do not know the meaning of the language, I shall be a foreigner to the speaker and the speaker a foreigner to me. So, with yourselves; since you are eager for manifestations of the Spirit, strive to excel in building up the church.

"Therefore, he who speaks in a tongue should pray for the power to interpret. [Personal, private prayer in tongues is effective and proper, but to edify the community, someone must interpret what was said.]

"For if I pray in a tongue, my spirit prays but my mind is unfruitful. [The senses are all at rest, but the spirit is alert and active when praying in tongues.] What am I to do? I will pray with the spirit and I will pray with the mind also; [pray in tongues and with regular speech.] I will sing with the spirit and I will sing with the mind also. Otherwise, if you bless with the spirit, how can anyone in the position of an outsider say the 'Amen' to your thanksgiving when he does not know what you are saying? [How can one support the prayers in tongues with their own prayers, if they do not understand what was prayed?] For you may give thanks well enough, but the other man is not edified. [the other man is not taught or blessed.]

"I thank God that I speak in tongues more than you all; nevertheless, in church I would rather speak five words with my mind, [normal speech] in order to instruct others, than ten thousand words in a tongue.

"Brethren, do not be children in your thinking; be babes in evil, but in thinking be mature. [Take life seriously.]

"In the law it is written, 'By men of strange tongues and by the lips of foreigners will I speak to this people, and even then, they will not listen to me, says the Lord.' Thus, tongues are a sign not for believers but for unbelievers, while prophecy is not for
36

unbelievers but for believers. [Unbelievers are <u>impressed</u> by tongues, but believers are <u>taught</u> by prophesy.]

"If, therefore, the whole church assembles and all speak in tongues, and outsiders or unbelievers enter, will they not say that you are mad? [Everyone will sound like they are uttering gibberish] But if all prophesy, and an unbeliever or outsider enters, he is convicted by all, he is called to account by all, the secrets of his heart are disclosed; and so, falling on his face, he will worship God and declare that God is really among you. [Prophesying in normal language will both benefit the stranger and be received by all.]

"What then, brethren? When you come together, each one has a hymn, a lesson, a revelation, a tongue, or an interpretation. Let all things be done for edification. If any speak in a tongue, let there be only two or at most three, and each in turn; and let one interpret. But if there is no one to interpret, let each of them keep silence in church and speak to himself and to God. [Private prayer]

"Let two or three prophets speak, and let the others weigh what is said. If a revelation is made to another sitting by, let the first be silent. For you can all prophesy one by one, so that all may learn and all be encouraged; and the spirits of prophets are subject to prophets. For God is not a God of confusion but of peace. [Accomplish all worship in an orderly manner.]

"As in all the churches of the saints, the women should keep silence in the churches. For they are not permitted to speak, but should be subordinate, as even the law says. If there is anything they desire to know, let them ask their husbands at home. For it is shameful for a woman to speak in church. What! Did the word of God originate with you, or are you the <u>only</u> ones it has reached? [Note: Paul does not exclude or prohibit women from the charisms, but from leadership of public worship in the church.]

"If anyone thinks that he is a prophet, or spiritual, he should acknowledge that what I am writing to you is a command of the Lord. [Paul wants affirmation of his teaching from everyone.] If

37

any one does not recognize this, he is not recognized. [If anyone fails or refuses to affirm his teaching, there is something wrong.] So, my brethren, earnestly desire to prophesy, and do not forbid speaking in tongues; but all things should be done decently and in order."[5]

In other words, St. Paul taught that to have others pray for us to have tongues. Our own prayers are sufficient to release the charisms and we should take care to use them properly.]

Reading *A Key To Charismatic Renewal In The Catholic Church* opened an entirely new spiritual vocabulary to me. It also provided my first insight into what was described as a "movement" of the Holy Spirit in Christian communities around the world.

I was not always a Catholic. I was taught nothing of religion by my parents and had little social exchange with Christians during my young life. Since the circumstances of my youth were unusual, perhaps it is best if I tell you some things about my personal history, so you will better understand my situation when the experiences began.

---

[5] 1 Cor 14:1-40 (RSV)

Chapter 5. Personal History.

My parents were divorced when I was eight years old and, from that time forward, my mother reared me. She was very bright, but only had a ninth-grade education and no particular skills with which to make a living for us.

She worked as a bookkeeper at one time, but mostly as a waitress in various restaurants in and around Houston, Texas. From the time of my parent's divorce, mother and I moved about within the city quite often. From the time of their separation, until I entered the University of Houston, I did not go to any school longer than one academic year and usually went to more than one school in any given year. In the second half of the ninth grade, I went to five different schools.

To this day, I do not know why we moved around so much. It did not occur to me to ask. I liked it. I did know that it was unusual. I actually looked forward to going to new schools. I did not realize and I am sure mother did not realize that going to so many schools would be a social handicap for me, later in life. I simply never learned how to develop long term friends.

I had no trouble keeping up with studies when we moved and I didn't feel a need for lasting friendships. I now feel that I was somewhat socially stunted by the time I reached adulthood. To this day, I am uncomfortable around people.

My parents were both children of very poor share croppers, in Oklahoma. Neither of them went beyond the ninth grade in school and no demands were put on me to obtain an education or to do well in studies. I never did homework, unless there were assignments which had to be turned in. Then, I usually managed to do them during class at school.

I always made A's and B's, but remember feeling embarrassed by the good grades. In those days, in the schools I attended, mostly girls made the good grades. I remember wishing I could reduce them in some way, but didn't want to cheat. We boys wanted to excel at sports.

My mother re-married and divorced several times during her life. I remember, during the summer between the tenth and eleventh grades, I worked all one summer. I saved every penny of my pay, except for bus fare. Finally, at the end of summer, I had accumulated $100.00 and bought a really beat-up old car. Its transmission didn't even have a first gear.

When I signed up for eleventh grade, I was allowed to take half-day training classes to be an auto mechanic in a program called "distributive education" courses. These courses were designed for boys who knew they would never go to college. The hope was to train us for some sort of skilled labor. As for me, I had no idea whether I wanted to go to college or not. I signed up for auto mechanics so I could work on my old car during school. After six-weeks, I could see that the program was really "mickey mouse" and actually designed to have some place to park the "dumb" boys until graduation. The classes were extremely boring.

Therefore, I went to the school counsellor and discussed the issue of my boredom with her. We decided that I could drop out of distributive education and take up a college preparation program, which included algebra. However, because I had missed the first six weeks, I was required to take two classes of the same algebra course. This was a technical thing that I had to have a certain minimum amount of algebra class time to qualify for the college prep program. I had no problem catching up with the class.

In the meantime, I was also required to continue the basic math course I had originally started in distributive education. It was so easy, I had a real problem staying interested and tended to talk with other boys seated nearby. One day, during a simple little test in which I knew I had all of the answers down right, I was

40

chatting with a boy nearby. My teacher came over, turned over my paper and wrote a big zero at the top of it. This not only surprised me, it infuriated me. At that point in my young life, I was very rebellious and resented any unfair treatment. When the period was over, I tore up my exam paper, put the pieces in a neat pile on the floor beside the trash can and walked out. The next day, I was expelled.

My mother sent me to stay with an old friend of hers in a nearby town, which was in another school district. She and her husband had one son, who was one year older than me. This boy's name was Glynn and we formed the only life-long friendship that I ever had. I was a year ahead in school, so we went to the same classes. He is dead now, but I still remember him often.

The new school was in Baytown, Texas. I noticed on the transcript that my math teacher did not give me a failing grade, and rightly so, because all of my test grades had been perfect until the last one. I also saw that the Algebra teacher had assigned me an "A." I still had no thought that I was above average in intelligence.

After my parents divorced, I grew away from going to church. We moved around so much, that going to church was difficult. I had been a Baptist from the time I was six. When I was thirteen and in junior high school, I still thought of myself as a Baptist. But, some unfortunate incidents made me change my mind.

I had been taught in Sunday school that Baptists did not believe in drinking alcohol, including wine, and my teacher discouraged us from going to movies on Sunday. Her reasoning was that, if Jesus came back on Sunday, we did not want him to find us at the show. I secretly thought that was silly and I remembered that my parents' entire Sunday school class drank wine at our house at a Christmas party before. Later, I saw people that I knew were Baptists who were going to dances, which was also forbidden. And, they were going to shows on Sunday.

Actually, my parents were not really Baptists. My mother had been reared as a Nazarene and my father had no religion. At that

41

time, I did not even know there were different denominations of religions. They became Baptists because I began going to the Baptist church by myself when I was six years old. It was one block down the street from our house, on the next corner from us. I saw the crowd there on Sundays and asked permission of my mother to go. She said it was OK and I would walk to church on Sundays, by myself.

I do not know why I did that. I was too young to fully understand the sermons. I still remember the first time I understood something and it was after I had already been going to church for a while. It was a story told by a visiting evangelist. I remember sitting at the very top of the balcony as I listened.

He was telling about a time he went through a hurricane in a friend's house. He and the friend were on their knees praying in the living room as the storm threatened to blow the house down. The evangelist wanted to go down into the basement, where it was safer, but the friend would not go. He stayed in the living room, praying. So, the evangelist went down by himself. The house blew down and the friend was killed. The evangelist said that the first time he told that story to a congregation, someone spoke up and asked where the evangelist's faith had been. The evangelist said he replied, "I took it with me." I got it.

He told more stories, which I also got, then he made an "altar call" for anyone who wanted to join the church to be baptized. I made the altar call, but came down very slowly from the balcony. The evangelist spotted me slowly descending and extended the call until I made it down to the altar. I had no idea why I went down there, but and one of the deacons sat down in the front row with me and helped me fill out an application for baptism.

My parents eventually joined a Sunday school group at the church. This was after the elders of the church personally called on them to advise that I had made the altar call and filled out the application to be baptized. The elders had called on my parents to make sure it was okay with them. I remember my parents giving

42

me some strange looks during that conversation. Soon, they, and my big brother, also joined the church.

It was after this that I saw my parents drinking wine with their Sunday school group during a Christmas celebration at our house. I remember one of the men saying something about a little wine did not hurt anything at Christmas. I was confused and scandalized by that, but I did not mention it to my parents. Also, I continued to go to the movies on Sundays and dances at school, despite feeling conflicted.

Later, during my first semester of junior high school, I decided I was no longer a Baptist. I had been taught how to dance the waltz at primary school in the sixth grade, and I enjoyed it a lot. It had not occurred to me that this might be against my religion at that time. I remember the girl I especially liked to dance with was named Jane Anderson. Her brother was a star football player in high school. But, I really discovered girls by the seventh grade, and wanted to go to the school dances. I discussed the dance issue with one of the boys in my grade and who was also a Baptist. He said it was okay to go, but I decided anyway that I did not want to be a Baptist any more.

From then on, I looked for another church to join. Soon, I made it a point to ride my bike to churches of different denominations each Sunday, seeking the "true church." Once, I even attended an all-black church with my friend Glynn. This was in the early 1940s and Texas was still segregated. The church allowed us to attend, but we did not feel comfortable there. It was not because everyone else was black. It was because they had us sit up on the stage with the elders, in front of everyone else. Believe it or not, I had never been told anything about segregation, by my parents or anyone else. I just knew they kept to themselves and we kept to ourselves.

Remember, my parents had grown up in Oklahoma as share croppers and most share croppers in Oklahoma were black. Mother talked about playing with children of a black family that lived

43

down the road from them. They simply did not talk about segregation. Mother also said she had an aunt that was a Cherokee Indian and I was 1/32nd Cherokee. At that time, being a Cherokee in Oklahoma was probably worse than being black. They called them "Blanket Buts." At any rate, I had no qualms about going to a black-church. We knew we were getting special treatment and that made us uncomfortable. We didn't go back.

None of the elders or preachers in the churches I visited seemed to realize that I needed to hear them say that theirs was the "right" church. I usually sought out pastors after the services and asked them whatever questions were on my mind from their sermons. They always seemed to have other things going on after the services were over and no one ever took the time to actually explain or teach me about their denomination. Two of them did have me over for lunch after church, but did not talk with me about the merits of their denominations.

I bounced around in this manner, from church to church, for all of my teen years. But, the remainder of my spare time was spent chasing girls or in competitive sports. I thought of myself as "happy."

I left home immediately after graduation from high school at Berkeley, California. It was not because I did not love my mother or she did not love me or take care of me. It was because I wanted to be a "man" and have adventures. I graduated at the age of 17, a year younger than my classmates. I had twice been advanced one semester because of the circumstances of moving and my grades seemed to indicate that I should be moved forward rather than backward in grade level.

At graduation, I hoped to go to Alaska and homestead 640 acres of land. That state was trying to attract new citizens with a homestead act. I thought of myself as a lone wolf by this time and made no companions or friends. Glynn was back in Texas and mother and I were in California and I had read a lot of Jack London adventure books in high school. The idea of living alone in

44

the wilderness did not seem strange to me at all. I did not know it, but the constant moving about had left me isolated, like my mom. She called herself "fiddle footed" and I thought of myself in the same way, but also as "adventuresome."

This is how we moved to California: During summer, between my junior and senior years of high school, mom was going to California for a vacation, by herself. She wanted to visit one of my father's sisters, whom she loved. I was staying with my aunt at the time and was working as a plumber's helper with my uncle in Houston. On the day she was leaving, I decided to go with her, just for the adventure of the trip. We visited one of her girl-friends in San Diego and then with her former sister-in-law in Oakland. We had a good time.

After a little more than a week, I suggested to her that we stay. She agreed. Mother found a job as a waitress and I enrolled in high school at Berkeley, for my senior year. I went to Berkeley because I had a cousin who went there also. Therefore, as one can see, I had no roots whatsoever and thought it perfectly normal that I wanted to go out on my own when I graduated. Mother did not stand in my way. Young men were expected to leave home in those days.

After graduation, I worked in California as an un-skilled laborer, an oiler on a dragline, through the summer. At the end of an extremely hot July, I was moved from my job as oiler to what they called a "sacker." My new job was to climb into slowly moving railroad cars, called gondolas. They carried gravel, which my company sold. The cars became damaged from loading and offloading the gravel, which they called "aggregate" because it had been segregated into various sizes. The idea was that I should caulk any holes or cracks in the bottom of each car with sackcloth, to make sure gravel did not leak or vibrate out during its transport to market.

This was an extremely hot, dirty and demanding job. I could see why the other guy quit. I had to stay ahead of the over-head loading chutes because the cars moved forward all of the time. They were pulled by a switch engine. It was like we were on a conveyor belt. I had to throw sack cloth over the sides of the cars, climb up and in and caulk the damages. Then, I had to climb out and down and go to the next car, staying ahead of the forward progress of the entire train. I had to hurry to keep up.

One day, as I was scurrying up the ladder of a car and swinging my leg over the top, I banged my knee very hard. I had to keep going, because to stop would cause a serious delay in the process of loading the cars. At the end of the day, after continuing for the remainder of the day in extreme pain from my knee, I decided there must be a better way to make money. So, I quit my job and returned to Texas to stay with my aunt. Mother stayed in California. I enrolled in night school at the University of Houston, determined to eventually get a college education and a good job. I never did make it to Alaska.

At the same time, I found a day job as an unskilled laborer for the local light company. I kept that job for one year. Usually, I worked as a lineman's helper, but not always. On a particularly hot day, I was dropped off at an alleyway with another young man to dig a series of utility pole holes. The holes needed to be 8 feet deep. They had to be dug by hand because the large digger truck could not get into the alley-way. We dug those holes with long-handled shovels and a tool which they called a "spoon". Both tools had 12-foot-long handles. The spoon was used to remove the dirt from the bottom of the holes, loosened while digging them with the shovel.

Toward the end of the day, the large, creosote soaked utility poles arrived and we, joined by several other men, wheeled them down the alley on two wheeled carts and set them in the holes. Creosote got on my skin in several places and, working in the hot sun, it burned me rather badly.

At the end of the day, I drove home, truly exhausted and uncomfortable. As I listened to music on the radio in the rattletrap car I had purchased, the disc jockey mentioned that anyone who wanted to get the Korean G.I. Bill had better join up soon because eligibility would cease at the end of that week.

As in California with my banged-up knee, my creosote burns and exhaustion made me think that there must be a better way to get a college education and make a better living. I knew the G.I. Bill would be a good way to pay for college. The financing of tuition was proving to be a heavy burden. Therefore, I took the next day off and went to the recruiting station, downtown.

My thought was simply to join up in order to get the G.I. Bill. I intended to join the Navy, because I had two uncles who were in the navy. But when I arrived, recruiters from the Army invited me to test for flying helicopters and recruiters for the Air Force wanted me to test for flying airplanes. That sounded like fun. I learned that at the end of helicopter school, I would automatically become a "flying sergeant." At the end of pilot training, I would automatically become a pilot, an officer and a gentleman. Officers make more money. They both qualified me for the G.I. Bill I opted to test for pilot training school because I could become an officer and a gentleman by act of Congress. At least, that is what the recruiter said.

The tests at Houston were basic IQ and physical coordination examinations, but they took all day. I was able to pass the tests and that qualified me for three days of more extensive testing in San Antonio, Texas. But first, if I wanted to take the three-day tests, I had to be sworn in as an airman basic. If I failed the testing in San Antonio, I would have to go to boot camp and remain in the Air Force for four years. Either way, I would get the GI Bill. If I passed the tests and passed flying school, I would remain in for three years as an officer and a pilot. But first, I had to successfully complete the 1 ½ year pilot training program. So, it was 4 years as an enlisted man or 4 ½ years as an officer. In either case, this sounded like a good idea to me. Unskilled labor had taught me that much.

After the swearing in at Houston, the recruiting officer gave me a train ticket to San Antonio and told me to report to Lackland Air Force Base.

The three days of testing was quite severe and in depth. It was intended to determine physical and mental capacity and psychological stability. During the three days, the Air Force also provided extensive motivational activity, including movies of very happy-go-lucky enlisted men and very heroic pilots in a movie called "Twelve O'clock High." They even added special footage to the movie. It was all designed to make us to want to be Air Force pilots or navigators and, if we didn't make it, to be happy and motivated enlisted men. We all wanted to be heroic pilots and navigators and not to revert to airman basic. On our bunks, we even had Air Force magazines filled with "gung ho" flying stories.

At that particular time of my life, I was quite skinny. I was 6'3" tall and weighed 124 pounds. But, I was told that my muscles were like piano wire. By the third day of testing, I was so motivated to make the cut, that I went into the cafeteria and drank several malted milks and several glasses of water to increase my weight. This wasn't my idea. I was told to do it by the testers whispering over the backs of their hands, in feigned secrecy. Obviously, other skinny boys had preceded me.

Before I could reach the scales, I had to leave the line 3 separate times to relieve myself. Then, I would drink more water and get back in line. Finally, I was the last in line for the day and did not have to wait. But, I barely managed to hold myself in long enough to be weighed. Happily, I weighed the minimum of 132 pounds for my height, with eight pounds of liquid in my belly. I stepped down from the scale and went straight to the rest room from there.

At the end of the three days, my group was ushered into a large room to wait. We were called into an adjacent private room, one by one. Our waiting to be called into the room was actually quite tense. We all wanted to be qualified for something, either navigator or pilot training. The worst of all possible worlds would be to watch the others going off to pilot or navigator school as an airman basic. They had motivated us well.

When I was finally called in, I saw two men. Both wore captain's bars on their collars. I could see that the wings on their chests were different, but I didn't know what that meant. Later, I learned that one wore navigator wings and one wore pilot wings. One of the captains told me that we could be qualified for navigation school or pilot school, or both. If we were found to be qualified for both, we were allowed to make our own choice about which school to attend.

One of the officers consulted my test grades and told me that I could go to either pilot or navigator school. Of course, I knew absolutely nothing about either position and had no idea what to choose. So, I asked who was in charge of the plane. They told me the one in charge of the aircraft was the pilot and I told them that is what I wanted to be. So, they signed me up and said to go home and wait, that they would soon be in touch.

I was given a train ticket back to Houston, packed my bag and left. There, I awaited notification to report for active duty as an aviation cadet, with a permanent grade of airman basic. I was told that upon graduation, in a year and a half, I would be a second lieutenant and awarded my wings.

Earlier, when I first arrived in Texas from California, I enrolled in night school at the University of Houston. The first semester, I enrolled for six credit hours, two three-hour courses, and made an "A" and a "B". At this rate, I knew it would take me a long time to accumulate the 120 hours for a bachelor's degree and I seemed to be able to do the work. In the second semester, I doubled my academic load to 12 hours. It was during the second semester that I was put in the alley to dig post holes and decided to try for the GI Bill.

As outlined above, I was sent to San Antonio for the Air Force testing, but, as fortune would have it, it was right at the beginning of final examinations at the University of Houston. This forced me to decide whether I was serious about getting the GI Bill. I opted to go to San Antonio, knowing that there could be problems about my classes in Houston.

When I returned to Houston from testing for cadets, the first three exams had already taken place. The fourth exam was in progress as I walked in. I told the professor my situation and asked to be allowed to make up the exam. His reply was that his exam was going on right then and I could take it at that time or forget about taking it. I walked out and forgot about it.

After all, I thought, I was just waiting to be called by the Air Force. Passing the exams didn't seem very important. I thought I could simply make them up when I got out. The professor who ordered me to take the test, recorded an "F" on my transcript, as did one other. The other two recorded incompletes. Later, when I separated from the Air Force and returned to college, I found that all four grades had reverted to "F" because I had not taken the exams within one year, as was required, unbeknown to me.

Therefore, although I was allowed readmission when I separated from the Air Force in 1958, I was placed on academic probation with one "A", one "B" and four "F's" on my transcript. I had to bring my average up to "C" the first semester in order to be removed from probation and placed in academic good standing. This required at least four "A's" and one "C" with a normal 15-hour load. Despite this, I signed up for an overload of classes of 18 hours.

I did this because the academic counselor I had been assigned calculated for me how I could, with overloads and going in the summers with full loads, receive a Bachelor of Science degree and a Doctor of Laws degree in four calendar years. It was called a "combination degree program."

I eagerly undertook the additional accelerated courses. This would qualify me for the Bar Examination in four years, and get me two degrees, just as the G.I. Bill ran out. I did not know it, but I

50

was to pay a heavy price in eye strain and emotional stress before the four years were over. Academic probation was just the first hurdle.

At the end of the first semester, I descended into the basement of the main administration building to prove that my grades allowed me to be removed from probation. At the little cubbyhole in the wall which was designated for that purpose, I rang the bell and there appeared an unusually stern-faced woman, to whom I handed my papers.

I supposed to myself that she looked so stern because of the nature of her job. As she looked at my records, reflecting all "A's", she wrote something in her record book and then looked back up into my eyes. Her face seemed to crack slowly and then to shatter into the brightest, most sunny smile that I have ever seen. Part of it may have been my imagination, but I remember it like that to this day, 58 years later, and I still feel her sunshine.

During the regular school years, I consistently made all A's. Although, for some reason, during the summers, I always made A's and B's. At the end of the first two years, my grades qualified me to be admitted to their phi beta kappa fraternity, even with my old F's factored into my grade average. But, the fraternity refused to admit me because the four F's on my transcript scandalized them. That upset me quite a bit. By that time, I had become proud of my grades and I hungered for recognition because of them. Now, I see it as just human nature that they did not want me, with my 4 F's, to be able to strut around, point at my academic key and brag about getting it despite the 4 F's. They were right. That is just what I would have done.

Eventually, I was able to complete both degrees in four years, the BS and Doctor of Laws. The BS was cum laude, but not Phi Betta Kappa. Even though I was gratified by this success, I was not satisfied with myself. I suppose I was suffering like someone suffering with anorexia. They cannot believe they are thin enough and I cannot believe I am smart enough, even today.

51

Secretly, I was afraid I didn't have what it takes to go to college. I anguished for four years that I was going to flunk out. By the beginning of the fourth year, my eye strain was so bad that I had to wear an eye patch over one eye to relieve the muscle strain. In the latter part of my last year, I simply could not read without getting sick to my stomach and having migraine headaches. Someone had to read my case assignments to me. I was doing all that I could do.

The only encouragement for higher education I remember having was from the administrator of an I.Q. test that I took when I was shifting from distributive education to an academic curriculum in the eleventh grade. The lady told me I was smart enough for college. But, secretly, I could not accept that fact. Even today, I feel inferior in intellect. It is like something inside me knows better than the results I experience. I almost stayed in the Air Force because of the fear and anguish I felt about school.

Despite everything, my older brother and I graduated law school together and took the bar exam together. He worked full time during the day. Although he originally started before me, we were together for my first 6-hour night course, before I tested for the Air Force. He continued in night school for a total of 10 years. Our father was a policeman. Other than his example, I do not know why either of us chose the law. We never discussed it with each other and we received no encouragement elsewhere, so far as I know. I do know my brother told me he tried to enroll in the police academy without our father's knowledge and my father, when he heard about it, had him removed.

We took the bar exams and oaths as attorneys together. Clayton is dead now and I remember our starting out together in the law best of all. Mother took pictures of the two of us with our hands raised, side by side, as we were being sworn in at the Supreme Court of Texas. Our paths had separated and then re-converged. He lived with my father and his new wife when we were children. I had it easier. I admired him greatly. Ten years requires a lot of determined commitment.

In 1955, while stationed at Dreux Air Force Base, France, I converted to Catholicism. I was still searching for a church at the time and stopped by the chaplain's office one evening to make my usual inquiry. I had done this on all the bases I had been stationed at before, just as I had done in private life. I was still looking for the right denomination. This chaplain happened to be Catholic and he knew how to respond to my questions. He simply handed me two books and told me to come back after I had finished them. They were both works of St. Thomas Aquinas, one was a condensation of the Summa Theologica by W. O. Farrell and the other was The Summa Contra Gentiles. The latter was a somewhat lesser known book by St. Thomas, which he wrote for the primary purpose of converting Muslims to Christianity. They were precisely what I needed. After reading them and being taught the Catechism of the Catholic Church, I joined. This was in 1955. I was then 20 years old. Three years later, in August, 1958, I separated from the Air Force and entered the University of Houston, in September, at long last, with the G.I. Bill.

Chapter 6. Patiently Toward Maturity.

Serious and Patient Growth Toward Maturity is what I have been trying to do for the last 32 years. Much has changed in my thought and attitude since I was given that command in the vision. I have 32 years of experience, straining in the harness for the Lord, plowing his fields and hoping to end up in heaven. Most of those years, I have been teaching the Bible and leading the practice of *Lectio Divina* (Divine Reading)[6] at my church. I also spent three years in a monastery as a postulant for the priesthood with a religious order, the Redemptorists. I'll tell you a little about that later. But this installment is about my difficulty in interacting with the transcendent realities of the experiences in my visions.

The difficulty stems from the fact that we only have five senses and none of them can detect the actual spirit world. We can neither see, hear, taste, smell or feel the reality of the spirit world. Nevertheless, our own spirits somehow know the spiritual world exists. In the last 33 years, it has been independently confirmed to me over and over again that God IS and that the Bible speaks the truth.

As to whether the Biblical truths are literal or symbolic, I am satisfied to allow the reader to sort out for himself. However, either way, I have satisfied myself that the truth is an absolute. It is what it is and it is the same for each of us. There is nothing that is relatively true. Your truth is my truth. All truth is our truth.

At first, I was totally mystified about how to be patient, to mature, and to take life seriously. Now, I am reasonably comfortable with my duty in this regard. For instance, I suspect

---

[6] *Lectio Divina* is a way to prayerfully read scripture through meditation and contemplation. It originated before the coming of Christ and was continued by Christians.

that one of my duties is to write this book. In view of my current age of 82, you will surely accept that I do not do this in order to become wealthy and retire to a beach somewhere. I have no personal hope, expectation, or desire for wealth and I retired long ago to sunny Florida.

I write to you out of love. It is the same love that moved me to kiss that distraught little housewife on the cheek and tell her she would never hear from me again. Since my first out of body experience, this love has deepened, without conscious emphasis on my part. It is the most merciful and fulfilling thing that has ever happened to me. It is asexual, entirely a response of the life within me to the life within other people. I reflexively communicate love to people, both male and female. I often tell them that I love them. Rarely, I do see looks of confusion or suspicion in their eyes, especially from men. Even those who do not at first understand, seem to quickly work out what I am talking about.

That said, I would like to give you a little critique about an important book I have mentioned, *A Key To Charismatic Renewal In The Catholic Church*. The book is a mid-level book about spirituality. It provides a large amount of vocabulary. But, it does not penetrate to the inner sanctum which drives the spiritual charisms and it does not provide a key to renew them. It is written from the stand point that we can do something to control the coming or use of charisms. Actually, we can do nothing other than to ask for them and to accept them when given.

Thirty-two years have passed since I first read *A Key To Charismatic Renewal In The Catholic Church* and it was an excellent place of beginning for the novice. I still have my copy and I recommend it to everyone. But, not as a key that opens a lock. There is no key and there is no lock, as the title implies. The charisms are truly indulgent gifts of the Holy Spirit, the result of his *agape* love. No one is righteous or worthy of them, not one,[7] and no one is especially able to exercise the gifts. The Holy Spirit

[7] See Rom 3:9 et seq

bestows his gifts on whomever and however he pleases and in whatever form or strength he pleases. His choices and methods and reasons are his own. It is beyond the capacity of man to understand or explain this.

This much I have learned, even though it is counter intuitive: Charisms are freely available to Christians. They are true gifts, but they are not gifts to the person who is enabled to exercise them.[8] They are gifts to his community.

They are, in effect, hot spots for serving *agape* love to those with special needs in the community. I felt *agape* love being individually applied to everything as I was being carried through the universe. I truly believe it is impossible for anyone, whether man or spirit, who has *agape* love to withhold any good thing from any of us who need or who ask. I also believe I have good reason for saying this.

Agape love transcends our naturally generated, selfish love. We are not, personally, its source. Once released, it mysteriously emanates from the Holy Spirit. We do not control it in any way. Charisms are gifts from the Lord, released from he who resides within us. *Agape* love is the motive force for feeding the sick, visiting prisoners or correctly exercising the charisms.

Direct inspiration and Inspired writings, such as the Holy Bible, are the only possible sources of knowledge concerning charismatic gifts, simply because they transcend our senses. We have no idea how to truly understand them. They are available to all Christians, but only from the Spirit within.

Books like *A Key To Charismatic Renewal In The Catholic Church* do help the reader resolve or remove some of the self-inflicted impediments to exercising the spiritual gifts, but they do not provide a key with which we can turn them on. There is no need of that. All we need to do is ask. Actual teaching about spiritual gifts may be reliably obtained from the writings of St.

---

[8] See 1 Cor 14:12

Paul. He explains that the spiritual gifts are according to God's grace.[9] They are all from the same Spirit for the edification, the moral, emotional, spiritual and intellectual growth and improvement of the Church.

This is in contradistinction to feeding the ego or lining the pockets of the recipients. The recipient of a spiritual gift actually and properly becomes a servant, a slave, of his community.[10] The church is always, and has always been, in need of such gifts.

Unfortunately, the nature of the beast which we call man is to aggrandize himself. Our nature is to try to be "No. 1". We were born with it. This nature is a flaw, not a sin. A baby wants to be fed and nurtured without regard for others. This is the flaw at work for good. A baby has no capacity to hurt others. Therefore, it is not a flaw at first. It is a necessity for survival. But, we never fully outgrow that selfish nature - none of us. We tend to protect "No. 1."

The entire Holy Bible, from cover to cover, reflects this truth. Man began in complete innocence with Adam, but, when tested, Adam and Eve had concern only for themselves, their own best interests, when they chose to disobey the commandment of God not to eat of the tree of knowledge of good and evil.

The reclamation of man toward resolving his selfishness and into loving and obedient service to our creator is a major thrust of all of scripture. And, we all fail to follow that thrust to perfection. Even so, we receive divine assistance from the example and sacrifice of Jesus Christ.

The spiritual gifts assist us during our lives because we are like sheep, following our noses, straying and seeking self-satisfaction from everything that appears good, like Adam and Eve. The fleshly interactions of the spiritual gifts for healing, learning, etc., inspire us toward spiritual maturity. They transform us from believing "friends" of Jesus into his willing and aspiring

---

[9] Cf Rom 11:29-12:8
[10] Cf 1 Cor 12:1-14:12

"servants". The charisms are like beacons in the fog, helping and guiding the entire community, so we can all gain the benefits of Jesus' sacrifice and get to heaven together.

We are told by Paul to seek the spiritual gifts.[11] But, caution and humility are necessary for those who do so. This is because our natural tendency to think that we have some ownership or control over them gets in the way.[12] For instance, one may pray for a gift of prophesy or of healing. Then, believing he is "stepping out in faith," begin to prophesy and lay hands on others, doing nothing more than feeding his ego. Errant prophesies and lack of healings could then undermine the faith of others and degrade the legitimate functioning of charismatic gifts in the community. In the meantime, those who have legitimate spiritual gifts, but are shy in using them, hold back and do not help others.

John, in the book of Revelation, told how entire churches of professing Christians go astray, even to the extent that the Lord will abandon them until they correct their course.[13] We are told in Revelation to repent and do good works;[14] do not fear suffering and be faithful;[15] repent of false teachings, giving bad examples, repent of fornication and do not deny God's faith;[16] Do not suffer the fornication or sacrificing to idols of others[17]

The books of Hebrews, James and Peter tell us how to stay on course <u>after</u> becoming Christians. If we do not pay attention to them, we <u>will</u> <u>naturally</u> go astray as we await either death or the second coming of the Lord.[18]

---

[11] Cf 1 Cor 14:1 *et seq*
[12] See 1 Cor 14:12
[13] See Rev 2:1-3:22
[14] Rev 2:5
[15] Rev 2:10
[16] Rev 2:19
[17] Rev 2:23
[18] IBID

Chapter 7. The Holy Land.

On May 27, 1985, a group of my fellow parishioners and I departed for the holy land. By this time, I had become sufficiently comfortable with urgings from the Holy Spirit to entrust myself to them and to obey. Many examples of these come to mind. The urgings can be quite strong and insistent, such as the urge to go to the perpetual adoration room at the time of my first "out of body" experience.

I had such an urge one Sunday at church as I passed a "sign-up" table for the trip to the Holy Land. It was the final week-end to sign-up and I obeyed. The next week-end, I found myself on an airplane, bound for New York, then Tel-Aviv. During this trip, I had the first experiences of others being healed through my hands. Actually, there were only three such experiences during the trip. I felt the mysterious and powerful urges to pray for healing each time.

Surprisingly for me, I received no personal gratification or recognition from any of the recipients of these miracles. They frightened me. I truly believe that this was through the merciful action of the Lord. The acclaim and adoration of spiritual healers such as Oral Roberts or Benny Hinn would have crushed me underfoot, like a bug. Then, the compensating flair of my ego would have probably stolen my salvation. This is what I thought at that time, for which I thanked God, and this is what I still think. A full release of the gift could very well crush me. Perhaps I am unconsciously diminishing or restraining the gift out of fear.

Nevertheless, there was a giant personal benefit from participating in these healings. They were so dramatic and so authentic in nature that they confirmed to me privately the absolute validity of the visions in the perpetual adoration room. There had already been many other confirmations, several of which are in my notes, but these three healings confirmed the actuality of the charism with which I was told I had been endowed.

They occurred like this: The first healing was on Sunday, June 3, 1985, during mass. Our group attended mass in a little church at the place in Jerusalem of Jesus' scourging. It is actually a rather small chapel and the seating was very limited, not enough to accommodate all of us. Nevertheless, a priest began bringing in extra chairs and I assisted him. Our tour guide was the parish priest of Galilee, a Franciscan, and he presided at the mass.

Before mass, he instructed us to place our crucifixes on the altar and identify in our minds the personal crosses we bear. While engaged in the calming prayers of the mass, I sensed that the Holy Spirit was all around me. Then, I looked up and saw a woman, whom I knew casually, seated in front of me. I noticed she did not place a cross on the altar before mass. I had two crosses with me and had placed both of mine in the pile on the altar.

During the mass, I could see she was being moved by the Lord. After the initial prayers, as we were sitting down, I leaned forward and whispered that Jesus loves her very, very much. As we were sitting, I placed my hand on the left shoulder blade of her back and asked the Lord, through Jesus Christ, to heal his poor unhappy servant.

I felt the Holy Spirit move through me gently and slowly, feeling like electricity. Eventually, the electricity flowed from the right side of my chest, down through my left arm, through my hand, to her. I knew the Holy Spirit was healing her. It was a very small thing and I realized my attitude, sincerity and sensitivity toward this lady was very important, but I did not realize she was estranged from the church.

During communion, we picked up our crosses. I took one of mine from its chain and handed it to her, whispering for her to keep it, that it would be important to her later. She accepted it readily, but not eagerly.

62

I had not consciously chosen, or planned, to do any of these things in conjunction with the prayer for healing. After mass, the lady thanked me most sincerely, but not effusively or excessively. I remember suspecting that if that was a healing, it was very weak.

Two days later, on June 5, 1985, a friend from church who had been in the perpetual adoration room on the occasion of my first out of body experience, walked up and told me that I should talk to the lady to whom I had given the cross during mass two days before. She said the lady had talked to her confidentially and needed to talk to me, but that she would not approach me. I would have to approach her. I told the lady that I did not want to talk to her about this. I said that I know what happened to her without talking to her and that she should go to a priest for guidance.

My friend said that the lady had a bad experience with a priest before and would not talk to them. That was the end of that conversation, except I said again that I did not want to talk to her. I was afraid that I would mess things up. I then told my friend part of the healing experience. I even described the feeling of electricity, but said that I am an infant in these things. I expected that as I matured, the healing will gain more power. My friend told me I had underestimated the power of this healing and again asked me to talk to the lady. I still declined.

Later in the day, I realized that the lady was going to have to have someone guide her to avoid losing the benefits of the healing. I suggested that my friend ask the lady to talk to another friend of mine, but there seemed to be some problem there also. I asked my friend to tell the lady about my side of the experience to help validate her healing, but my friend said that was too great of a responsibility. I was thoroughly thwarted.

When I finally realized that the lady was able to validate that the Holy Spirit had truly endowed me with the gift of healing, I thought perhaps the reason I was being so thoroughly thwarted was that the Lord required me to talk to her as part of the process. At the end of dinner that evening, I went to the lady and told her I thought we should talk. She said she thought so too; however, she was on her way to a prayer meeting and it would have to be another time. I never saw her again. I learned that being shy is not the way to go.

The other two healings occurred the next evening after dinner, at our hotel. Two ladies, who were in a group separate from mine, and I were lingering at the dinner table, chatting. I did not know them, but had seen them at various places on our separate tours.

One of the ladies indicated she had some sort of problem with her eye and that the doctor had told her she would be permanently blind in that eye if it did not resolve itself within a certain number of days. The days had already gone by and she still could not see. This lady was not young and she seemed to be trying to accept being blind in one eye.

In response to a strong urging, I asked permission to look closely at her eye and, when she granted it, placed my fingertips around the socket and prayed secretly for her healing. I thanked her for the opportunity to look at her eye. Nothing more was said on the subject and we soon arose and went our separate ways.

As I approached the hotel elevator, another lady from the other group was waiting for the elevator to come. She was obviously in great pain and her friend turned to me and said that she had fallen in the bathtub and tomorrow was the last day of their tour. She was not only in great pain but was also in great anguish because she could not complete the tour.

With a strong inner urging, I asked the lady if I could see her hand, inviting her to place her open hand on the back of my hand. She did so, but with obvious great pain. It was badly swollen and discolored. She could not even open her fingers as she placed her hand on mine. I said a short silent prayer for her healing, then gave her a few hopeful and encouraging words as the elevator doors opened. Then, we all went about our business.

The next morning, the other group and my group were all in the lobby of the hotel, about to sally forth on our separate ways for the day. I asked the lady with the blind eye how her eye was doing. She replied happily that her sight had returned during the night, later than the doctor had said. I experienced an inner thrill that the Lord had been so kind to her and thanked him profusely for allowing me to serve him. She had no idea.

I also saw the lady who had suffered the fall in the bathtub. She seemed to be quite happy and excited, chatting and anticipating a full and final day on the tour. Her hand had also healed overnight. Both the swelling and the discoloration were gone. She did not seem to realize that this was impossible, but for a miracle.

Again, I was overjoyed and thanked the Lord for his mercy. I have never seen any of the ladies again and am confident that only the one from the little chapel where Jesus was scourged is aware of the merciful workings of the Lord in their lives.

As for me, I was totally convinced by these healings that my endowment with the gift was actual and of the intervention of my creator. I have realized since that time that I would be an absolute fool to either doubt him, or his existence, or his love, or his mercy. His love continues to abide in me. My most ardent desire since that time is to supply the same assurance to as many others as he will allow.

Chapter 8. Beginnings of Growth.

As our day of departure approached, the drama continued to play out before me. Occurrences regularly unfolded that made me feel protected, loved, nurtured. For instance, one evening, while praying in my room, my mind's eye saw myself in a vortex of some kind, with evil spirits swimming and circling, snapping, but not able to reach or harm me. To me, this seemed to mean that I was protected from evil while praying for the healing of others. Obviously, I was ravenously hungry for help and guidance.

On June 4, 1985, our tour guide and I sat together at table during dinner. He was very charismatic and I wanted his guidance. I asked if he would have time to talk with me that evening, before bedtime. He agreed and said that we should meet at his room, but later, because he had to go and pray over someone.

I returned to my own room to pick up my notes and then went down to the chapel to pray for guidance about how to proceed. While praying, I received a strong feeling that I should simply ask him for information about how to contact him and his superiors and then offer to answer any questions he might have of me. Immediately after this, my mind's eye saw a tall icon-like figure appear between me and the tabernacle for the holy Eucharist. The figure was graceful, feminine, wearing a cloak of vertical brown and black shadings. It had a flesh colored face and the eyelids were demurely lowered. It was extremely beautiful. As I watched admiringly, the image began to morph into a different shape. Its head changed into a very repulsive canine configuration, with bloodshot eyes, gaping, tooth-filled mouth and large white fangs. In the meantime, large leathery, graceful wings unfurled from behind it and it began to lunge straight at my face.

I blurted an amazed exclamation of some kind and started falling backward to avoid it. But, it continued coming toward me. My mind flashed out a command, "I demand in the name of God that you leave." It continued to come.

These things were happening very quickly, as I frantically cast about in my mind for something to say or do. Then, it seemed to engulf my head in darkness and I began to pray over and over again "Holy Spirit protect me", fearing that I was too late. I imagined that my body was impacted with great force by something, but not the evil attacker. I suspected that it was the Holy Spirit, or an angel, and felt that it had begun to protect me, but I could not tell for sure. I was horrified and desperately afraid.

The evil apparition then withdrew in retreat, the same as it had come. It paused where it had been, once again assuming the appearance of a serene icon with eyes cast down and hands demurely clasped in front. Then, it collapsed into itself and disappeared. I suspected it was mocking me as if I was an inexperienced novice.

I tried to look inside me with my mind's eye, hoping I had encountered protection from the Holy Spirit, but I could not tell. I was thoroughly shaken. I thought there was a possibility that it had entered me and I had no idea what to do. Almost by default, and in desperation, I began to continually repeat, "Holy Spirit protect me."

I wondered where to go and what to do. Should I leave the presence of the Holy Eucharist? Should I stay there and call out for help of some kind? But, who could I call? I decided to leave the chapel and tried to make it to the priest's room. During the journey, I was filled with fear and continually prayed for protection, over and over again. I had no idea what had happened to me, if anything, but the apparition had seemed very real and I wanted no part of it. When I arrived, the priest was not there. I waited in the hallway, outside his room, for about 15 minutes, continually repeating over and over again, "Holy Spirit protect me." Finally, he returned.

I was afraid to stop my prayer and I did so only in order to talk to him. I told him I was very frightened and that I thought it was possible an evil spirit had entered me. I asked if anything could be done. Instead of answering my question, he asked me what had happened. I told him everything, including what I was praying continually afterward. He still gave me no response. Instead, he asked me what approach to our meeting I had settled on. This confused me even more. I was then seeking help, protection or advice, not a discussion about the planned meeting.

I told him I merely wanted to get his address and that of his superiors, so I could stay in touch. And, if he had any questions of me, I would try to answer them. Immediately, he began to quiz me in a way that I thought very unfair. As a trial lawyer, I recognized that he was trying to control and interrogate me. It was very different than I had anticipated. He was aggressive and seemed hostile.

Rightly or wrongly, the thought kept going through my mind that this must have been the way they jumped on Jesus. I had no chance to demonstrate the bona fides of my spiritual messages, no comfort, no guidance, nothing concerning the fears I had brought with me. He didn't seem interested in what I wanted. He was on a mission of his own.

He began to interrupt me with questions that were aggressive and dismissive. When it became obvious that he was driving toward a preconceived goal, I told him that I would prefer to more accurately respond to his questions from the notes I had brought with me. However, he raised his hand to stop me and would not let me refer to them, saying that I should be able to answer his questions from memory. With this, I had the sinking feeling that he had gained control in our exchange, despite me. I abandoned my hopes and began to answer him in the way he wanted.

Then, he seemed to reconsider for a few seconds, abandoning his own goals and returned to the very beginning of our conversation. He told me that evil spirits could not enter my body in the manner I had described, that I had to do something wrong that would give them an opening. I told him that was a great relief.

Next, he criticized me for "avoiding the name of Jesus." It had not occurred to me that I was doing so. I thought that perhaps this is what set him off so aggressively. He said he suspected there was something wrong in me that made me avoid using the name of Jesus. He was very suspicious. He asked me to tell him who Jesus is

I told him that Jesus is my Lord and Savior, who was crucified and murdered for me. That he is my personal ticket to heaven, that I cannot earn entrance on my own merit, that he is part of the holy trinity. Then, I slowed down as if to ask if he was satisfied that I had answered his question. I think he was testing to see if I was in the control of an evil spirit.

I now recognize that he was testing the spirits as set out in the first letter of St. John. Of course, I was concerned about an evil spirit because of my experience in the chapel. So, I wanted to be tested. Finally, he seemed satisfied and began to relax.

He then told me that to protect myself from evil spirits, I should do so in the name of Jesus, that they could not care less if I do it in the name of God because it could be any God, such as the God of tin, etc., and my admonition would have no effect. Then he added that I should ask to be covered with the blood of Jesus, saying they cannot stand the blood of Jesus.

He advised me not to bear witness to the community about this. He suggested that when I get back home I should join a prayer group and learn. I admitted to him that I was almost totally ignorant in these matters and assured him that I would tell my parish priest of his views.

70

He had stung me with the observation that I should not witness and I told him that his feelings could be summed up that he was afraid I would do something stupid, that those were invalid fears, that I was no fool and was not surrounded by fools, that I would have full approval from the clergy in whatever I do or say and avoid being speculative or controversial.

I did not know that cooperation or approval such as I envisioned is next to impossible for the clergy. Therefore, what I said was invalid and not binding because it was not made with knowledge of that fact. I did not intend to muzzle or mute myself. I merely intended to bind myself to be obedient. The entire interview left a bad taste in my mouth and I was glad when it was over.

Now that many years have gone by and I know much more about these matters, I continue to feel that his advice was not appropriate. For instance, I do not know what authoritative support he could possibly have for telling me that my invocation of protection from God was inadequate. His thought was that I could have meant any god, such as the god of tin, etc. and therefore God would not protect me from attack. He said I must invoke the name of Jesus Christ.

However, I was not undertaking to frighten the evil spirit away by invoking divine protection, so it would hear me and flee. I was trying to invoke divine protection, per se! I had demanded in the name of God that the spirit leave me. It would not matter whether the spirit heard me. It would matter whether the only God in whom I believe, heard me. I was trying to do an exorcism! Then, I continually prayed, "Holy Spirit protect me."

God knows my mind and my heart, and always does. The prayer was not to run the beast off. I later learned that the Church does not approve of the laity doing exorcisms. But, I doubt that either my spiritual Father or the Holy Spirit would fail to come to my assistance because of this, or any other technical failure on my part. I prayed from the bottom of my heart and in great fear and trembling. Neither God nor the Holy Spirit would have withheld his protection. He loves me. I have faith in this. And, I submit that scripture supports me in this:

"And I tell you, Ask, and it will be given you; seek, and you will find; knock, and it will be opened to you. For every one who asks receives, and he who seeks finds, and to him who knocks it will be opened. What father among you, if his son asks for a fish, will instead of a fish give him a serpent; or if he asks for an egg, will give him a scorpion? 13 If you then, who are evil, know how to give good gifts to your children, how much more will the heavenly Father give the Holy Spirit to those who ask him!"

"Now he was casting out a demon that was dumb; when the demon had gone out, the dumb man spoke, and the people marveled. But some of them said, 'He casts out demons by Beelzebul, the prince of demons'; while others, to test him, sought from him a sign from heaven. But he, knowing their thoughts, said to them, 'Every kingdom divided against itself is laid waste, and a divided household falls. And if Satan also is divided against himself, how will his kingdom stand? For you say that I cast out demons by Beelzebul. And if I cast out demons by Beelzebul, by whom do your sons cast them out? Therefore they shall be your judges."[19]

I did not set out the foregoing to show that the priest was wrong or that I had been mistreated. Such a demonstration would have no proper place in this story. Instead, I set it out to show the most basic flaw in all of us at work.

This human flaw first surfaced when Adam and Eve committed the first sin by disobeying a commandment of the Lord.

Adam and Eve opted to eat the apple because it seemed good to them, even though it was contrary to God's command. Because they correctly judged that the apple was good. It opened their minds to know the difference between right and wrong. But, they

---

[19] Luke 11:9-19 (RSV)

72

were prohibited from eating it, regardless of whether or not it was a good to them. Obedience is what was required by God and they fell short of the requirement.

Adam and Eve were not, and we are not, entitled to do something simply because it is good for us personally, or seems good to us. Only God has that privilege. We are mere creatures, subject to his laws and we must be obedient if we are to become parts of his body in eternity. Likewise, if our finger disobeys us, we could, and should, cut it off.

If we remain like Adam and Eve, we will all choose what seems best for us, to be the head of the body, just like I chose to go to pilot school in the Air Force. Everyone could not be pilots. Some had to be navigators. Pilots are not made better by becoming pilots. They are merely placed in control.

In the creation story, Adam and Eve chose to eat the forbidden fruit simply because it was good for them. They followed their self-interest, rather than obey. What could be more natural? The flaw was inherited by Cain, but not by Abel. Abel pleased God, which means that he obeyed God and unselfishly gave unto him of his flocks. Cain slew Abel because he was jealous. It seemed good for him to remove the competition for God's pleasure. Obviously, Cain inherited the faulty gene from his parents and Abel did not. Abel chose not to sin, Cain did not. We are descendants of Cain and we all inherit the faulty gene. This epitomizes our problem. We must grow and mature into love, despite this weakness. We must die to self to gain the blessings of eternal life.

St Paul taught us what to do:[20] "Now there are varieties of gifts, but the same Spirit; and there are varieties of service, but the same Lord; and there are varieties of working, but it is the same God who inspires them all in every one. To each is given the manifestation of the Spirit for the common good. To one is given through the Spirit the utterance of wisdom, and to another the

---

[20] Please forgive the length of this quotation.

utterance of knowledge according to the same Spirit, to another faith by the same Spirit, to another gifts of healing by the one Spirit, to another the working of miracles, to another prophecy, to another the ability to distinguish between spirits, to another various kinds of tongues, to another the interpretation of tongues. All these are inspired by one and the same Spirit, who apportions to each one individually as he wills.

"For just as the body is one and has many members, and all the members of the body, though many, are one body, so it is with Christ. For by one Spirit we were all baptized into one body - Jews or Greeks, slaves or free - and all were made to drink of one Spirit.

"For the body does not consist of one member but of many. If the foot should say, 'Because I am not a hand, I do not belong to the body,' that would not make it any less a part of the body. And if the ear should say, 'Because I am not an eye, I do not belong to the body,' that would not make it any less a part of the body. If the whole body were an eye, where would be the hearing? If the whole body were an ear, where would be the sense of smell? But as it is, God arranged the organs in the body, each one of them, as he chose. If all were a single organ, where would the body be? As it is, there are many parts, yet one body. The eye cannot say to the hand, 'I have no need of you,' nor again the head to the feet, 'I have no need of you.' On the contrary, the parts of the body which seem to be weaker are indispensable, and those parts of the body which we think less honorable we invest with the greater honor, and our unpresentable parts are treated with greater modesty, which our more presentable parts do not require. But God has so composed the body, giving the greater honor to the inferior part, that there may be no discord in the body, but that the members may have the same care for one another. If one member suffers, all suffer together; if one member is honored, all rejoice together.

"Now you are the body of Christ and individually members of it. And God has appointed in the church first apostles, second prophets, third teachers, then workers of miracles, then healers,

74

helpers, administrators, speakers in various kinds of tongues. Are all apostles? Are all prophets? Are all teachers? Do all work miracles? Do all possess gifts of healing? Do all speak with tongues? Do all interpret? But earnestly desire the higher gifts.

"And I will show you a still more excellent way.

"If I speak in the tongues of men and of angels, but have not love, I am a noisy gong or a clanging cymbal. And if I have prophetic powers, and understand all mysteries and all knowledge, and if I have all faith, so as to remove mountains, but have not love, I am nothing. If I give away all I have, and if I deliver my body to be burned, but have not love, I gain nothing.

"Love is patient and kind; love is not jealous or boastful; it is not arrogant or rude. Love does not insist on its own way; it is not irritable or resentful; it does not rejoice at wrong, but rejoices in the right. Love bears all things, believes all things, hopes all things, endures all things.

"Love never ends; as for prophecies, they will pass away; as for tongues, they will cease; as for knowledge, it will pass away. For our knowledge is imperfect and our prophecy is imperfect; but when the perfect comes, the imperfect will pass away. 11 When I was a child, I spoke like a child, I thought like a child, I reasoned like a child; when I became a man, I gave up childish ways. For now we see in a mirror dimly, but then face to face. Now I know in part; then I shall understand fully, even as I have been fully understood. So faith, hope, love abide, these three; but the greatest of these is love."[21]

OF COURSE!! As for me, this scripture contains everything I need to correctly respond to the commands I received from the Spirit. I was instructed to be patient, to mature, to take life seriously. The scripture also explains the why and wherefore of the command. Love is patient. (1 Cor 13:4) Until I love, I am nothing! (1 Cor 13:3) *AGAPE* LOVE IS MATURITY!! (1 Cor 13:1-2) We

---

[21] 1 Cor 12:4-13:13 (RSV)

are told to make <u>love</u> our aim. (1 Cor 14:1) Whether we are aspiring to the office of bishop, of deacon or a lowly man or woman in the community, we serve <u>seriously</u> and with great confidence in the faith we have in Jesus Christ, becoming pillars and bulwarks of the truth."[22]

Why did it take me so long to see this? Could it be because I was not aware of our genetic flaw? Actually, the early church did recognize the problem of our genetic flaw at the counsel of Trent, but it did not soak in on me before reading the above scripture.

These days, the problem is often referred to as "original sin." Original sin is discussed in the Catholic Catechism and in the Catholic Encyclopedia. But, the term Original Sin does not appear as such in the Holy Bible. A Wikipedia article on that term sets out the positions of both Protestants and Catholics.

The simple fact is that we cannot, and, even if we could, we are not entitled to, think like God. For one thing, we do not have all of the information which he has, to work with. Our own best interests are not the paramount interests. This lack of ability limits our function, even though in a limited sense we are gods.[23] Often, a sacrifice of our own best-interests is required for the good of the whole, like cutting off a gangrenous finger to protect the whole body. This is also true as to spiritual gangrene, but we cannot sense it.

Back to my interview with the priest in Jerusalem, the priest and I both lost sight of that fact. It should not have mattered to the priest whether or not I had become possessed by an evil spirit. His questioning satisfied nothing more than his curiosity. If I was possessed, it was the possessing spirit that was evil, not me. He could have provisionally prayed for the spirit to be cast out. Actually, that is what he ended up doing. He also told me to cough,[24] to expel any evil, just in case.

---

[22] See 1 Tim 3:1-16
[23] John 10: 34-36

For my own part, with a little faith, I had nothing to fear from an evil spirit. If it had managed to possess me, a simple prayer and fasting would have dispossessed it.[25] If I had faith, even a little, that I was endowed with the power to heal with my hands, any evil spirit could not have stayed within me.

In the spiritual life, success requires that we capture and strive to retain the attitude and perspectives of little children. They begin life full of faith. Jesus said: "Verily I say unto you, Except ye turn, and become as little children, ye shall in no wise enter into the kingdom of heaven."[26] Again, "Jesus said, Suffer the little children, and forbid them not, to come unto me: for to such belongeth the kingdom of heaven."[27]

As little children, we are not entitled to disavow the authority of the church which Jesus established through St. Peter: "And I also say unto thee, that thou art Peter, and upon this rock I will build my church; and the gates of Hell shall not prevail against it. I will give unto thee the keys of the kingdom of heaven: and whatsoever thou shalt bind on earth shall be bound in heaven; and whatsoever thou shalt loose on earth shall be loosed in heaven."[28] We are to render unto Caesar what is Caesar's and unto God what is God's.[29] We are not given a choice. Scripture explicitly says that the Church of Peter is God's church. Nothing could be more clearly said.

That is why I joined the Catholic Church, not because it is the "right." Church. It is not my purpose to convert anyone to the Catholic Church. God knows it has its problems. However, it is my purpose to unearth and expose the most deadly and pernicious flaw

---

[24] He said that an exiting evil spirit often causes one to cough. He explained that he wanted me to cough, just in case.

[25] Matt 17:21

[26] Matt 18:3 (ASV)

[27] Matt 19:14 (ASV)

[28] Matt 16:18-19 (ASV)

[29] Matt 22:21

which we have as humans. It requires the attention and the effort of everyone to overcome and correct by following the new commandment given us by Jesus: "A new commandment I give unto you, that ye love one another; even as I have loved you, that ye also love one another."[30] This is *agape* love. The commands in my vision tell me how to become *agape* love. They have to do with attitude, rather than specific acts that I control.

But, I have raced ahead of myself. Regardless, I submit that correcting this flaw will remove the major impediment to the workings of the Holy Spirit in carnal man, making him a charismatic son of God and brother of Christ, able to move mountains through faith. Now, I will return to my narrative and the first clear indication that the Holy Spirit was intervening in my life in a real and concrete way. It occurred immediately upon my return from the holy land.

---

[30] John 13:34 (ASV)

Chapter 9. Prophesy Encountered.

When I returned from the Holy Land, the Lord demonstrated to me that prophesy is real. I was full of joy and love, as I checked my mailbox at home. It contained chilling news, a notice to appear before the Office of Professional Responsibility (OPR) in Washington DC.

A hearing had been scheduled to inquire into whether I had abused my power and authority as an attorney in the Organized Crime and Racketeering Strike-force. Attorneys in the Strike-Force were vested with great authority and leeway in their activity. For instance, all law enforcement personnel were at our disposal. The states all cooperate with this power and furnish assistance when requested. I could fly anywhere in the world on my own authority and with a full expense account, in pursuit of an investigation. Each attorney generated his own investigations from any source whatever. If an investigation was opened concerning any individual, the chances were more than 90% that he would spend the rest of his life behind bars. One can imagine that with such awesome authority, came awesome responsibility to avoid its abuse. Even the slightest hint that I was making an official inquiry of a charity concerning the deductibility of a donation, was suspect. That is why my supervisor had turned the matter over to the OPR without any investigation or inquiry on his own part. His knee-jerk reflex protected his own position.

I had to appear in Washington at the end of the week. I knew this was an extremely serious matter. It could ruin my career and even cost me my license to practice law. I had no idea what the accusation concerned, since I had not yet returned to work.

When I reported for work the next morning, I learned that my supervisor in Washington D.C., the main office of the strike-force,

79

had made the accusation. I learned that a co-worker of mine, the temporary head of our Miami office, had told our Washington supervisor that I had contacted a charitable organization concerning a donation I had made, but he had not mentioned that it was on his orders. Unbeknown to either of us, contact of this nature for the personal benefit of the attorney is specifically prohibited by the Code of Federal Regulations.

I had made the contact pursuant to specific instructions by the head of the Miami office and over my own protest because I knew it was a waste of time. I knew the charity was a valid 501 C(3) charity, because I had checked before making the donation.

The head of our Miami office wanted everything to remain squeaky clean until his confirmation. Therefore, he wanted to make sure that the donation was above reproach and that it was made to a qualified charitable organization.

When he reported it to Washington in his regular weekly report, our supervisor, knowing of the prohibition, immediately turned it over to the OPR. Of course, the contact could be construed as an effort to insure, <u>after the fact</u>, that my donation was tax deductible. This inquiry could be construed by the charity as an attempted black-mail. I was very uneasy about this and considered my entire career to be in jeopardy.

In the middle of the week, I attended a charismatic worship and prayer meeting at my church. While participating, I began to feel a powerful urge to open my Bible. In response, I got up from my chair and went to the back of the room, to do so in privacy. I had heard that some people "cut the Bible" by opening it randomly for a "word of knowledge" from the first passage that their eyes fall upon. I had never done this, but felt urged to do so at that time.

The Bible opened and my eyes fell upon the following passage at Psalm 3:6-8, "I will not be afraid of ten thousands of the people that have set themselves against me round about. Arise, O Jehovah; save me, O my God: for thou hast smitten all mine enemies upon the cheek bone; Thou hast broken the teeth of the wicked.
80

Salvation belongeth unto Jehovah: Thy blessing be upon thy people." I must admit that the comfort I felt from this was a bit tenuous. Dare I rely upon it?

When I attended the hearing that Friday in Washington D.C., I found that it was actually a preliminary examination and not a full-blown hearing. I was examined by one man in a small room, with a desk between us. There was no court reporter or other trappings of a formal hearing. He simply told me about the accusation and invited me to explain myself. I told him that I had only made the contact because of specific orders from the head of the Miami office and that I had done so under protest. I also handed him a copy of a provision in the Code of Federal Regulations (CFR) which I had discovered the day before. It indicates that any charitable organization, organized under section 501 C(3) of the CFR and who was listed as being such in the current annual publication of the CFR was entitled to accept charitable donations from the public and the public could rely upon such listing in making donations.

Therefore, my contact could not have worked to my benefit because this charity was listed. They could not be black-mailed, falsely accused of something or otherwise abused by the simple inquiry I was alleged to have made! The contact could only have worked to my detriment. I then handed the examiner a copy of the current listing in the CFR, which included the 501 C(3) charity to which I had donated my boat.

The examiner looked at the papers carefully, picked up his telephone and called his superior and explained the entire matter to him. Upon hanging up the phone, he looked at me with a smile and told me to go home and forget all about this. I did so, but thanked the Lord all the way. I am not sure who my enemies were that caused me to be reported, but their teeth were surely broken. This is not an endorsement of cutting the Bible, but it is an endorsement of responding to the urgings of the Holy Spirit and conformation that prophesy is real!

Chapter 10. A Place In the Community.

After my trip to Washington, I believed that the Lord not only loved me and blessed me with his charisms, but that he would protect me so that I could do his will. During the following two years, I tried all that I knew to discern his will for me.

Please note, I gradually realized that God does not need me to know his will and he does not need my help to do anything. My independent efforts, especially those aimed at discernments such as going into the seminary, were actually attempts to control the will of God.

True, my motives were pure, but attempting to discern was a mistake. I had already experienced his urgings and had obeyed. I knew that if he wants me to do something, he knows how to tell me so. My efforts were actually manifestations of the basic flaw first exhibited by Adam and Eve, original sin! I wanted to decide what to do. I now realize that this is nothing more than a lack of patience. Will I never learn? Can patience be learned?

Without realizing I was making a mistake in pursuing discernment, I obtained a spiritual director, a well-respected and experienced priest, and went to him regularly. Also, I learned to formally practice Ignatian Discernment of Spirits. I even did a month-long retreat, but I was not good at it. Nothing seemed to work.

I knew I wanted to serve the Lord in the best possible way and thought that the best and highest service was to become a priest. I told this to my spiritual director and, after several sessions, he suggested that perhaps I should become a postulant for the priesthood with some religious order, as a late vocation. When he opined that I could discern while pursuing my postulancy.

This seemed impossible at the time. Although my marriage had been annulled, I had three children under the age of 18 and was obligated to support them during their minority. No religious order would accept me under those circumstances. However, I contacted my former wife and told her of my hopes. Since our divorce, she had married a successful contractor to NASA and I found her sympathetic and agreeable to my becoming a priest if I could work the other obstacles out.

I proposed to set aside, in trust, sufficient funds to meet my child support obligations for the remainder of the minority of my children. This, I did, and both my former wife and the Redemptorist Order of Priests, after extensive interviews and examinations, accepted me. I was sent to Washington D.C. for my postulancy. They had me attend classes at Catholic University, mostly in philosophy and logics, looking to an eventual doctor's degree in theology.

Without burdening the reader with a long discussion about the Catholic seminary system, I will simply say that I continued my discernment with the Redemptorists for three years before it was made clear to me that the Lord did not want me for the priesthood. I have never regretted my decision to enter their system and hope they have never regretted having me with them. I left with their permission in lieu of taking vows. Having put my hand to the plow, I did not want to return to secular life as a quitter. They said it was Okay.

I would like to add that about a month, perhaps a month and a half, before I went away to join the Redemptorists, I met a very spiritual and beautiful young lady at a prayer meeting. At that time, I was feeling insecure and lonely. I needed company, someone to talk to and share my aspirations with. I called the young lady, who was years younger than I, and told her my situation. I asked if she would please just socialize with me, knowing that I was going into the seminary and not available romantically. She said that she would willingly do so and that when the time came, she would put me on the train herself.

That is the way it happened. But, by the time I left, I knew in my secret heart of hearts that I had fallen in love with her, but did not say so. I was determined to serve my Lord as a priest, if that was his desire. Without my realizing it, by exercising my flaw I had put God in the back seat, so I could drive. I knew he had not told me to be a priest, but stumbled ahead, gushing love and preferring my own judgment to his.

Upon arrival in Washington, I went into the chapel of the Redemptorist's house, kneeled in front of the holy Eucharist, spread my arms and said sub-vocally, "Here I am Lord. I am yours." With that, a vision came before my eyes of a giant white bird, with wings spread, and I could see my face and eyes, round with excitement, peering out from the feathers beneath its wing. I took the bird to be symbolic of the Holy Spirit and was dismayed to see that beside me, also peering excitedly out from the feathers, was the young lady with whom I had fallen in love.

I immediately opened my eyes and said apologetically to the Lord, "No, no, this is a mistake". With that, I closed my eyes again and saw the same vision. After opening my eyes a second time and closing them for the third time, the vision remained. I did not know what to do. So, instead of going back to Florida, I got up and went to my room, disgusted with myself. Despite all of my prior experiences, I did not believe that vision. My faith in them was shaken for three years because of that vision. I did not know how else to react. I was determined not to leave (Adam and Eve all over again) and intended to see it out.

Upon leaving the seminary, three years later, I returned to Texas. Actually, I had no choice, it was the only state in which I was licensed to practice law and I had to make a living. Five more years went by, and I could not get that Florida girl out of my mind. Finally, I decided to try to contact her. I located her telephone number and she answered my call.

On August 6, 1996, Jennifer and I were married. We have been peering out from beneath the wing of the Holy Spirit together, ever since. We lived in Houston for three years, but, somehow, never settled-in.

In January, 1999, we returned to Florida and our home parish, permanently. I took the Florida bar exam and set up my practice. We have remained there to this day. After a few years, I do not have the exact date, I began to lead a Bible study one evening a week. Eventually, that morphed into *Lectio Divina*. I am long retired now, but Jenny works. She is younger than I and will be able to retire soon. How much easier it would have been to simply leave things alone and wait upon the Lord.

All of the foregoing brings us to an explanation of how I was undertaking to comply with the Lord's command to be patient, to mature, and to take life seriously and what it taught me. I did not surface as a great or famous healer. But, the charism has never left me. Occasionally and regularly, authentic healings do occur. I do not make a big deal out of it and do not ballyhoo the occasions, or encourage others to do so. I have simply tried to serve my community, when asked.

During the last 20 years, many people have experienced healing power flowing from my hands and I have regular opportunities to serve the community.

For example, recently, I was enjoying coffee and a snack in a small meeting room, made available for that purpose by my parish. There are usually two long tables at which we sit and chat. In the midst of a chat, one of the men who has observed several healings during my prayers, called out to me. There was a young lady seated beside him whom he had told to go to me for healing prayer. As she arose and came toward me, a friend of hers got up also.

The young lady told me that she had recently suffered unconsciousness from anxiety, that she was a mother and that she was afraid. She asked if I would pray with her. I agreed. I instructed her to take a seat, moved diagonally behind her, placed

86

my hands upon her head and began to pray. At this, I felt the hand of her friend upon my own shoulder. I could feel healing power flowing from my hands and completed my prayers fairly quickly. As I did so, I leaned over, kissed the lady on the head and reclaimed my seat.

The friend of the young lady started to stammer behind me. She had a look of astonishment on her face and began to speak as I turned and looked at her. She said, "I don't know how to say this, so I will just blurt it out. As I put my hand up on your shoulder and you prayed, I could feel electricity going into my body." I sort of acknowledged her experience by nodding my head, then continued to sit down and resumed chatting with my friends.

The next day, I saw the young lady and asked her how she was feeling and she replied that she had been cured. I have noticed her several times since then, at mass. She always looks happy and at peace. Her friends, strangers before the prayers, all greet me now, with smiles on their faces and occasionally stop by to chat.

God designed us to function with the charisms. Scripture shows this and it comports with the practices of St. Paul. They need not be a big deal. All of the charisms have a rightful place in the congregations of all Christian communities. The charisms reflect God's love, guidance and protection for the community. Only our preference for self and a lack of faith inhibits them.

Chapter 11. Gifts Are For Servants.

At first, I confused the announcement that I would heal with my hands with the commands to be patient, to mature and to take life seriously. I was slow to recognize the one as an announcement and the others as commands. Now, I realize that there is a distinction between the announcement and the commands. I was endowed with the gift of healing. That was the announcement. I have no choice about it and I cannot enhance or diminish it. It is what it is and it only requires prayer in faith for me to exercise it.

Much is said about faith in the Bible. With just a little faith, anyone can move mountains or perform miracles of healing. Faith unlocks the healing charism.[31] In short, faith is the key to this charism. We can all do it. The difference is that I was gifted, perhaps, so others can discover it from my example.

The three commands are a different matter. They require both belief and faith on my part, but I cannot cause or control them. I know I gain patience and become mature as I take life seriously. Yet, I cannot gain patience or maturity by <u>choosing</u> to do them. Forcing myself to be patient does not make me patient.

Put in another way, faith enables the functioning of charisms that already reside within us. I was told while in the spirit that I have the gift of healing, forever. It has been turned loose within me. I was endowed with it.

Whether I have sufficient faith to allow the charism to function on any given occasion, is up to me. The flood gates have never opened. I know my faith is weak. I must help it grow. But, the Lord makes the healing power somehow squeak past the quenching power of my weak and insipid faith.

---

[31] Luke 18:1-8

How loving and merciful that he should do such a thing. The gift does not benefit me, but is for everyone else. Despite the uncontrollable pride that gushed from and sloshed about within me at first, I cannot discern any physical benefit to me. Still, that does not make me a humble servant. True, the unmerited gift strengthens my own faith, but that is a spiritual thing. The healing charism works a <u>physical</u> benefit to others with bad egoistic pressures and implications for me.[32]

From the Bible, world literature, and from personal experience, I am convinced the gift of healing can function with or without the knowledge of the recipient. It can also function with the laying on of hands or from a distance. Human touch is a plus, as is the faith and hope of the recipient.

Unfortunately, the recipient of healing prayer can easily mislead himself into believing that he has been healed, when he has not. Therefore, the recipient's belief is clearly not a criterion for whether healing has occurred. Often, time is required to truly tell whether healing occurred.

The faith-filled belief of he who prays and the healing power of God is what are important. The sick person himself, and the passage of time, are the best determinates of whether or not a healing has taken place.

Some pretenders encourage the recipient to believe or to "step out in faith." This merely encourages him to disregard faith in God and to idolize the purported healer. Encouraging a recipient to "step out" shifts the focus from what is helpful, faith in God, to the will of the recipient. It also shifts blame for any failure to the recipient and away from the prayer. Thus, the charlatan generates a scape-goat to take the blame for failures.

Clearly, the Holy Spirit does not need assistance from any personal power we have to heal ourselves. His healing action flows from his *agape* love, unleashed by the faith of he who prays. This

---

[32] Matt 9:5 *et seq*

is simply because the sort of prayed for healing is always miraculous, an <u>exception</u> to the natural process of healing. Although miraculous intervention was predestined by God before we were born, it is nevertheless, a miracle.

Its divine purpose is patently to bring people closer to belief in the love and power of God, not belief in some sort of healing power of a charismatic person. All of the charisms have this same purpose. Miracles make us perceive that there is a creator God with absolute power over nature, that he loves us and that he will change things for those who love him. He is like a doting father favoring his child. Why do we denigrate them? But for our original flaw, how do we <u>dare</u> denigrate them?

According to scripture, the ordinary use for charisms is to serve the church community, to feed and maintain its faith. <u>Faith</u> in the healing power of God is what is important.[33] Faith is a gift. It grows out of belief. Little children automatically believe in the existence of things which they cannot sense. We were all born with faith. It was a gift. It is what made us believe unquestioningly in Santa Claus and the tooth fairy. As we become independent and able to survive the dangers of the world, we learn to test things first, rather than believe them in faith. This becoming independent and able to survive tends to quench faith. We demand to know for ourselves what is good and what is bad for us. That is a manifestation of the basic flaw of Adam and Eve at work in us.

By a simple change in attitude, the seeds of faith can be rejuvenated and made to grow. Faith can be awakened and made to grow by unquestioning acceptance of something. This is what is referred to as a "leap" of faith. It is belief in something that cannot be seen. Belief does not require faith if one insists on testing first. But faith requires belief because one cannot have faith in something if he is able to test it.

---

[33] Acts 3:16

The relation between faith and belief is difficult to grasp. This is mostly because of our natural self-interest. True, self-interest is needed for survival, but it frustrates the working of the charisms. Jesus explained the requirement of faith to his disciples. Again, matter enclosed in brackets is added for clarity. Underling or italics are also supplied to help clarify. The reader to test what appears brackets, but should try to have faith in what is quoted:

"And the disciples came to the other side [Of the lake where Jesus was preaching] and forgot to take bread. And Jesus said unto them, 'Take heed and beware of the leaven of the Pharisees and Sadducees.' And they reasoned among themselves, saying, 'We took no bread.' [They were worried because they had nothing to eat.] And Jesus perceiving it said, O ye of <u>little faith, why reason ye among yourselves</u>, because ye have no bread? <u>Do ye not yet perceive</u>, neither <u>remember</u> the five loaves of the five thousand, and how many baskets ye took up? Neither the seven loaves of the four thousand, and how many baskets ye took up? [His miraculous power to provide bread had already been shown to them. They should have had faith that he would feed them as a matter of course.] <u>How is it that ye do not perceive</u> that I spake not to you concerning bread? [Why do you subvert the actual thrust of my parable to the selfish needs of your belly?] But beware of the leaven of the Pharisees and Sadducees. [Their teaching grows among you <u>like</u> leaven in bread. This is the original sin of Adam and Eve at work.] They understood that he bade them not beware of the leaven of bread, but of the teaching of the Pharisees and Sadducees."[34]

The disciples understood and believed Jesus' teaching after he explained the subtleties to them. However, there is nothing in the text to show that they began to have <u>faith</u> in him, no matter what, or that they no longer suffered from original sin. They wanted to understand for themselves. Despite his prior demonstration of his

---

[34] Matt 16:5-12

miraculous power to feed them, they had no faith that he would take care of their needs. They did not have child-like faith in him

Then, Scripture shows that Jesus tested the faith in their faith by asking, "Who do you say that I am?" There were various faithless replies, but St. Peter responded that Jesus is the Christ, the son of the living God. Jesus then said, "Blessed art thou, Simon Bar-Jonah: for flesh and blood hath not revealed it unto thee, but my Father who is in heaven."[35]

Thus, Peter's faith in Jesus allowed him to accept spiritual knowledge, not based on reason, but as it was revealed to him by the Father. This is an example of man's ability to put aside self-interest and listen with his spirit, in faith. If faith was not involved, Peter would not have made his declaration. None of the disciples understood that Jesus was teaching in parables, that the erroneous teaching of the Pharisees and the Sadducees could spread error among them all like yeast in dough.

Child-like belief avoids reasoning in a self-interested mode and allows us to have righteous understanding from God. The key to grasping Jesus' parables is clearly signaled from within the parable itself, every time. Pre-existing belief in Jesus is always required in order to have faith that what he said is true. True faith is the absolute, child-like knowledge that the belief is true.

The mistaken perception of the disciples in the parable was caused by the same flaw in reasoning as Adam and Eve. They reasoned from the standpoint of their own interests. Seeing that the fruit was good did not mean that it was permissible for Adam and Eve to disobey God's command to leave it alone. This same self-interested, flawed reasoning applies to the commission of any sin.

Actually, what would have been good for them was to obey God. There is nothing in scripture that says either Adam or Eve were hungry, or otherwise needed to partake of the forbidden fruit. This same selfish error is consistently made by man throughout

---

[35] See Matt 16:16 *et seq* (ASV)

history because it is based upon love of self over love of God. To automatically subject love of self to love of God is the very basis of faith in him. Jesus said so:

"And Jesus answered and said unto them, Verily I say unto you, If ye have faith, and doubt not, ye shall not only do what is done to the fig tree, [Jesus had withered the fig tree by a simple word of command.] but even if ye shall say unto this mountain, Be thou taken up and cast into the sea, it shall be done. And all things, whatsoever ye shall ask in prayer, believing, ye shall receive."[36] NOTE: Jesus is talking about faith-filled belief, see the first sentence. He is talking about faith-filled belief in what is unseen-the willing power of God to grant what is asked.

Concerning our propensity for self-interest, it is clear that baptism does not remove our flaw. Baptism removes the stain of original sin and makes us pure. But, it does not correct our common flaw concerning future sin. Our propensity for self-interest, our constant desire to control circumstances and protect ourselves at all costs, our love of self, remains. Jesus teaches us that to have faith is our solution. We can protect ourselves better through faith than any other way. More than purity, faith brings about justification and faith is something we can control. We can decide to have faith, just as we can choose to be patient. If we believe, it will grow.

We are taught that all who have been baptized in the Spirit have the Holy Spirit residing within them, forever. All who have the Holy Spirit within them, of necessity, have the charisms also, for the charisms come from the Holy Spirit. Faith is the tool that opens the spiritual faucet of the charisms already residing in us, just like Jesus said.

We cannot control the amount of faith we have, but we can decide to believe in order to have and grow faith. Belief is not faith, but faith begins to grow from, and out of, belief. One must

---

[36] Matt 21:21-22 (ASV)

simply <u>trust</u> the Holy Spirit, relying upon the *agape* love he has for us and he <u>will</u> move mountains, because he loves us.

As for me, what a fool I was. I was given urgings more powerful and accurate than any Ignatian discernment and I constantly tried to impatiently throw their benefit away. I merely had to faithfully wait for urgings.

Why, you may ask, if I know so much and if I am endowed with the gift of healing, am I not a famous healer, like St Peter? The answer is probably my lack of faith. That is why I referred to it earlier as "insipid.":

"And Jesus rebuked him; and the demon went out of him: and the boy was cured from that hour. Then came the disciples to Jesus apart, and said, Why could not we cast it out? And he saith unto them, Because of your little faith: for verily I say unto you, If ye have faith as a grain of mustard seed, ye shall say unto this mountain, Remove hence to yonder place; and it shall remove; and nothing shall be impossible unto you."[37]

Earlier, Jesus had given the disciples power to dispel evil spirits. Implicit in this scripture is the teaching that all Christians have the charisms within them, for Jesus implies that is separate from the power he had given them. And, with <u>sufficient</u> faith, <u>anyone</u> can move mountains. This is not mere speculation. The Holy Spirit, the source of charismatic power, resides within Christians, but faith is what gives us access to the <u>power</u> of the charisms of the Holy Spirit.

Despite a lack of faith to move mountains, the Holy Spirit often chooses some of us, enabling them to especially exercise specific charisms. These are people <u>he</u> chooses. However, <u>any</u> of us can prayerfully seek the charisms and induce the Holy Spirit to release them to us, if we are zealous.[38]

---

[37] Matt 17:18-20 (ASV)
[38] 1 Cor 14:12

Therefore, it is clear that those with charisms or even with faith sufficient to move mountains are special. It means they have gained the faith which is available to us all or they have a special dispensation.

All of this leads to a discussion of love. Without love, we are personally nothing, even if we benefit others in every way.[39] Each person in whom the Holy Spirit resides contains the entire Spirit, including the power of all charisms. Whether one drop of water or a whole ocean, each particle of water is entirely HO^2. Likewise, the Holy Spirit residing in us is 100% Holy Spirit. The charisms are in us just as much as he is in us. It is merely a matter of asking for their release and empowerment through faith.

The gifts are given for service, not for ego-filled ownership. Self-interest, the original flaw, makes us want to control the power of the charism. If we cannot be the source of healing power, the flaw makes us seek the ability to turn it on and off. It makes us want to possess and control the power of God. This is not faithfully serving, it is service that is flawed by self-interest. Anything can be made to serve God. Everything does. The only thing we can create by ourselves, is love. Love is God-like and fills up what is lacking of the afflictions of Christ on our behalf.[40] It is *agape* love perfected in us that is our own personal reward for loving God. If we have love, faith will grow.

[39] 1 Cor 13:1-13
[40] Col 1:24

Chapter 12. Toward Maturity.

To test whether the commands to be patient, mature and take life seriously have borne fruit, I submit the following observations: The most difficult of all is the command to be patient. Patience is not my long-suit. I realize I needed the command. The command for patience has kept me in harness as I stumbled and fell through the years since receiving it. The footprints I leave during my life have never been in a straight line, but I do believe they have followed a generally straighter track since receiving that command. Even so, I still have to <u>consciously</u> seek patience. It allows us to savor the urgings of the Holy Spirit, rather than automatically responding to whatever is in my path and allows me to minimize self-interest.

Painting with the broadest brush possible and narrowing to the finest line possible, my journey as a Christian has proved the right one for me. I have studied the great religions with a critical approach, sufficient to finally adopt Christianity. I am not proselytizing. I am merely undertaking to show that there is reasoning in the path I have followed. Most religious conviction is a matter of geography. Where we live largely determines what religion we practice.

The Lord said, "And other sheep I have, which are not of this fold: them also I must bring, and they shall hear my voice: and they shall become one flock, one shepherd."[41] I do not know what this truly and fully means, but I do know that the Lord also said, "Judge not, that ye be not judged."[42] Therefore, I am content to allow him to guide us into an appropriate flock for the journey into

---

[41] John 10:16
[42] Matt 7:1 (ASV)

heaven. God willing, I will learn contentment in all things. I am content about Christianity.

As for choosing Catholicism, I did so primarily because Catholics have a special advantage over others. I consider it manifest that Protestants follow a path to heaven and the Catholic Church agrees. However, the head of our church was specifically granted authority to bind and loose sins on the earth.[43] I am aware that this authority was also granted elsewhere in the Bible to all of the apostles and to the church community as a whole. Nevertheless, I do not want to squander any advantage that is available to me. All of the apostles and all of the churches charismatically responding to the Holy Spirit were "Catholic" originally.

A second, and more important, advantage is that the Lord specifically licensed the apostles to commemorate his sacrifice at the Lord's supper, for our physical nourishment (The bread-his body) and the forgiveness of our sins (The wine-his blood). Consuming them in remembrance of him is the highest form of worship the Lord gave us.[44]

"Whoever eats the bread and drinks the cup of the Lord in an unworthy manner is guilty of the body and the blood of the Lord, bringing judgment of condemnation on himself if he does not discern the body. If a man is mistaken in his own judgment, he will be chastised at the final judgment, but not condemned with the rest of the world. The Last supper is not a normal meal. That should be taken at home before coming together to eat of it and to drink."[45] By partaking unworthily, we can be condemned. Yet, we partake in response to a specific command that we do so.[46] This means we have to do the best we can to do so worthily.

---

[43] Matt 16:18-19
[44] See 1 Cor 11:23-32
[45] See 1 Cor 11:17-34 (RSV)
[46] IBID

98

Spiritually speaking, this is an extremely serious and obligatorily business. I feel that, sinner that I am, I require all of the help that I can get to obey Jesus' command worthily. Jesus commanded the 12 disciples, whom he later bade his apostles, to eat the bread and drink the wine in memory of him.[47] Therefore, the blessings of commemorating the last supper, I dare not abandon. Nor, dare I undertake to obey the command without the assistance of those specifically authorized to conduct the meal while we are accordingly gathered together as the church of Jesus Christ.[48] To me, I have no choice but to be Catholic, despite and of its shortcomings, caused by men. Mine is to obey, despite my protests. I have been given no right to reject.

As for the rest, we are all obliged to do more than obey the command of Jesus at the Last Supper. We have an obligation to do what we can to help each other and ensure that we all get to heaven together. I have tried to do what everyone has the right to expect of me, heal with my hands. In discharging this obligation, I point to the entire legacy of writings and traditions of the apostles. They fill up what is lacking in the afflictions of Christ to fulfill the word of God[49] Each of us must separately travel down the way to justification and righteousness.

We have been blessed by being taught the manner and means to reach toward the light which brightens our path. The manner and means have been taught since the Scriptures were first written. Even so, the basic flaw is within us all and it interferes with our reach toward the Lord and his wisdom.

The highest and best way to reach toward the Lord and his wisdom was beautifully taught by St John of the cross, especially in his poem, "Stanzas Of The Soul." It is extremely difficult for anyone who does not already practice contemplative prayer to understand this poem. But, basically, it teaches and shows that we

---

[47] IBID
[48] IBID
[49] Cor 1:24

must bring our senses to quiet in order to allow our spirit to love and learn from the Lord. The senses interfere, like noise, with the focus and hearing of the spirit.

This may sound like gobbledygook, at first, but St. John of the Cross did not make it up. He teaches a legitimate method of prayer. And, it was first taught by the Lord.[50] It is the only way I know to consistently address the Lord in spirit. When doing so, our basic flaw cannot interfere, for it is couched in the senses. With the senses quiet, we can truly hear without self-defeating self-interest.

Putting the "Stanzas of the Soul" aside until we are more mature, St. Paul described the beginnings of mature worship in the second through fourth chapters of his first letter to the Corinthians. With all that is within me, I urge the reader to carefully study these Scriptures, if he seeks to become a spiritual man. They contain the common teaching of all the apostles about the Holy Spirit's action within us and guide us in how to become spiritual men. These lines of scripture require and deserve careful and introspective examination preliminary to all else.

To assist in that end, I set these scriptures out in Chapter 12 in the American Standard translation. The archaic language should slow the reading down and cause greater introspection. If the reader feels urged to delve more carefully into the teachings of these scriptures, he may consult Strong's Exhaustive Concordance for a word by word translation from the Latin, in context. To avoid any human dilution whatever, one must consult the original writings, which are in Greek.

At any rate, the teaching of St. Paul for those who would follow the path to righteousness, sanctification and redemption, the path to acquiring the power of a spiritual man is in that scripture sequence. Not knowing the reader's level of familiarity with scripture, I have also placed succinct comments on the scripture, in brackets, as an additional aid.

---

[50] Matt 6:6

In addition to regular prayer and participating in community worship, we should join an ongoing study of Scripture through *Lectio Divina*. This is the best possible beginning on the path to spiritual manhood. Like the disciples in the upper room at Pentecost, the first steps include receiving the gift of tongues.[51] Praying in tongues is extremely important for those who seek to become a spiritual man.[52] It is also the most easily attainable of the charisms.

It maximizes direct communication between the man and the Lord through the Holy Spirit which resides within us.[53] The importance for the unspiritual man to pray in tongues cannot be over-stated. The Holy Spirit, residing within us with *agape* love, helps us in our infirmity to mature.

When we pray in tongues, we release the Spirit to intercede for us with sighs too deep for words intelligible to ourselves. He who searches our hearts knows the mind of the Spirit for he makes intercession for us according to the will of God.[54] In this way, we can wait for salvation with patience, because we know in faith that the Holy Spirit is interceding on our behalf with the best possible prayers for healing our infirmity, for our salvation and for responses to our supplications.[55]

Therefore, praying in tongues is a much-needed charism, easily attainable by all. We have spiritual men pray over us for the gift, or we simply ask for it of the Holy Spirit, in faith.

Even so, we must learn how to employ the gift, for it is easily quenched by beginners. Release of the charism normally includes a relaxation of the will, a release of control. We are trying to allow the Holy Spirit to pray on our behalf in a tongue that is foreign to us.

---

[51] See Acts 2:1 et seq
[52] See 1 Cor 12 et seq
[53] IBID
[54] Rom 8:26-27
[55] Rom 8:18-33

The relaxation and release can most easily be attained by going inside of our person with the inner eye to seek peace. As we begin to find peace, the will relaxes its rigid control and the intercession of the Holy Spirit begins to bubble out of us in words that only the Lord understands.

One should not be concerned if this charism is not released instantly. It will happen, often when least expected, in prayer or meditation or even during peaceful relaxation.

When I was prayed over for the gift, nothing happened for a couple of weeks. Then, one evening while I was watching TV alone, the prayer in tongues began to bubble out.

I know another who received the gift while in the shower. After receiving the gift, caution is advised to ensure that prayer in tongues does not degenerate into a mere repetitious mantra. We are not in control of the mysterious groanings of the Holy Spirit and we want to release his prayers on our behalf, not quench them with the willful control of a mantra. Let the spirit soar. If there is repetition by the Spirit, that is his business.

We are instructed to seek all of the gifts, especially the higher gifts. Imagine the peace available to the mother who can, with faith, seek and receive physical healing for her child or husband. Entire families and communities benefit from the charisms. We can allow the gift of tongues to encourage us to go further. The twelfth chapter of Paul's first letter to the Corinthians can be our guide. We cannot even imagine the depth and breadth of the love the Lord has for us:

"For the gifts and the calling of God are not repented of [Not regretted]. For as ye in time past were disobedient to God, but now have obtained mercy by their [through the Jews'] disobedience, even so have these [The surviving Jews] also now been disobedient, that by the mercy shown to you they [The Jews] also may now obtain mercy. For God hath shut up all [Jews and Gentiles alike] unto disobedience, that he might have mercy upon all. O the depth of the riches both of the wisdom and the

102

knowledge of God! how unsearchable are his judgments, and his ways past tracing out! [No one can understand or discover his plans] For who hath known the mind of the Lord? or who hath been his counsellor? or who hath first given to him, and it shall be recompensed unto [repaid to] him again? For of him, and through him, and unto him, are all things. To him (be) the glory forever. Amen."[56]

Dare we turn away from such generosity without seeking the gifts? I think not. They are more precious than gold. The gifts are avenues to converse with God in a two-way conversation; to learn authoritatively and accurately from the teacher; to repair our bodies and fulfill the desires of our spirits.

A preparatory prayer in tongues seems preparing to pray for the healing of others, or activating any of the gifts, begins a two-way dialog between the Lord and the Spirit, who entreats on our behalf. The Lord knows what we need, but we are expected to ask for it in faith. How better can a dialog be maintained, than through an interpreter speaking in his native tongue?

This story will not end until my life on earth ends. But, at least, this writing brings it down to date. God bless you.

Chapter 13. Mature In Spirit.

My fervent prayer is that the reader may find himself drawn to the spiritual life the same as I. Come, get aboard that great white bird. Allow your eyes to become wide with wonder as we soar away from the precipice. He will bear us up to our places in the body of Christ. St. Augustine spoke for us all when he acknowledged to our God that our hearts are restless until they rest in him.

As St. Peter observed about Paul's writing, "So also our beloved brother Paul wrote to you according to the wisdom given him, speaking of this as he does in all his letters. There are some things in them hard to understand, which the ignorant and unstable twist to their own destruction, as they do the other scriptures. You therefore, beloved, knowing this beforehand, beware lest you be carried away with the error of lawless men and lose your own stability. But grow in the grace and knowledge of our Lord and Savior Jesus Christ."[57]

I close this confession with a quote from 1 Corinthians, Paul's invitation to begin the spiritual life in the power of God, and an admonition to prayerfully seek the charisms. They are a bridge between the carnal and the spiritual. He makes it manifest that we are all one in love. Here are Paul's difficult words with my iterations in brackets:

"When I came to you, brethren, I did not come proclaiming to you the testimony of God in lofty words or wisdom. For I decided to know nothing among you except Jesus Christ and him crucified. And I was with you in weakness and in much fear and trembling; and my speech and my message were not in plausible words of

---

[57] 2 Peter 3:15-18 (RSV)

wisdom, but in demonstration of the Spirit and of power, that your faith might not rest in the wisdom of men but in the power of God.

"Yet among the mature [Spiritual men] we do impart wisdom, although it is not a wisdom of this age or of the rulers of this age, who are doomed to pass away. But we impart a secret and hidden wisdom of God, which God decreed before the ages for our [We believers'] glorification. None of the rulers of this age understood this; for if they [Both the Jews and the Roman Gentiles] had, they would not have crucified the Lord of glory. But, as it is written, 'What no eye has seen, nor ear heard, nor the heart of man conceived, what God has prepared for those who love him,' God has revealed to us through the Spirit. For the Spirit searches everything, even the depths of God. [The Spirit knows and communicates to us the deepest truths of God and of man.] For what person knows a man's thoughts except the spirit of the man which is in him? So also no one comprehends the thoughts of God except the Spirit of God. Now we have received not the spirit of the world, but the Spirit which is from God, that we might understand the gifts bestowed on us by God. And we impart this in words not taught by human wisdom but taught by the Spirit, interpreting spiritual truths to those who possess the Spirit. [The apostles speak directly from, and only from, God.]

"The unspiritual man does not receive the gifts of the Spirit of God, for they are folly to him, and he is not able to understand them because they are spiritually discerned. The spiritual man judges all things, but is himself to be judged by no one. 'For who has known the mind of the Lord so as to instruct him?' But we have the mind of Christ."[58]

"But I, brethren, could not address you as spiritual men, but as men of the flesh, as babes in Christ. I fed you with milk, not solid food; for you were not ready for it; and even yet you are not ready, for you are still of the flesh. For while there is jealousy and strife among you, are you not of the flesh, and behaving like ordinary

---

[58] 1 Cor 2:1-16

men? For when one says, 'I belong to Paul,' and another, 'I belong to Apollos,' are you not merely men?

"What then is Apollos? What is Paul? Servants through whom you believed, as the Lord assigned to each. I planted, Apollos watered, but God gave the growth. So neither he who plants nor he who waters is anything, but only God who gives the growth. He who plants and he who waters are equal, and each shall receive his wages according to his labor. For we are God's fellow workers; you are God's field, God's building.

"According to the grace of God given to me, like a skilled master builder I laid a foundation, and another man is building upon it. Let each man take care how he builds upon it. For no other foundation can any one lay than that which is laid, which is Jesus Christ. Now if any one builds on the foundation with gold, silver, precious stones, wood, hay, straw - each man's work will become manifest; for the Day will disclose it, because it will be revealed with fire, and the fire will test what sort of work each one has done. If the work which any man has built on the foundation survives, he will receive a reward. If any man's work is burned up, he will suffer loss, though he himself will be saved, but only as through fire.

"Do you not know that you are God's temple and that God's Spirit dwells in you? 17 If any one destroys God's temple, God will destroy him. For God's temple is holy, and that temple you are.

"Let no one deceive himself. If any one among you thinks that he is wise in this age, let him become a fool that he may become wise. For the wisdom of this world is folly with God. For it is written, 'He catches the wise in their craftiness,' 20 and again, 'The Lord knows that the thoughts of the wise are futile.' So let no one boast of men. For all things are yours, whether Paul or Apollos or Cephas or the world or life or death or the present or the future, all are yours; and you are Christ's; and Christ is God's.

"This is how one should regard us, as servants of Christ and stewards of the mysteries of God. Moreover it is required of stewards that they be found trustworthy. But with me it is a very small thing that I should be judged by you or by any human court. I do not even judge myself. I am not aware of anything against myself, but I am not thereby acquitted. It is the Lord who judges me. Therefore do not pronounce judgment before the time, before the Lord comes, who will bring to light the things now hidden in darkness and will disclose the purposes of the heart. Then every man will receive his commendation from God.

"I have applied all this to myself and Apollos for your benefit, brethren, that you may learn by us not to go beyond what is written, that none of you may be puffed up in favor of one against another. For who sees anything different in you? What have you that you did not receive? If then you received it, why do you boast as if it were not a gift?

"Already you are filled! Already you have become rich! Without us you have become kings! And would that you did reign, so that we might share the rule with you! For I think that God has exhibited us apostles as last of all, like men sentenced to death; because we have become a spectacle to the world, to angels and to men. We are fools for Christ's sake, but you are wise in Christ. We are weak, but you are strong. You are held in honor, but we in disrepute. To the present hour we hunger and thirst, we are ill-clad and buffeted and homeless, and we labor, working with our own hands. When reviled, we bless; when persecuted, we endure; when slandered, we try to conciliate; we have become, and are now, as the refuse of the world, the offscouring of all things.

"I do not write this to make you ashamed, but to admonish you as my beloved children. For though you have countless guides in Christ, you do not have many fathers. For I became your father in Christ Jesus through the gospel. I urge you, then, be imitators of me. Therefore I sent to you Timothy, my beloved and faithful child in the Lord, to remind you of my ways in Christ, as I teach them everywhere in every church. 18 Some are arrogant, as though I were not coming to you. But I will come to you soon, if the Lord wills, and I will find out not the talk of these arrogant people but their power."[59]

Chapter 14. Belief.

The following brings down to date the confession about my life, that Jesus Christ is Lord, and what the author believes about the charism of healing. Therefore, the autobiography is complete. This final chapter pulls them together.

Again, books like *A Key To Charismatic Renewal In The Catholic Church* assist us in how to seek the gifts, but they cannot make us understand them. This is a difficult and crucial, concept for potential servants of the churches, regardless of denomination. Baptism of the Holy Spirit gives us more than a ticket into heaven. It also gives us the charisms. They are part of the warp and woof of the Spirit that came to reside in us.

It is a basic truth that spiritual gifts transcend human understanding. They <u>relate</u> to human experience, but the essence does not relate to human knowledge. Every true charismatic gift and every experience of them is actually miraculous, emanating from the Holy Spirit that abides in us. Even so, the spiritual gifts are available to every individual of every church which is composed of worshipers who have been baptized in the name of the Holy Spirit. But, the gifts can be lost, or retracted by the Holy Spirit because of a lack of faith.

This was made clear during the first and second journeys of St. Paul, described in the book of Acts. There, we learn that the apostles would establish churches through prayer and baptism, then they would appoint leaders from the congregation. The climate was right at this time in history for man to be spiritually nurtured and to grow. People could readily accept that the Holy Spirit is real and abides in them. They did not quench the Spirit. He manifested freely among them, guided, taught and prophesied through them. This allowed Paul and the other apostles to establish churches and move on, leaving the teaching to the Spirit.

Looking back to the beginning of man, the breathing of life into Adam and Eve was the inception of the body of Christ. From its inception, the incipient body multiplied and grew freely, but it was not perfect. It was a wild and defiant creature, but its genes adapted to the environment as it pursued its survival through self-seeking.

The first great plateau was reached with the birth of Noah, the offspring of Lamech, the son of Methuselah. Lamech called his son Noah, saying, "This same shall comfort us in our work and in the toil of our hands, (which cometh) because of the ground which Jehovah hath cursed." This curse was upon the descendants of Cain because he slew Abel. All of the world was wiped out in a great flood, except the Lord saved and retained Noah, his wife and their children. They possessed the first genes that contained the seeds of sacrificial service, prophesied by Lamech.

They built the ark, not only for himself, but also for his family and a representative sampling of God's creatures. Their progeny was to carry on the fleshly development of man to the service of the Lord.

If the wiping out of all of mankind, except for Noah, seems overly extravagant and excessive, the reader is invited to consider the extravagance of matter created by the Lord with the Big Bang. Even though he may have additional plans or uses for the remainder, all of the barren matter which we can see in the universe does imply that we do not understand his purposes or his manner or the means of accomplishing them. Nevertheless, God's plan is described by Paul and God did not forget those before Noah, for Jesus descended into hell to salvage them and all of creation.

The second great plateau was with the coming of Moses, through whom the Lord handed down instructions and rules of living which are designed to eventually make man an obedient

112

servant. The instructions and rules were accompanied by appropriate manifestations of the presence and existence of the Lord God sufficient to prove that there is but one God. He taught through Moses that the one God is to be obeyed and disobedience is to be appropriately punished.

Man labored under the burden of God's rules until he was relieved by the coming of Jesus. It was clear that man could progress in holiness, but could never become justified by his own will. This called for the third plateau, the coming of the predicted anointed one, the savior of the world, Jesus Christ.

Jesus Christ was prophesied to be a suffering servant of the people, but it was not understood that he was the example par excellence of the perfect man; that we are all called to become his brothers; or that he is the head and we are the body in eternity, ruling with him at the right hand of the Father.

In order to accomplish our salvation into everlasting life as his brothers, it was necessary that he prepare the way for us. As the perfect and ideal example of man, Jesus was incarnated as a human to take upon himself all of our sins. He received punishment on our behalf, like the whipping boys of old, which purifies us. This opened the way to our salvation. The mere fact that his sacrifice on our behalf purified us is not sufficient to justify us before his father. More than purification is required. This occurs at the last judgment. Jesus' sacrifice presents us to the Father, but each of us must present our petition for justification to the judgment of the Father. Justification is not withheld from those who seek it by repentance and turning away from their past short comings, their sins.

Jesus' sacrifice on our behalf did not sully his own justification in any way because his perfection is infinite, able to absorb and annihilate all of the sins of mankind with no detrimental effect to him whatsoever. Jesus Christ, the anointed one, is the third plateau from which mankind is currently moving forward as his brothers, toward and into eternal life.

However, our salvation is not yet accomplished or automatic. We must fill in through the working of our free will what is still lacking. Although Jesus purifies us before his father, and abides in those who believe in him, the believers must become like little children, relinquishing individual attempts to control their destiny, and be steadfast with faith in Jesus Christ. This relinquishment of self-seeking on our part as we become parts of the body of Christ in eternity is somewhat like our own fingers, toes, eyes, nose, etc. It is unthinkable that our own eyes, nose, etc. could or would refuse to sacrifice itself for the good of the whole. Or, seek to sacrifice the whole for its own preservation.

To those of us who persevere and become the body of Christ, God is pleased to make known what are the riches of the glory of Jesus Christ in us, so that every man may be presented perfect in Christ, knit together in love and into all the riches of the full assurance of understanding the mystery of God, in whom all the treasures of wisdom and knowledge are hidden. Herein lies the key to the charisms – faith, becoming like the finger is to the body in full and true service.

During the entirety of the mysterious and beautiful journey, hope, inspiration, healing and teaching can be facilitated and assisted through the charismatic gifts. Unfortunately, in these educated and sophisticated days, we quench their fire through our world experience, egocentricity and pride.

We quench and suppress the spirit which drives the charismatic gifts. This reflects the gradual retraction of the gifts by the Spirit. We are extremely handicapped in becoming spiritual men by scientific advancement. We then to think that is all there is. We prefer the workings of our own wills to those of the Spirit. Relinquishing this personal preference and reclaiming spirituality is no small task, even after a soul shaking conversion experience. And, it gets more and more difficult with the advancement of man during the passage of time. This is predicted in the Bible.

Progressively, since the days of the apostles, our society has become more and more effective at rejecting the spiritual, despite evidence supporting it. Today, in the more "advanced" societies of the world, the gifts and the spirit are simply not tolerated because they are not understood and not thought to be needed. Our scientifically oriented and educated world rejects what we do not understand and cannot observe. This rejection promotes agnosticism and atheism. It is almost impossible for us to admit that we cannot eventually know everything.

Without occasional divine intervention, we choose to do and know things ourselves, thinking we can eventually exhaust progressive learning. Occasionally, the Holy Spirit jars some individual out of this spirituality-destructive rut by forcefully calling his attention to the charisms and endowing him with some.

Then, it is clearly that person's duty to accept the charisms and exercise them for the benefit of his brothers. That is what happened to me. I have put my hand to the plow and will not look back at the way I was. Perhaps this writing will call attention to my situation. The charism clearly exists within me. I see it regularly. But, so what, if the world does not know it. I believe St. Thomas More was right when he encouraged the world by his own self sacrificial courage and saying, "Let's all get to heaven together."

This is much of what the author believes about why he is to heal with his hands and this is much of what he now believes he is to do. I wait (patiently?) to learn whether or not my gift is to be fully unleashed. I admit that my lack of faith causes me to fear the full unleashing, with a force sufficient to move mountains, is through some fault or failure on my part. Yet, in my more quiet and rational times, I know that I was predestined to receive this gift and to heal with my hands. I cannot think that the Lord would have so predestined me in vain. Why bother?

Abandoning rational thought and clinging to inspired scripture, I choose to stand upon his word:

"He will cover thee with his pinions (wings), and <u>under his wings shalt thou take refuge</u>: His truth is a shield and a buckler."[60]

Amen. Come, Lord Jesus.

---

[60] Ps 91:4 (ASV)

Epilogue.

As you read this story, I hope you found yourself on a journey with me. I know I was on one, as I wrote. After writing this book, I stepped away from it for a few days. My purpose was to allow the text to "cool off", in anticipation of a final edit. During that time, I re-read an allegorical book by Ms. Hannah Hurnard entitled *Hinds' Feet On High Places*. On the cover, it alleges itself to be "An allegory dramatizing the journey each of us must take before we can live in 'high places'." The heroine of the book is named "Much-Afraid". At the end of part one, Much-Afraid had laboriously climbed into the mountain of the Lord and been laid upon an altar, in obvious imitation of the crucifixion of Jesus. The high priest of the mountain (Jesus) performed a sacrificial operation upon her. He removed her old heart and replaced it with a new one.

During the reading of this, the meaning of the Spirit's command for me to be patient came to fruition. Finally, after so many years, I understood most of the visions with which I had been blessed. One of the visions, which I did not write about earlier, came as part of the "package" of visions I received in the spring of 1985. I did not include this vision earlier, because it had no special significance for me, except to expose my selfishness. It supplied proof to me that I had not "died to self" at that time. Of course, dying to self is necessary to heal self-interest, the original flaw of Adam and Eve. For some reason, I was embarrassed to expose this fact in the book; however, the vision did bring this fact home to me and I have borne it in my heart ever since – to my shame.

During one of the 1985 visions, the Spirit asked me a series of questions, obviously designed to test my willingness to serve God. Of course, the Spirit knew the answers to the questions before they were asked. When I approached the limits of my willingness, I

117

knew they were actually to demonstrate <u>to me</u> that I did retain within myself certain limits, rather than to assure him.

The questions asked whether I would be willing to do certain things. They began with simple little things, acts of love, etc. They were presented rapidly, like hammer blows, and I replied willingly and lovingly with my "yes", at first. Like a machine gun, the questions continued to pound at me with ever increasing demands. Toward the end, I hesitated more and more to give my yes, until the final question. I did answer yes to the final question, but my heart was heavy because I knew that the spirit had plumbed the depths of my self-giving.

The final question was whether I was willing to proselytize the Lord in the deepest, darkest, heart of Africa, all alone. I admit that the idea of this question frightened me greatly and that my yes to it was grudging and insincere. I have borne that grudging insincerity like an albatross about my neck ever since. However, as I read about the giving of a new heart to Much-Afraid on the sacrificial altar in the high places of God's mountain, the purpose of my visions so many years ago literally dawned upon me.

I now realize that the questions were not merely to show me that my love for the Lord had limits or that my original flaw was not yet healed. It was more than that. My unquestioning willingness to serve the Lord in any possible way was to be a gauge by which I could measure whether and to what extent I had <u>matured</u>. There may be more to <u>taking life seriously</u> than imitating Jesus, but I am confident that imitating him is sufficiently serious for a sinner such as me. As for being <u>patient</u>, it is the needle on the gauge which shows the <u>extent</u> of maturity. I know that once the needle hits the stop at the top of the gauge, I will have become totally mature, totally patient. I will have become *agape* love. My will shall await the will of the Lord <u>as His true servant</u>.

Words formed by the Spirit dwelling within me will flow from my belly with inexpressible prayers on my behalf. The Holy Spirit will entreat the Father directly and nothing will be impossible to

118

me as his servant. If I say unto a mountain, "Be thou taken up and cast into the sea, it shall be done."[61] And, I shall unreservedly heal with my hands. On that day, I know I will pray with true faith at least the size of a mustard seed. Whatever I ask in Jesus' name, he will do, that the Father may be glorified in the Son.[62]

But, where shall I go to express these things or to mature into such faith? Certainly, not to men, but to holy scripture through *Lectio Divina*. There, the still small voice of the Lord speaks to my ears.

"And as for you, the anointing which ye received of him abideth in you, and ye need not that any one teach you; but as his anointing teacheth you; concerning all things, and is true, and is no lie, and even as it taught you, ye abide in him."[63]

Some years later, after discerning whether the Lord had called me to religious life, after leaving my job with the Federal Government, after marrying Jenny, the light of my life, after teaching the Bible for many years and writing the lessons myself each week, I was asked to establish a *Lectio Divina* practice group in my church. I did so.

It was in pursuing *Lectio Divina* that I discovered the pearl of great price written about in the Bible. In parable, Jesus said, "[t]he kingdom of heaven is like a merchant in search of fine pearls, who, on finding one pearl of great value, went and sold all that he had and bought it." Not only I, but the majority of those practicing with me also found the pearl through *Lectio Divina*. For that reason, I have included a version of our Handbook for *Lectio Divina* to enable the reader to share our joy. It is not an easy read. Study it until it becomes difficult. Then, lay it aside and proceed to the Ruminations in Chapter 5. Read the ruminations and the pertinent scriptures while practicing *Lectio Divina*, as best you can. No

---

[61] Matt 21:21 (ASV)
[62] John 13-14
[63] 1 John 2:27 (ASV)

119

matter how far you have progressed in *Lectio*, if you read the Ruminations with a good heart, your life will be changed.

Return to the Handbook when you are moved to do so. No one understands *Lectio Divina*, or its workings, not one. It is the pale blue light going into and out of your belly, the passageway to heaven. This is my gift to you, my reason for writing. As a saintly lawyer, St. Thomas More, said many years ago, "Lets all get to heaven together." Amen. Come, Lord Jesus.[64]

---

[64] Rev 22:20

Exhibit A.

At the turn of the Nineteenth Century, a famous philosopher and psychologist, Dr. William James, gathered anecdotal evidence concerning religious experiences as a phenomenon and lectured on the subject at the University of Glasgow. The lectures were gathered into a book that is available for download from the Gutenberg Project for free. I have no idea how to better describe the feelings I had because of my experiences than as set out in these lectures. All of the anecdotes he included in his lectures were of "successful" men and women, many of them famous. The lectures on Conversion and Mysticism are especially penetrating, even though more than a century has passed since the book was written. Although the discipline of psychology has grown and matured since that time, this book still forms the foundation for current understanding of the religious experience phenomena.

Two of the anecdotes from his book are set forth here as examples for comparison with my own ongoing Twenty First Century experiences. Dr. James' closing of his second lecture on conversion deals interestingly on the permanence of the conversions.

Inside the front cover of the book, is written, "One of the greatest philosophical minds America ever produced, William James had a genius for the concrete and vivid phrase. He could make the most abstruse of theories at once clear and vivacious. The Varieties of Religious Experience is one of his most brilliant works. In this classic on the psychology of the religious impulse, William James studies such religious phenomena as conversion, repentance, mysticism, saintliness, the hopes of reward and the fears of punishment. He presents his arguments with boldness, sympathy, and the common sense of science."

James' book survives as a classic to this day. It shows that experiences such as the subject of this book are actually commonplace. The Varieties of Religious Experience is in the public domain. It is available from the World Wide Web as an eBook in various formats, including Kindle, and as a free Audiobook from The Guttenberg Project. Simply Google Guttenberg free ebooks and you will be taken to the site for download. It is also available for free from Amazon Books. Of course, Amazon will also be happy to sell you a paperback or hard cover version, if you prefer.

These experiences may test the credulity of anyone who has not had personal encounters of a similar nature. We highly recommend that any reader who is not personally familiar with similar experiences should, at the very least, read Chapter 10, "Conversion," for an initial grounding in the phenomenon.

The author first read this book some five years after his own experiences began. It helped me realize that they are more than mere illusions and that the changed direction of my life was to be expected. I still have the copy, now yellowed with age, given to me by a Redemptorist priest in Esopus, New York, while I was a postulant in seminary. Until then, I thought my experiences were unique, or at least, very rare. They are neither of these.

Here are two examples:

"Dr. Starbuck gives an interesting, and it seems to me a true, account—so far as conceptions so schematic can claim truth at all—of the reasons why self-surrender at the last moment should be so indispensable.

"To state it in terms of our own symbolism: When the new centre of personal energy has been subconsciously incubated so long as to be just ready to open into flower, "hands off" is the only word for us, it must burst forth unaided!"

"Conversion," writes the New England Puritan, Joseph Alleine, "is not the putting in a patch of holiness; but with the true convert holiness is woven into all his powers, principles, and practice. The sincere Christian is quite a new fabric, from the foundation to the top-stone. He is a new man, a new creature."

"The most curious record of sudden conversion with which I am acquainted is that of M. Alphonse Ratisbonne, a free-thinking French Jew, to Catholicism, at Rome in 1842. In a letter to a clerical friend, written a few months later, the convert gives a palpitating account of the circumstances.[121] The predisposing conditions appear to have been slight. He had an elder brother who had been converted and was a Catholic priest. He was himself irreligious, and nourished an antipathy to the apostate brother and generally to his "cloth." Finding himself at Rome in his twenty-ninth year, he fell in with a French gentleman who tried to make a proselyte of him, but who succeeded no farther after two or three conversations than to get him to hang (half jocosely) a religious medal round his neck, and to accept and read a copy of a short prayer to the Virgin. M. Ratisbonne represents his own part in the conversations as having been of a light and chaffing order; but he notes the fact that for some days he was unable to banish the words of the prayer from his mind, and that the night before the crisis he had a sort of nightmare, in the imagery of which a black cross with no Christ upon it figured. Nevertheless, until noon of the next day he was free in mind and spent the time in trivial conversations.

"I now give his own words. [121] My quotations are made from an Italian translation of this letter in the Biografia del sig. M. A. Ratisbonne, Ferrara, 1843, which I have to thank Monsignore D. O'Connell of Rome for bringing to my notice. I abridge the original.

'If at this time any one had accosted me, saying: "Alphonse, in a quarter of an hour you shall be adoring Jesus Christ as your God and Saviour; you shall lie prostrate with your face upon the ground in a humble church; you shall be smiting your breast at the foot of a priest; you shall pass the carnival in a college of Jesuits to prepare yourself to receive baptism, ready to give your life for the

Catholic faith; you shall renounce the world and its   and pleasures; renounce your fortune, your hopes, and if need be, your betrothed; the affections of your family, the esteem of your friends, and your attachment to the Jewish people; you shall have no other aspiration than to follow Christ and bear his cross till death;"—if, I say, a prophet had come to me with such a prediction, I should have judged that only one person could be more mad than he— whosoever, namely, might believe in the possibility of such senseless folly becoming true. And yet that folly is at present my only wisdom, my sole happiness.

'Coming out of the cafe I met the carriage of Monsieur B. [the proselyting friend]. He stopped and invited me in for a drive, but first asked me to wait for a few minutes whilst he attended to some duty at the church of San Andrea delle Fratte. Instead of waiting in the carriage, I entered the church myself to look at it. The church of San Andrea was poor, small, and empty; I believe that I found myself there almost alone. No work of art attracted my attention; and I passed my eyes mechanically over its interior without being arrested by any particular thought. I can only remember an entirely black dog which went trotting and turning before me as I mused. In an instant the dog had disappeared, the whole church had vanished, I no longer saw anything, … or more truly I saw, O my God, one thing alone.

'Heavens, how can I speak of it? Oh no! human words cannot attain to expressing the inexpressible. Any description, however sublime it might be, could be but a profanation of the unspeakable truth.

'I was there prostrate on the ground, bathed in my tears, with my heart beside itself, when M. B. called me back to life. I could not reply to the questions which followed from him one upon the other. But finally I took the medal which I had on my breast, and with all the effusion of my soul I kissed the image of the Virgin, radiant with grace, which it bore. Oh, indeed, it was She! It was indeed She! [What he had seen had been a vision of the Virgin.]

124

'I did not know where I was: I did not know whether I was Alphonse or another. I only felt myself changed and believed myself another me; I looked for myself in myself and did not find myself. In the bottom of my soul I felt an explosion of the most ardent joy; I could not speak; I had no wish to reveal what had happened. But I felt something solemn and sacred within me which made me ask for a priest. I was led to one; and there alone, after he had given me the positive order, I spoke as best I could, kneeling, and with my heart still trembling. I could give no account to myself of the truth of which I had acquired a knowledge and a faith. All that I can say is that in an instant the bandage had fallen from my eyes, and not one bandage only, but the whole manifold of bandages in which I had been brought up. One after another they rapidly disappeared, even as the mud and ice disappear under the rays of the burning sun.

'I came out as from a sepulchre, from an abyss of darkness; and I was living, perfectly living. But I wept, for at the bottom of that gulf I saw the extreme of misery from which I had been saved by an infinite mercy; and I shuddered at the sight of my iniquities, stupefied, melted, overwhelmed with wonder and with gratitude. You may ask me how I came to this new insight, for truly I had never opened a book of religion nor even read a single page of the Bible, and the dogma of original sin is either entirely denied or forgotten by the Hebrews of to-day, so that I had thought so little about it that I doubt whether I ever knew its name. But how came I, then, to this perception of it? I can {222} answer nothing save this, that on entering that church I was in darkness altogether, and on coming out of it I saw the fullness of the light. I can explain the change no better than by the simile of a profound sleep or the analogy of one born blind who should suddenly open his eyes to the day. He sees, but cannot define the light which bathes him and by means of which he sees the objects which excite his wonder. If we cannot explain physical light, how can we explain the light which is the truth itself? And I think I remain within the limits of veracity when I say that without having any knowledge of the letter of religious doctrine, I now intuitively perceived its sense and spirit. Better than if I saw them, I FELT those hidden things; I felt them by the inexplicable effects they produced in me. It all happened in my interior mind, and those impressions, more rapid than thought shook my soul, revolved and turned it, as it were, in another direction, towards other aims, by other paths. I express myself badly. But do you wish, Lord, that I should inclose in poor and barren words sentiments which the heart alone can understand?'"

I might multiply cases almost indefinitely, but these will suffice to show you how real, definite, and memorable an event a sudden conversion may be to him who has the experience. Throughout the height of it he undoubtedly seems to himself a passive spectator or undergoer of an astounding process performed upon him from above. There is too much evidence of this for any doubt of it to be possible. Theology, combining this fact with the doctrines of election and grace, has concluded that the spirit of God is with us at these dramatic moments in a peculiarly miraculous way, unlike what happens at any other juncture of our lives. At that moment, it believes, an absolutely new nature is breathed into us, and we become partakers of the very substance of the Deity.

That the conversion should be instantaneous seems called for on this view, and the Moravian Protestants appear to have been the first to see this logical consequence. The Methodists soon followed suit, practically if not dogmatically, and a short time ere his death, John Wesley wrote:—

"In London alone I found 652 members of our Society who were exceeding clear in their experience, and whose testimony I could see no reason to doubt. And every one of these (without a single exception) has declared that his deliverance from sin was instantaneous; that the change was wrought in a moment. Had half of these, or one third, or one in twenty, declared it was GRADUALLY wrought in THEM, I should have believed this,

126

with regard to THEM, and thought that SOME were gradually sanctified and some instantaneously. But as I have not found, in so long a space of time, a single person speaking thus, I cannot but believe that sanctification is commonly, if not always, an instantaneous work." [122] Tyerman's Life of Wesley, i. 463.

Here is part of the closing of Dr. James' second lecture on Conversion. It includes observations on the transiency or permanence of abrupt conversions:

"I just now quoted Billy Bray; I cannot do better than give his own brief account of his post-conversion feelings:—

'I can't help praising the Lord. As I go along the street, I lift up one foot, and it seems to say 'Glory'; and I lift up the other, and it seems to say 'Amen'; and so they keep up like that all the time I am walking.' [141]

"I add in a note a few more records:— 'One morning, being in deep distress, fearing every moment I should drop into hell, I was constrained to cry in earnest for mercy, and the Lord came to my relief, and delivered my soul from the burden and guilt of sin. My whole frame was in a tremor from head to foot, and my soul enjoyed sweet peace. The pleasure I then felt was indescribable. The happiness lasted about three days, during which time I never spoke to any person about my feelings." Autobiography of Dan Young, edited by W. P. Strickland, New York, 1860.

'In an instant there rose up in me such a sense of God's taking care of those who put their trust in him that for an hour all the world was crystalline, the heavens were lucid, and I sprang to my feet and began to cry and laugh.'

"H. W. Beecher, quoted by Leuba. 'My tears of sorrow changed to joy, and I lay there praising God in such ecstasy of joy as only the soul who experiences it can realize.' —'I cannot express how I felt. It was as if I had been in a dark dungeon and lifted into the light of the sun. I shouted and I sang praise unto him who loved me and washed me from my sins. I was forced to retire into a secret place, for the tears did flow, and I did not wish my shopmates to see me, and yet I could not keep it a secret.'—'I experienced joy almost to weeping.'—'I felt my face must have shone like that of Moses. I had a general feeling of buoyancy. It was the greatest joy it was ever my lot to experience.'—'I wept and laughed alternately. I was as light as if walking on air. I felt as if I had gained greater peace and happiness than I had ever expected to experience.' Starbuck's correspondents.

"One word, before I close this lecture, on the question of the transiency or permanence of these abrupt conversions.

"Some of you, I feel sure, knowing that numerous backslidings and relapses take place, make of these their apperceiving mass for interpreting the whole subject, and dismiss it with a pitying smile at so much "hysterics." Psychologically, as well as religiously, however, this is shallow. It misses the point of serious interest, which is not so much the duration as the nature and quality of these shiftings of character to higher levels. Men lapse from every level—we need no statistics to tell us that. Love is, for instance, well known not to be irrevocable, yet, constant or inconstant, it reveals new flights and reaches of ideality while it lasts. These revelations form its significance to men and women, whatever be its duration. So with the conversion experience: that it should for even a short time show a human being what the high-water mark of his spiritual capacity is, this is what constitutes its importance—an importance which backsliding cannot diminish, although persistence might increase it. As a matter of fact, all the more striking instances of conversion, all those, for instance, which I have quoted, HAVE been permanent. The case of which there might be most doubt, on account of its suggesting so strongly an epileptoid seizure, was the case of M. Ratisbonne. Yet I am

128

informed that Ratisbonne's whole future was shaped by those few minutes. He gave up his project of marriage, became a priest, founded at Jerusalem, where he went to dwell, a mission of nuns for the conversion of the Jews, showed no tendency to use for egotistic purposes the notoriety given him by the peculiar circumstances of his conversion—which, for the rest, he could seldom refer to without tears—and in short remained an exemplary son of the Church until he died, late in the 80's, if I remember rightly.

"The only statistics I know of, on the subject of the duration of conversions, are those collected for Professor Starbuck by Miss Johnston. They embrace only a hundred persons, evangelical church-members, more than half being Methodists. According to the statement of the subjects themselves, there had been backsliding of some sort in nearly all the cases, 93 per cent. of the women, 77 per cent. of the men. Discussing the returns more minutely, Starbuck finds that only 6 per cent. are relapses from the religious faith which the conversion confirmed, and that the backsliding complained of is in most only a fluctuation in the ardor of sentiment. Only six of the hundred cases report a change of faith. Starbuck's conclusion is that the effect of conversion is to bring with it "a changed attitude towards life, which is fairly constant and permanent, although the feelings fluctuate…. In other words, the persons who have passed through conversion, having once taken a stand for the religious life, tend to feel themselves identified with it, no matter how much their religious enthusiasm declines."[142][65]

---

[65] James, William. Varieties of Religious Experience, a Study in Human Nature. Kindle Edition.

LECTIO DIVINA,

A PEARL OF GREAT VALUE.

~~~

By Bohn Phillips

Prologue: Why Lectio Divina?

"The unspiritual man does not receive the gifts of the Spirit of God, for they are folly to him, and he is not able to understand them *because they are spiritually discerned.* The spiritual man judges all things, but is himself to be judged by no one. For who has known the mind of the Lord so as to instruct him? But we have the mind of Christ."[66]

Lectio Divina is the outstanding way to mature and strengthen faith, to become a spiritual man. It can give us the same experience as the Apostle John, who said: "That which was from the beginning, which we have heard, which we have seen with our eyes, which we have looked upon and touched with our hands, concerning the word of life - the life was made manifest, and we saw it, and testify to it, and proclaim to you the eternal life which was with the Father and was made manifest to us - that which we have seen and heard we proclaim also to you, so that you may have fellowship with us; and our fellowship is with the Father and with his Son Jesus Christ. And we are writing this that our joy may be complete."[67]

This is not some reading about what the Teacher says, but a direct teaching by the Lord, "This prayerful reading, well practiced, leads to an encounter with Jesus the Teacher. [...] To the knowledge of the mystery of Jesus the Messiah...to fellowship with Jesus the Son of God."[68]

"Among the many ways of approaching the Sacred Scripture, there is a privileged one to which we are all invited: Lectio Divina

---

[66] 1 Cor 2:14-16

[67] 1 John 1:1-4

[68] Aparecida 249. [Letter of His Holiness Benedict XVI to the Bishops of Latin America and the Caribbean], Apprecida, Brazil, May, 2007]

or exercise of prayerful reading of the Sacred Scripture. This prayerful reading, well practiced, leads to an encounter with Jesus the Teacher, to the knowledge of the mystery of Jesus the Messiah, to fellowship with Jesus the Son of God, and to the testimony of Jesus, Lord of the universe. With its four steps (reading, meditation, prayer, contemplation), prayerful reading encourages a personal encounter with Jesus Christ in the same way so many other persons found in the Gospel: Nicodemus and his desire for eternal life (cf. John 3.1-21), the Samaritan woman and her longing for true worship (cf. John 9), the pathway of growth in maturity conformed to the fullness (cf. Ephesians 4.13), the process of discipleship, fellowship with brothers and sisters and social commitment. Zacchaeus and his longing to change (cf. Luke 19.1–10). All of them, because of this encounter, were illuminated and refreshed because they opened up to the experience of the Father's mercy that is offered through his Word of truth and life. They didn't open their hearts to something about the Messiah, but to the very Messiah ...[69]

This is an opportunity for each of us to have the same encounter. We encounter the very Messiah, the pathway of growth and maturity to the full stature of Christ. The practice of Lectio Divina is a first stage in a real spiritual journey, a pilgrimage, in which the soul grows and matures into the full stature of Christ. Jesus said, "To you it has been given to know the secrets of the kingdom of heaven..."[70]

Through practicing Lectio Divina, Jesus offers to us the same knowledge of the secrets of heaven which he offered to His first disciples. The Holy Bible offers the same parables and other teachings which they heard with their own ears more than two thousand years ago. Jesus said to them, "Have you believed because you have seen me? Blessed are those who have not seen and yet believe."[71]

---

[69] See Joseph, Card. Ratzinger, Letter On Meditation, Appendix II
[70] Matt 13:11

Lectio Divina, was handed down from Origen, through St Gregory, Ambrose, St Augustine and eventually, to us. Pope Benedict XVI shows us that this happened powerfully and naturally: "He (Origen, 184/185 – 253/254) was convinced that the best way to become acquainted with God is through love, and that there is no authentic *Scientia Christi* without falling in love with him. (...) In his Letter to Gregory, Origen recommends: "Study first of all the lectio [reading] of the divine Scriptures. Study them, I say. For we need to study the divine writings deeply... and while you study these divine works with a believing and God-pleasing intention, knock at that which is closed in them and it shall be opened to you by the porter, of whom Jesus says, 'To him the gatekeeper opens'.

"While you attend to this Lectio Divina, seek aright and with unwavering faith in God the hidden sense which is present in most passages of the divine Scriptures. And do not be content with knocking and seeking, for what is absolutely necessary for understanding divine things is *oratio* (prayer) and in urging us to this the Saviour says not only 'knock and it will be opened to you', and 'seek and you will find', but also 'ask and it will be given you'" (Ep. Gr. 4). [...]

"The 'primordial role' played by Origen in the history of Lectio Divina instantly flashes before one's eyes. Bishop Ambrose of Milan, who learned from Origen's works to interpret the Scriptures, later introduced them into the West to hand them on to Augustine and to the monastic tradition that followed. [...] according to Origen the highest degree of knowledge of God stems from love. Therefore, this also applies for human beings: only if there is love, if hearts are opened, can one person truly know the other.

"So, the practice of Lectio Divina is to become acquainted with God through love. It offers us not only knowledge of the secrets of heaven, wisdom and understanding of the things Jesus

---

71 John 20:29

taught, it teaches and empowers us to correctly pray, to ask aright, and enables us to receive what will be given. *It allows us to understand as spiritual men*."[72]

Clearly, Lectio Divina is worth doing well. But, who am I to be writing to you in this manner? What weight should you give to what I say? Surely, that is a matter for the reader to decide. To establish credibility for my words, I included Book I. It is a true and accurate rendition of my life experiences, so far as they relate to Lectio Divina. Additionally, so far as hands-on experience is concerned, I have been lecturing on the Holy Bible and Lectio Divina for more than 10 years. I have written this book because I am compelled to do so. It tells of the greatest discovery of my life and relates the manner and means of the private worship which the Lord seeks.

---

[72] Benedict XVI, General Audience, St Peter's Square, Wednesday, 2 May 2007

Chapter 1. Physical and Mental Preparation.

Lectio Divina is a Latin term meaning "Divine Reading." It means that, in *Lectio Divina*, one receives spiritual words directly from God. It is a Spiritual way of reading. God is Spirit. Our senses do not detect him. Yet, all Christians who have had a conversion experience know without doubt that he IS and that He has communicated with them. It is sort of like foot prints appearing in the sand, one by one, without being able to see the body that is making them. When such things happen, it seems like a miracle, or a delusion. But, such occurrences are neither miracles nor delusions. They are natural spiritual phenomena and they are real.

The Christian goes beyond the scope of scientific inquiry. He is called into the presence of the Lord.[73] He has eyes to see and ears to hear which are not possessed by unbelievers.[74] He transcends the limits of science. But, that doesn't mean Christianity is speculative, untrue, or that it is not scientifically based. It means that Christian belief is beyond the scope of science.

The practice of *Lectio Divina* demonstrates that Christian belief is true. This is because, in *Lectio Divina*, one learns from the word of God, the transcendent reality to which it relates. That is, anyone can read the Bible as the words relate to the world, but *Lectio Divina* allows us to relate those same words to the transcendent reality of *agape* love. *Lectio Divina* is a bridge, a point where transcendent and worldly realities intersect. It empowers us to learn. Just because science has not observed transcendent words as spiritual entities does not mean they do not exist.[75] There are other ways of knowing than knowing through

---

[73] John 6:44
[74] See Matt 13:16
[75] See Eph 3:14-19

science. For instance, Christians believe Jesus Christ is the <u>Word</u> of God. Our spirits know this.

"God is a Spirit: and they that worship him <u>must</u> worship <u>in</u> <u>spirit</u> and truth."[76] The Bible says so, in black and white. As worldly creatures, we can worship God. But, as we mature into spiritual men, we become capable of worshiping Him in spirit and truth. True worship <u>must</u> be in spirit and truth. That is what the Lord leads us to: "Yet a time is coming and has now come when the true worshipers will worship the Father in spirit and truth, for they are the kind of worshipers the Father seeks. God is spirit, and his worshipers <u>must</u> worship in spirit and in truth."[77]

Our difficulty is obvious. Scripture teaches us that we are helpless to think, or perceive, transcendent reality in spiritual ways without first becoming "spiritual men." This is something we mature into.[78] If, during *Lectio Divina*, we seek to worship with our mind's eye, an <u>image</u> of Jesus as God, i.e.: If we <u>envision</u> Jesus as a blond, blue eyed, long haired Caucasian on a cross, we are in danger of idolatry because we are relegating his spirit, as God, to our own world. This is something other than worship in spirit and truth. That is not what we seek. Jesus is <u>all</u> spirit and <u>all</u> man and <u>all</u> God as part of the Holy Trinity. We must worship this God in spirit and truth, as spiritual men. Practicing *Lectio Divina* brings the maturity to do so.

Scripture not only says that we must worship in spirit and in truth, it tells us why: "The Spirit searches all things, even the deep things of God. For who among men knows the thoughts of a man except the man's spirit within him? In the same way, no one knows the thoughts of God except the Spirit of God. We have not received the spirit of the world but the Spirit who is from God, that we may understand what God has freely given us. This is what we speak, not in words taught us by human wisdom but in words

---

[76] John 4:24 NIV
[77] John 4:23-24 NIV
[78] 1 Cor 2:11-14

138

taught by the Spirit, expressing <u>spiritual</u> truths in <u>spiritual</u> words,[79] and it is not praying in tongues. "[t]he Spirit helps us in our weakness; for we do not know how to pray as we ought, but the Spirit himself intercedes for us with sighs too deep for words. 27 And he who searches the hearts of men knows what is the mind of the Spirit, because the Spirit intercedes for the saints according to the will of God."[80]

This is not just *hocus pocus*. This response to God's desires is attainable. But, we cannot merely choose to be spiritual men. It is a matter of spiritual maturity and it is taught through Holy Scripture. But, *how* does one mature into being a spiritual man or woman and how is *Lectio Divina* the very best method of doing so?

That *Lectio Divina* presents the manner and means of growth into spiritual maturity through spiritual exchanges with God is the very nubbin of truth. It is the fruitful means by which we can all travel the road to spiritual manhood. Its practice brings us to the contact point, an encounter, with God himself. It is the only sure and certain way to the spiritual manhood about which Paul teaches and which God seeks.

It teaches transcendent truths. Anyone can read the Bible, but only the grace of God causes us to understand the transcendent truths contained in its words. He actually sends the Holy Spirit to serve us in our need for this learning! The only thing that we can control during the process is the manner in which we receive the grace of the Spirit. The necessary manner is to be as humble as a little child.

Joy, consolations and spiritual growth come to us during the practice. Spiritual manhood is beyond description and totally out of our control. We undertake the journey to spiritual manhood with a good and faithful heart, knowing that God is faithful and with the words of St. Paul to the Romans and Corinthians ringing in our

---

[79] 1 Cor 2:10-16 (NIV)
[80] Rom 8:26-27

ears, we can be confident that will learn to worship in spirit and truth.

The teaching of St. Paul to the Corinthians was to the immature. His words were merely milk, not solid food for the mature. But, we are also immature! Scripture is the place of beginning for us. To transform our minds into the mind of Christ without scripture is simply beyond us. The Holy Spirit is the laborer in the vineyard of spiritual maturity, not us, and not Paul.

That is why *Lectio Divina* is an intricate part of our maturation. First, we come to quiet, then we meditate, then we contemplate. Coming to quiet is a natural skill which we can master. Meditation applies God's word to our worldly reality, but it does bring us toward the encounter we seek. It only prepares us to receive the mind of Christ. Contemplation allows us to receive the unspoken, transformative and transcendent teaching of God's word. This is done in silence, without normal words and without the intervention of the natural senses.

The final product, a spiritual man, is the very man from whom God seeks worship, perfected spirit to perfect spirit. The resultant peace and joy, the fruit of our prayer, is the sure sign that the Lord has been maturing and molding us to have the mind of Christ.

This is precisely what Paul told the Corinthians: "Yet among the mature we do impart wisdom, although it is not a wisdom of this age or of the rulers of this age, who are doomed to pass away. But we impart a secret and hidden wisdom of God, which God decreed before the ages for our glorification. None of the rulers of this age understood this; for if they had, they would not have crucified the Lord of glory. But, as it is written, 'What no eye has seen, nor ear heard, nor the heart of man conceived, what God has prepared for those who love him,' God has revealed to us through the Spirit. For the Spirit searches everything, even the depths of God. For what person knows a man's thoughts except the spirit of the man which is in him? So also no one comprehends the thoughts of God except the Spirit of God. Now we have received not the

140

spirit of the world, but the Spirit which is from God, that we might understand the gifts bestowed on us by God. And we impart this in words not taught by human wisdom but taught by the Spirit, interpreting spiritual truths to those who possess the Spirit. The unspiritual man does not receive the gifts of the Spirit of God, for they are folly to him, and he is not able to understand them because they are spiritually discerned. The spiritual man judges all things, but is himself to be judged by no one. 'For who has known the mind of the Lord so as to instruct him?' But we have the mind of Christ."[81]

We cannot contemplate about God with our senses or our imagination. If we truly try, the best we can manage is a totally blank mind, because the thoughts we require are not of our world. We must go beyond this in order to contemplate the transcendent presence of God. That is why our spirit must go out unseen by our senses, as explained by St. John of the Cross. True contemplation is a matter for the spirit alone. Contemplation allows our spirit to soar into the transcendent presence of God, unfettered by our senses or any of the things of this world.

There is a process by which we can cause our senses to come to rest, so they do not interfere with the spirit "going out unseen" and unnoticed. Once our senses are at rest, our intention allows the spirit to soar into the presence of the imminent God, so long as the senses remain at rest. This is in a different dimension than the physical world. There, we receive the teaching which Paul refers to above. Indeed, Jesus himself, while on this earth, spoke only what the Father taught him and said only what the Father told him to say.[82] Such a mind is the mind we seek through *Lectio Divina* and such a mind is the mind the Father seeks to worship him.

Now, let us consider how to allow our spirit to go out unseen and unfettered by our senses or by any worldly concerns. The gist of this Chapter is that several methods are very effective aids for

---

[81] 1 Cor 3:6-16
[82] John 8:23-33

relieving the distractions to our consciousness and the fetters to our spirit. Once we are proficient at bringing our senses to stillness, our spirit is free to go out "unseen" by them into a dark night, guided by sheer grace as a lover to his beloved, the one who awaits us.

Stillness of the senses, called "quiet" by St Teresa of Avila, is a basic prerequisite to allowing the spirit to go into the transcendent. This is a condition of true darkness, called the Dark Night by St. John of the Cross in his poem, "Stanzas of the Soul." One can pray without this stillness, but the distractions are very frustrating and even discouraging to the prayer. In those distractive circumstances, it is most difficult to learn. The process of attaining stillness is aimed at bringing activities of the senses under control and then assisting them to be still and to stop bringing information to the brain. Normally, the senses are not controlled at all.

The state of stillness is not a special gift from God. It is a normal physical condition that anyone can attain. It simply allows one to pray "in the spirit" without interruption or distraction from the senses. It is a physical state, like being awake or asleep. It helps us abandon the distractions of the cares of the world and it is preliminary to allowing the spirit to go out unseen and unfettered. There is no technique for "conjuring up" or "making contact" with the Lord. We do not control the encounter. He always hears us. He is always in and all around us, always ready to be heard, but He is the master of the encounter with our spirit. We must learn to be truly docile and to listen. Someday, with growing maturity, we will experience an encounter with the Lord that is different. It is startling to our senses in the flesh. This is an encouragement for beginners who have not yet left their "cares among the lilies," as did St. John of the cross in the dark night. The encounter itself is awesome. Indeed, the experience can be so awesome that if we were standing, we would automatically fall to our knees in reverential adoration. The exquisite, pure, total and absolutely selflessness of His love for the entirety of the universe, including our unworthy selves, is so much more than we can encompass that we will realize His love is divine, and that we are not. The mystics call this experience a "consolation."

"In the state of beginners, the soul is often favored by God with what are called 'sensible consolations' because they have their beginning and are felt chiefly in the senses or sensible faculties. They consist in sensible devotion and a feeling of fervor arising from the consideration of God's Goodness vividly represented to the mind and heart; [...]"[83]

The reader is being told about these consolations simply so he will not be alarmed or frightened if one, or more, of them should happen. The experience is perfectly natural, normal and common among Christians. It is not insane or extraordinary for beginners who meditate. If unanticipated, the first experience can be very surprising, even frightening.

When consolations, or other experiences occur, there are two sure ways to know whether or not one's experiences are of God:

First, they will, in themselves, be love. Our goal in practicing *Lectio Divina* is to begin finding the spiritual springtime, rendering reciprocal love through divine reading. To worship in spirit and in truth is to truly love. If the experience is not love, it is highly suspect. One will know if it is not love.

Second, have what the words said come true? This can require patience, but God does not forget giving and neither will we forget receiving such a profound experience as encountering the Word of God. It will manifest itself as true over time. Until this happens, one must suspend accepting it as authentic.

Third, meditation, prayer, contemplation, and action, not hearing words in the ear or in our heads, is the thrust of the practice of *Lectio Divina*. If the master of the encounter wants to speak to us, He will do so in his own way. We practice to become

---

[83] Catholic Encyclopedia, Consolations

able to worship in spirit and truth. In the meantime, merely practicing brings great joy to the heart.

We will know that we have been practicing well when we can say of ourselves something equivalent to St. John of the Cross saying, "One dark night, fired with love's urgent longings- ah, the sheer grace! - I went out unseen, my house being now all stilled." Eventually, one becomes accustomed to contemplation and as a mere transition from a physical focus into a spiritual one.

The stillness of St. John of the Cross allows the prayer to have and retain the focus of his/her full attention on the subject of his choice, one subject at a time. For instance, one who is proficient in attaining stillness for practicing *Lectio Divina* gains an advantage for worship, both in reasoning and in memory. It allows one to pray clearly, without distractions. The act of living life causes us to build up a reservoir of distractions, unresolved issues or memories. These issues and memories are what concern and pester us when we try to attain stillness.

Laying this on-going accumulation of active issues and memories to rest is a skill that must be learned. Otherwise, they are a cacophony of distractions, preventing us from being at peace during our practice. When one has come to stillness, he can address one thought at a time to his conscious mind. This skill is a prerequisite in spiritual prayer and it is also a powerful tool for mental function and focus in the physical world.

The extent of attained stillness of the senses can be measured by an electroencephalogram. Simply put, the electroencephalogram plots our electrical brain activity in the form of three waves, called Alpha, Beta and Theta. The mental condition of "stillness" plots out as an Alpha wave only. The Beta and Theta waves normally also occurring are plotted as essentially flat. This condition is usually called the "Alpha state." Master works by painters, musical scores by musicians and other strokes of genius are often reported to occur when one is in the Alpha state. The Beta and Theta waves seem to represent intrusive, disruptive thoughts which distract us

144

from the thrust of Alpha inspiration. Hearing a door slam or a person coughing shows up on an electroencephalograph as a Beta or Theta wave. Sudden or unexpected movement, light, sound or noise can very easily disrupt a hard earned "stillness," as measured by an electroencephalogram.

Attaining stillness allows *Lectio Divina* to be "well practiced". Stillness allows us to meditate on, pray and contemplate about the words of the Lord with minimal physical and mental distraction. This also "opens us" to the Word of God. To the extent that our attention is focused on other things, we diminish our ability to hear the Lord speaking to us, or experience Him loving us. Of course, God's voice has more than enough power to make Himself heard. But, why should he raise His voice if we are not interested in being transformed? He does not gain by speaking to us.

By attaining stillness, we are doing all that we can to be serious about practicing *Lectio Divina* well. We do not have to be able to come to stillness before we can reap benefits from *Lectio Divina*. Everyone must begin somewhere. The benefits begin immediately, even amid distractions. Simply make the effort. As St. Teresa of Avila said, "Mental prayer (in which she specifically includes *Lectio Divina*) in my opinion is nothing else than an intimate sharing between friends; it means taking time frequently to be alone with him who we know loves us."[84] Simply attempt to become still and then lovingly begin reading the chosen scripture. Attaining stillness greatly assist us, but it is not required. The Lord assists us, even in our ineptness.

Of course, beginners should use whatever works for them in coming to stillness. Stillness is not prayer. It is a technique proper to Christian, Muslim, Buddhist, or any meditative practice for minimizing physical sense interference. After one becomes proficient, no technique is required. Attaining stillness becomes largely a matter of learned, intentional relaxation and focus.

---

[84] Life of Teresa of Avila, 8, 5

Physical:

A relaxed body and mind is where we begin. This skill is very difficult for many beginners to attain, initially. Simply give it time. Patience will pay off in the long run and it is worth it.

Begin by bringing the body, from the feet up, to a relaxed state.

Focus attention on the toes first. Relax them.

Likewise, sequentially focus on the ankles, calves, knees, thighs, mid-body, shoulders, arms, hands, Trapezius muscles, and neck. Relax them one by one.

During the process, return to the toes and go back up, making sure that everything remains relaxed. If not, cause it to relax anew. This may take several times before remaining relaxed, especially the legs and Trapezius muscles.

The head requires the greatest attention. Make sure the jaw muscles are relaxed. Do not grind or clench the teeth. This is difficult to maintain and may need to be repeated several times. Open the jaw a little, keeping the lips closed.

Relax the mouth. Pay special attention to whether the lips are relaxed. It may be necessary to open them just a little. Give attention to the lips until the lips and the jaw muscles are fully relaxed. Go back and re-check the entire body.

Relax the area around the mouth. This area of relaxation is very difficult to retain. Go from the eyes, to the lips, re-relax the shoulders, the Trapezius muscles, down through the arms and to the hands, then back to the eyes. After this entire area becomes relatively relaxed, and stays that way, return to the toes and work your way back up to the eyes.

Relax the forehead. Return to the eyes, lips, etc. down to the fingers.

Relax scalp and the back of the neck. Quickly and gently check the rest of the body and return to the forehead.

Mental:

Once the physical senses remain stable and still, or relatively so, focus on bringing the mind to stillness. One may discover that he has a massive number of thoughts running around in his head, totally out of control. Not to worry. With time and patience, the thoughts can be brought to stillness also. This is simply a skill which must be acquired. The process is very relaxing, much better than chemical sedatives, or even music.

Imagine sitting on the bank of a small stream.

The water is flowing from left to right.

Imagine a series of small, toy boats floating slowly and gently down the stream.

Place each of the rampant thoughts on a boat. (You can do this!)

If the thoughts will not stay on the boat, imagine placing them each in a bubble, sort of like words in a cartoon. Allow them to gently and slowly float off, out of sight. Then, go back to the stream for the next one.

Eventually, all of the rampant thoughts will be gone, either floating up and away or down the stream.

Go back and check the entire body to make sure everything is at rest. Go back to the mind. When everything remains relaxed, you have attained a level of stillness. You will probably be surprised at how awake and alert you are. Now, one is advantageously positioned to pray and worship in the spirit. Once sufficiently relaxed, the spirit can go out in secret from the senses.

Retaining the Condition of Stillness. We must learn how to maintain ourselves in that condition. Our natural condition is to have many things going on in the mind and for our muscles remain prepared for action or to simply go about the business of living life. Keeping everything quiet takes effort. Otherwise, we will naturally allow competing and distracting thoughts and actions to awaken and begin anew.

Regardless of how skilled we become, the condition of stillness must be maintained by active intention of the will. We cannot get "stuck" in that condition. Stillness is like a bubble being held under water. If we turn it loose, it will rise to the surface on its own.

Maintaining Pure Meditation or Contemplation in the condition of stillness allows us to discover that we can present thoughts to the consciousness, one thought at a time. This is when *Lectio Divina* can begin, in its pure sense. We can focus the mind in loving adoration of God. Slowly and gently we present the chosen meditation scripture to the mind, try to identify its context in the Bible and ask the Lord to enlighten us as to what He was communicating with those words.

A new and surprising change in condition may occur. At some point, while developing skill at attaining stillness, we will, and should, experience a startling change. It feels as though we are coming out of our body! That is not what happens, but it feels like it. It is very startling and can even be frightening. Fear not, we cannot stay out there, even if we try. At first, while this experience is very different and new, we tend to "tense up." That alone will force us back out of the condition. What is happening is that we will be entering into the condition that St. John of the Cross calls the "dark night". St Teresa calls it the "Fourth Mansions". And the unknown author of The Cloud of Unknowing calls it the "cloud of unknowing." Scientists call it the "alpha state."

These conditions, the alpha state, the dark night, Fourth Mansions and the cloud of unknowing are gifts of the body. Man simply presents himself to them as the senses quieten. They will not lead to religious encounters. God is the master of the encounter and He will eventually lead us there. But, if we are persistent in

148

learning skill in the practice, we will eventually attain the out of body experience <u>whenever</u> we practice. It is merely the "spacy" way we physically feel when our senses have come to rest and our spirit is freed to go out in worship.

In this spacy way, the person praying creates an apprehension of space in which one can search for and address himself totally and lovingly to the imminent God. The emptiness, or quiet, which we attain is merely a renunciation of distracting personal attentiveness. We go out from ourselves, leaving all distractions behind. There is no doubt that in prayer one should concentrate entirely on God and as far as possible exclude the things of this world which bind us to our selfishness. To intentionally remain focused on oneself is a real <u>refusal</u> to practice well.

We must go out and present our spirits to the invisible, immanent God. We are not important, <u>He</u> is. Remember, an out of body feeling is merely a physical sensation that occurs early in learning the skill of bringing our senses to rest. There is no body, no physical "center" which contains God or upon which we can focus. What our spirit needs is to become free to transcend the physical. Only then, can we begin to worship in spirit and truth. Infused contemplation, the pure form of worship, comes later. For now, we merely seek to encounter.

If the surprising change in condition, the out of body feeling, or "spaciness" does not occur soon enough for you, the experience may be hurried as follows:

At the end of your attempts to attain stillness and when the feeling of peace is as good as it is going to be, focus your attention on the temples of your head. Imagine that you move the points of focus inward, <u>into</u> the skull. Quite probably, if you have not already done so at some point in your relaxation, you will feel that you are "coming out of your body!" Your house is now stilled. Do not be afraid. Your intentionally directed prayer to the Lord is, while in this condition, of the spirit because your flesh is totally stilled and at rest.

You will eventually discover that there is an even better way, for those who are sufficiently proficient. While bringing the senses to quiet, by focusing upon various parts of the body, pay attention to the thing that is focusing on the parts of the body. The thing that is focusing is the consciousness, which is spiritual. It accompanies the spirit at all times and provides the control which relaxes the flesh. When the senses are quiet, the consciousness remains alert, but seems to be suspended and independent of the body. It is no longer bound by the boundaries of the flesh. Allow it to expand, to "go out" and become immanent, as the Lord is immanent. You will then be conscious of the universe and in the presence of the Lord. The spirit which accompanies the consciousness can adore and worship the unseen Lord unfettered and in truth. The resultant interchange of love is absolute. It is at this time that the Spirit which dwells within us prays on our behalf concerning the subject of our meditations and the Lord responds by teaching us. Eventually, when full proficiency is achieved, "oneness" with the Lord can, at His discretion, occur.

Do not try to "see" or "sense" the Lord. It is a useless way of wasting energy. Instead, try to focus your attention on the invisible Lord and He will in a mysterious way allow you to know that He is there, in you and around you. His presence is indescribable, but you will know that He is love. You will know that you have come home to the presence of your Father! If you do not experience love, something is wrong, because God is love.

The Role of Free Will, Imagination and Love in *Lectio Divina* also deserves our attention. God absolutely honors our free will. We can always choose, always make up our minds, and always change our minds after they have been made up. With our minds, we can imagine things that we have never experienced. Indeed, imagination requires guidance or it will run amuck, envisioning fanciful things, such as talking animals and flying elephants. Imagination can be influenced to help us believe things we have been told, such as the size and shape of the universe, the depth of the sea, the roundness of the earth, etc. We all have beliefs about these things, even though we may be totally incompetent to know the truth for ourselves. Guided imagination is fruitful here. We want to use this in <u>meditation</u>.

Imagination is always based, in some way, on sense experience. For instance, we imagine the supernatural in worldly terms. We imagine that angels have wings and that God looks like us, only older. We innately know that we are not God because we recognize that we cannot create, in a God-like sense. Things we have not sensed, we cannot imagine. Our imagination, even the most fanciful imagination, draws upon prior sense experience. If imagination were creative, it would be like God. But, it is not. The creator is God. However, we can put imagination to work for us by imagining ourselves in the roles of the characters in scripture. This lays a predicate for contemplation.

There is only one thing that we can create. Given that God honors our free will to the extent that He will not, under any circumstances, take it away, we can freely exercise our will to love Him with an immortal love that is not natural to us, a love which He commands us to give. We do not create immortal *agape* love without his grace, but we can choose, when he gives his grace, to love in a selfless, God-like way. That is, we can independently respond to his *agape* love in kind and we can bestow it on others.

By stating that "charity (love) never falls away" (1 Cor 13:8), St Paul clearly intimates that there is no difference of kind, but only of degree, between immortal love here below and immortal love above. As a consequence, divine love reflects the inception of that God-like eternal <u>life</u> which never falls away, even though it reaches its fullness in heaven. Such a love is so humanly impossible that it identifies disciples of Christ. The truth of this is obvious from the witness of their lives, but it is also mysterious, so far as understanding, or doing it by ourselves, is concerned.

The implications of *agape* love are extremely important in conceptualizing eternal life in worldly terms, for there is no eternal life for our <u>physical</u> selves to experience. Imagination is useless to us here. That is, we are taught that God is love and he who does not love does not know God. We know from 1 John 4:12 that "No man has ever seen God; if we love one another, God abides in us and his love is perfected in us." There is some sort of circular connection between us, God's love and our *agape* love. From 1 Tim 15-16, we learn, "[a]nd this will be made manifest at the proper time by the blessed and only Sovereign, the King of kings and Lord of lords, who alone has immortality and dwells in unapproachable light, whom no man has ever seen or can see."

Perhaps the following will help tie the very difficult spiritual truths to the worldly vocabulary expressed in scripture; i.e.: "The eternal God, who is love, can be loved with an eternal love by us if we simply return His merciful love for us. To be with Him, to become love as He is love, is to have eternal life, but we do not become one with Him, such as a drop of water disappears and dissolves into the sea. Nowhere does the Bible state or imply this. We become His children and brothers of His only begotten Son, parts of his body, but always individuals. (Cf. "The Christian Way To Union With God)"[85] Because of this same difficulty in tying spiritual truths to the worldly vocabulary expressed in scripture, it is clear that the particular translation of the Bible used in *Lectio Divina* is not vitally important. The text of the Bible is a stepping stone. Then, the thrust of *Lectio Divina* goes beyond. It is an exchange of *agape* love with the Lord, in which He teaches us the full and true meaning of the scripture. This full and true meaning transforms and molds us. It becomes part of our being, just as the Holy Spirit dwelling within us becomes part of our being. There are no physical aspects or any human words involved.

---

[85] Cf. Catholic Encyclopedia, "Charity".

152

Lectio Divina leads us to union with God. But first, our souls must be perfected. St John of the Cross, so many years ago, gave us his answer to this question at the end of his poem, "The Stanzas of the Soul." All beginners in the practice of *Lectio Divina* can expect to thrill to the joy of discovering that their feet are on the path to singing the stanzas of this poem. All we have to do is to begin by taking the first steps.

He said: "Before embarking on an explanation of these stanzas, we should remember that the soul recites them when it has already reached the state of perfection - that is, union with God through love - and has now passed through severe trials and conflicts by means of the spiritual exercise that leads one along the constricted way to eternal life, of which our Savior speaks in the Gospel [Mt. 7:14]. The soul must ordinarily walk this path to reach that sublime and joyous union with God. Recognizing the narrowness of the path and the fact that so very few tread it - as the Lord himself says [Mt. 7:14] - the soul's song in this first stanza is one of happiness in having advanced along it to this perfection of love. Appropriately, this constricted road is called a dark night, as we shall explain in later verses of this stanza. The soul, therefore, happy at having trod this narrow road from which it derived so much good, speaks in this manner."[86]

The pearl of great price.

My dear one, you will recognize love in the practice of *Lectio Divina* and you will thrill at finding this pearl of great price through the transcendent Word in Holy Scripture. Isn't it obvious that the love which we offer in return to God's love cannot be touched, tasted, smelled, heard or seen, but that it IS? We cannot imagine or envision or construct it by our will or intellect. It is from grace. One can recall that one is <u>in</u> love, or savor or ruminate upon it. One can feel the presence of love or know that love is within us, but one cannot make love visible or locate it at any

---

[86] Dark Night Of The Soul, St John of the Cross, Barcelona, 1619. See Appendix I

particular place within the body. Therefore, it is clear that we cannot intentionally make *agape* love exist. Once it exists, such love is immanent and eternal. It is fruit of the Spirit. All of creation is saturated and permeated with the *agape* love of the Lord. We can open ourselves to receive and commune with it by our specific intent to do so. When we do, love grows within us because God, who is love, abides in and empowers us.[87] We do not "puff up", but are "built up".

We know this, not by choice, but by grace. God is love, and he who abides in love abides in God, and God abides in him. "Knowledge" puffs up, but love builds up. If any one imagines that he knows something, he does not yet know as he ought to know. But if one loves God, one is known by him.

God feeds, strengthens, nurtures and purifies the Love which abides in us, the same love which we have sullied and dishonored with our sins. We have the spiritual power to approach love transcendentally because the Holy Spirit prays for us in our weakness and human helplessness.

But, we can know that we are growing in love through *Lectio Divina* because we sense the changes within us. When we begin to sense these changes, we will also realize with great joy and shame that we have begun to be in the very presence of a brilliance so intense that our eyes are totally blinded. We will experience a love so intense that the Stanzas of the Soul will soar and sing with us. We will become harps and violins upon which it plays. We will live the dark night, proclaiming the Stanzas of the Soul with all of our strength. Each word of its last stanza summarizes and concludes the entire teaching of this Handbook: "I abandoned and forgot myself, laying my face on my Beloved; all things ceased; I went out from myself, leaving my cares forgotten among the lilies."[88] This is where the *Lectio Divina*, well-practiced, ultimately leads. Until we die and go to heaven, it is the best of all possible

---

[87] See John 15:5
[88] See Appendix I

154

worlds. It is a journey upon a divine road. In truth, we do not actually create *agape* love. It is created in us. But, our souls can magnify it and offer its essence back to our Creator. The mother of Jesus taught us this. Come, "Lets all get to heaven together." Amen. Come, Lord Jesus

Lectio Divina **is for everyone**.

Lectio Divina is a formulated way of savoring the scriptures with our souls. There are times in the life of everyone when the spirit soars, we know not where, but in exquisite joy we fly away toward an elevated and inexpressible place. This can happen when we see great beauty, thrill to the sound of great music, experience a beautiful day, see green grass or at any other time. We feel as though we can fly through the air or swim infinitely and deeply in an ocean of love. Moments such as these take us beyond our usual selves. We remember them and cherish them, but we cannot create them by acts of will, nor can we make ourselves stay within them. *Lectio Divina*, well-practiced, leads us there. We experience a veritable spiritual springtime which we recognize as the way, the truth and the life in which we were created to be.

Lectio Divina exposes the very warp and woof of our essence to the healing and calming, peaceful warmth of the loving presence of our creator. It is a form in which we meditate and contemplate the Words of the Holy Bible which God caused to be written for love of us. This is the way for our spirits to mature as we pass from milk to solid food. It is divine reading.

This has recently been affirmed by two generations of the highest leadership of the Catholic Church. Whether one is Catholic, Protestant, Orthodox or non-Denominational, such affirmation is worthy of notice by all Christians, because they affirmed a religious practice which goes back to the very beginnings of Christianity. *Lectio Divina* was well practiced when there was only one Church, one body of worshipers and no structures in which to hold services.

155

Saint Pope John Paul II taught that the Church in America must "give a clear priority to prayerful reflection on Sacred Scripture by all the faithful."[89] He was insistent about this, as was Pope Benedict XVI, his successor. For instance, Saint Pope John-Paul II said: "This reading of the Bible, accompanied by prayer, is known in the tradition of the Church as *Lectio Divina* and it is a Practice Session to be encouraged among all Christians. For priests, the *Lectio Divina* must be a basic feature of the preparation of their homilies, especially the Sunday homily."[90]

In another document, Saint Pope John Paul II said, "There is no doubt that this primacy of holiness and prayer is inconceivable without a renewed listening to the Word of God. Ever since the Second Vatican Council underlined the pre-eminent role of the Word of God in the life of the Church, great progress has certainly been made in devout listening to Sacred Scripture and attentive study of it. Scripture has its rightful place of honour (Sic) in the public prayer of the Church. Individuals and communities now make extensive use of the Bible, and among lay people there are many who devote themselves to Scripture with the valuable help of theological and biblical studies. [...] Brothers and sisters, this development needs to be consolidated and deepened, also by making sure that every family has a Bible. It is especially necessary that listening to the word of God should become a life-giving encounter, in the ancient and ever valid tradition of *Lectio Divina*, which draws from the biblical text the living word which questions, directs and shapes our lives."[91]

Note that in the foregoing, the Pope emphasized the primacy of holiness and prayer being inconceivable without a renewed listening to the word of God. This refers to meditation and contemplation which is an intrinsic part of *Lectio Divina*. Later, he said: "In this context, I would like in particular to recall and

---

[89] Proposito 32
[90] Cf. His Holiness John Paul II, Apostolic Letter Dies Domini (May 31, 1998), 40:AAS 90 (1998), 738 and Ecclesia in America 31
[91] Novo Millennio Ineunte, 39

recommend the ancient tradition of *Lectio Divina*: the diligent reading of Sacred Scripture accompanied by prayer brings about that intimate dialogue in which the person reading hears God who is speaking, and in praying, responds to him with trusting openness of heart."[92]

In affirmation of Saint Pope John Paul II, Pope Benedict XVI said, "If it [*Lectio Divina*] is effectively promoted, this Practice Session will bring to the Church – I am convinced of it – a new spiritual springtime. As a strong point of biblical ministry, *Lectio Divina* should therefore be increasingly encouraged, also through the use of new methods, carefully thought through and in step with the times. It should never be forgotten that the Word of God is a lamp for our feet and a light for our path (cf. Psalm 119[118].1105)."[93]

Without doubt, *Lectio Divina* was practiced by the first Christians. Then, by the Desert Fathers and subsequently in monasteries and abbeys throughout the world. From the earliest times, Christians have taken the teachings and commands of Jesus as binding. Literacy being sparse, the priests largely taught the laity from the pulpit. Indeed, independent lay reading of the Bible was affirmatively discouraged until Vatican II, in the 1960s. Now, having encouraged the reading of the Bible for a short time, the Church is telling us that the laity has grown up enough to practice the *Lectio Divina* on its own.

The "Great Religious Revolt" of the Protestants occurred because of three major historical events, lay education, the printing press and the teaching of Martin Luther. In the sixteenth century, the revolt was led by Martin Luther. It was preceded by the invention of the printing press in the fifteenth century, which let the grounds of the revolt be publicized throughout the world. Both

---

[92] Cf. *Dei Verbum* 25

[93] His Holiness Pope Benedict XVI, Address to the International Congress to commemorate the 40th anniversary of *Dei Verbum* Castel Gandolfo, (September 2005).

of these events were preceded by the spread of university level education beyond the priesthood and into the general population during the Renaissance of the thirteenth century, which meant there were plenty of lay scholars to take up Luther's banner. The writings which underpinned the revolt allowed the Protestant laity to leap far ahead of the Catholic community by encouraging wide spread Bible study. This was extremely important in teaching, maturing, enabling and equipping, the entire Christian laity to, individually and in community, respond to the command of Jesus to "go into your room" and pray.[94] Unfortunately, in their rebellion, the Protestants abandoned the practice of *Lectio Divina*, along with all other Catholic rituals, as being "Papist." To the extent that the Protestants abandoned *Lectio Divina*, they unwittingly abandoned a pearl of great price.

I say unwittingly, because they did not realize that *Lectio Divina* was taught by Jesus himself in the very Bible which they study so diligently. *Lectio Divina* is not some sort of "Papist Ritual." It comes directly from Jesus.

Summary.

In summary, an appropriate response to Jesus' teaching about prayer, both in common and in private is *Lectio Divina*. It is a scriptural approach to any form of prayer. *Lectio Divina* has been practiced from the very beginnings of Christianity as the way to talk to and listen to our Lord. It has been preserved through the years until Christians in general are ready for its use. Now, Popes Saint John Paul II and Benedict XVI have declared that the lay Catholic Christian public is ready. Even for beginners, it represents a means of "worship in spirit and truth" sought by our Lord: "[t]rue worshipers will worship the Father in spirit and truth, for the Father seeks such as these to worship him. God is Spirit, and those who worship him must worship in spirit and truth."[95]

---

[94] Matt 6:5-8.
[95] John 4:23-25

Now, in the Twentieth and Twenty first centuries, the laity has sufficiently matured in education and spiritual responsibility that it is being entrusted by the Church with what had long been the province of monastics and cloistered nuns. A great power for sanctity has been revealed and released to all of us!

Ultimately, each individual soul is responsible for its own salvation. The clergy obeys the commands to practice the Last Supper in remembrance of Jesus, to teach what Jesus taught, to bind and loose on the earth and to lead. But justification is effected through our personal faith. "But now, apart from law, the righteousness of God has been disclosed, and is attested by the law and the prophets, the righteousness of God through faith in Jesus Christ for all who believe. For there is no distinction, since all have sinned and fall short of the glory of God; they are now justified by his grace as a gift, through the redemption that is in Christ Jesus, whom God put forward as a sacrifice of atonement by his blood, effective through faith. He did this to show his righteousness, because in his divine forbearance he had passed over the sins previously committed; it was to prove at the present time that he himself is righteous and that he justifies the one who has faith in Jesus."[96]

---

[96] Rom 3:21-26

Chapter 2. Lectio Divina Described.

Lectio Divina is a diligent reading of Sacred Scripture, accompanied by prayer, which brings about an intimate dialogue. The person hears God speaking and responds to him with trusting openness of heart. It consists of prayerful reflection on Sacred Scripture. This prayerful reading, well practiced, leads to an encounter with Jesus the Teacher, to the knowledge of the mystery of Jesus the Messiah, to fellowship with Jesus the Son of God and to the testimony of Jesus, Lord of the universe.

One practices *Lectio Divina* by reading, then meditating upon, praying about it, then contemplating the Lord in its light. The practice improves with experience. It gradually improves into a loving human response to Love Itself, which is intrinsic in the words of Scripture. With *Lectio Divina* well practiced, Jesus the Teacher explains and leads one to the mystical knowledge of Himself. Jesus "opens the mind to understand the scriptures." This is described in the Bible by two disciples, who said to each other on the Road to Emmaus:

"Did not our hearts burn within us while he talked to us on the road, while he opened to us the scriptures?"[97] One is moved to loving worship and responds to the Holy Spirit with great joy, continually blessing God. At the beginning, the mere practice of *Lectio Divina* is, in itself, a response to the Holy Spirit. Eventually, with practice and experience, further appropriate action becomes clear, which is undertaken in reverence, with deep love and joy. This is worship in spirit and truth, sought and desired by the Lord.

Format:

First Step, Reading of Scripture.

---

[97] Luke 24:32

This is approached with diligence and docility of spirit. For beginners, the simple act of reading can have special difficulties. *Lectio Divina* well practiced requires focused concentration, mental peace and a quiet surrounding. We want to address the scripture in a way that prepares us for meaningful meditation. This preparation depends on minimal distractions by our own senses. At first, the senses cause a veritable cacophony of interruptions and distractions. Peace from these distractions is called "stillness". Depending upon the depth of stillness one has attained and any interruptions from surrounding distractions, the scripture will remain in our recollection more, or less, vividly. At first, it may even be difficult to retain the general subject matter of our meditation, much less any in-depth rumination about it. It may need to be repeatedly read, or have read to us if we are in a community practice, to properly focus on it. Do not be dismayed. This is a common problem.

Second Step, Meditation.

This addresses the actual words read in the scripture, plus the manner and the context in which they appear. We do not ask, "What is the scripture saying to me." That is, we do not "interpret" the scripture. The appropriate meditation is simply to review the scripture by mentally asking, "What is the Scripture saying". Do not "change" or "modify" the message to fit you as an individual. Instead, allow the scripture to modify you. This is extremely difficult at first and the opposite of allowing your thinking to discover what seems to be the "real meaning" of the scripture.

An over simplified explanation is that we simply allow ourselves to be newly taught by the Holy Spirit, ignoring what we believed before. We do not evaluate or judge, based on prior knowledge. We learn with a "clean page". We take the scripture into our minds as truth and permit the Holy Spirit to inspire our understanding. We do not re-define terms in order to understand.

This is very subtle. It is essentially a matter of relaxing our mental processes. We instruct our mental gate-keeper to keep the

162

gate wide open, rather than choosing whether to keep it open or closed. We attentively make ourselves available to the Holy Spirit the same as a little child carefully listens to the teaching of a parent about something entirely new. This can be accomplished by consciously intending it.

Third Step, Prayer.

We appeal to the Holy Spirit to teach us that truth which the Lord wants us to learn, our own reason having been laid to rest. We do this while bearing the words and subject of the scripture in mind, reviewing what it said.

Do not expect a "voice from above". The Holy Spirit does not normally teach in that way. Instead, expect to recall, the same as recalling an experience. The teaching encounter with the Holy Spirit is not normally a conscious thing. It is done in secret from our senses. Instead of rote recollection, the immediate fruit of the practice is experienced as "comfort" and "peace".

Learning from the Holy Spirit is similar to using our instincts. We simply "know" that we must eat, sleep, live and die. These things are learned in secret from our senses, but they are known very well. In time, love and joy, fruits of the teaching, begin to blossom within us, then manifesting as actions we take in the way we live our lives. This is what we watch for. The learning itself simply happens and actually changes who we are, unaware.

Fourth Step, Contemplation.

At the beginning level, it is beneficial to remind ourselves that we are merely learning, and not examiners or inquisitors of the text. We patiently place ourselves in the shoes of each character in the scripture. We try to receive the sense impressions that he or she was receiving. We emote and react in good faith to each occurrence mentioned in the scripture. As that character, we relate to and react to the other characters. We consciously open ourselves to the Holy Spirit and try to be docile to His teaching. We bring our *Lectio* to a close in a manner similar to basking in sunlight.

163

Contemplation is essentially the spirit being truly and completely at rest in the presence of the Lord. It is very difficult in the beginning because our senses are not used to being ignored.

Fifth Step, Action.

Bear in mind that for the beginner the practice of *Lectio Divina* is, in itself, action. Expect the Holy Spirit to begin to inspire you in a depth of love that is not natural to you.

Thinking the Thought of Christ.

Lectio Divina is not a Bible Class. But, only a believing Christian can practice *Lectio Divina* well. The Practice uses scripture to engage the believer in a dialogue with God. *Lectio Divina* is an <u>intentional</u> practice in which we seek to quell any and all impediments or interference to conversing directly with God himself. At its height, the exchange in the conversation is pure love. It is an exchange of living water (the Holy Spirit) which sustains, molds and matures us. This exchange is caused solely and allowed only by the grace of God.

Pope Benedict XVI said *Lectio Divina* is, "[t]hinking with the thought of Christ. And we can do this by reading the Holy Scripture where the thoughts of Christ are Words that speak with us. In this sense we should follow the *Lectio Divina*, listening in the Scriptures to the thought of Christ, learning to think with Christ, thinking with the thought of Christ and thus having the same feelings of Christ, being capable of giving Christ's thought and feelings to others."[98]

A few days later, Pope Benedict expanded this reflection: "Among the many fruits of this biblical springtime I would like to mention the spread of the ancient practice of *Lectio Divina* or "spiritual reading" of Sacred Scripture. It consists in pouring (Sic) over a biblical text for some time, reading it and rereading it, as it

---

[98] His Holiness Pope Benedict XVI, Reflection at the First General Congregation for the XI Ordinary General Assembly of the Synod of Bishops, (2 – 23 October, 2005)

were, "ruminating" on it as the Fathers say and squeezing from it, so to speak, all its "juice," so that it may nourish meditation and contemplation and, like water, succeed in irrigating life itself. One condition for *Lectio Divina* is that the mind and heart is <u>illumined</u> by the Holy Spirit that is, by the same Spirit who inspired the Scriptures, and that they be approached with an attitude of "reverential hearing".[99]

The worldwide opening of *Lectio Divina* to the Catholic laity was a new and significant shift toward spiritual maturity. It should extend to all of Christianity.

Directing Our Prayers to God.

Jesus said that we should seek, ask and knock on the door. Look carefully at the actual scripture that says this:

"So I say to you, ask, and it will be given you; search, and you will find; knock, and the door will be opened for you. For everyone who asks receives, and everyone who searches finds, and for everyone who knocks, the door will be opened. Is there anyone among you who, if your child asks for a fish, will give a snake instead of a fish? Or if the child asks for an egg, will give a scorpion? If you then, who are evil, know how to give good gifts to your children, <u>how much more will the heavenly Father give the Holy Spirit to those who ask him</u>!"[100]

This scripture does not suggest that we ask for a fish or an egg. It says we should ask for the Holy Spirit. It says the Father will give the Holy Spirit to those who ask him like a doting father gives good things to his child! St Paul assures us that we do not need to worry about "knowing what to say or how to say it." The Holy Spirit takes care of that. All we have to do, in our weakness, is to try to pray in good faith: "Likewise the Spirit helps us in our weakness; for we do not know how to pray as we ought, but that very Spirit intercedes with sighs too deep for words. And God,

---

[99] His Holiness Pope Benedict XVI, Angelus, (6 November 2005)
[100] Matt 7:7-8

165

who searches the heart, knows what is the mind of the Spirit, because the Spirit intercedes for the saints according to the will of God.[101]

Learning from the Holy Spirit.

Lectio Divina opens one to learning in a spiritual manner from the Holy Spirit. The Holy Bible is our means to access the things Jesus wants us to know. During *Lectio Divina* well practiced, the Holy Spirit teaches directly to our spirit in transcendent spiritual language, so there can be no mistake about what was taught. After his resurrection, Jesus sent the Holy Spirit to remind the Apostles of all things he had taught them. He also commanded them to teach all things to us. Both the Holy Bible and the Sacred Traditions are their response to the command, "Go therefore and make disciples of all nations, baptizing them in the name of the Father and of the Son and of the Holy Spirit, teaching them to observe all that I have commanded you; and lo, I am with you always, to the close of the age."[102]

Historical development of *Lectio Divina*.

Immediately after the crucifixion of Jesus, specific ways to worship were developing. The books of the New Testament were being written. A written formulation for worship with the meal in remembrance of Jesus, called the Didache, was created. Before the mass was developed, hermits, ascetics and monks began to live in the desert of Egypt, practicing *Lectio Divina*.

Anthony the Great, who moved to the desert in 270–271, became known as both the father and the founder of desert monasticism. Desert life allowed the Desert Fathers to be, in effect, "in their room and to pray in secret" much of the time. These people were the forerunners of the monks and religious who are now found throughout the world. These are the ones who nurtured and preserved *Lectio Divina* for the laity. Now, the entire lay

---

[101] Rom 8:26-27
[102] Matt 28:19-20

community is being called to take up the practice of *Lectio Divina*. It requires some initial learning to enable us to actually practice well, but the rewards are inestimable.

The first written form of regular religious practice after the apostles passed away, the Didache, called for praying the Our Father three times a day. In the time of the apostles and after their passing, original Christian communities met in homes of the laity for worship until churches began to be built for this purpose. There is no specific call in the Didache to private prayer. Private prayer, as a discipline, had a separate course of development. The lay community as a whole *did not read* and had difficulty devoting as much time as the desert fathers did to prayer. They had child rearing, families and livelihood to attend to.

This did not stop the Desert Fathers from urging the practice of *Lectio Divina* upon the laity. The first written indication that we have, which exhorts the lay Christian community to imitate the Desert Fathers in practicing the *Lectio Divina*, is a homily from St. John Chrysostom (343-407). He said that *Lectio Divina* is "medicine" sorely needed for those who are in the world, receiving wounds daily.[103] However, the laity was not able. Now we, a literate society, are being called to Biblically based prayer. *Lectio Divina* is being presented to the Christian laity throughout the world. The practice of *Lectio Divina* is now appropriate for the laity and it will bring a "spiritual springtime" to the *entire* Church, both Catholic and Protestant. *Lectio Divina* results in significant insight, wisdom and spiritual maturity. It is a proven road to salvation, sainthood and heaven. It is life changing.

The Coming of *Lectio Divina* to the Laity.

We do not know how much time will pass before the second coming of Jesus. We live our lives within the span of time between his death and his return, whatever it is, and tend to impatiently feel that it has already been a "long time". Nevertheless, we can trace a

---

[103] St. John Chrysostom, Homilies on St. Matthew, II

continual spiritual growth and maturing during the pilgrimage of mankind to the end. *Lectio Divina* accelerates the maturing process. It is <u>indispensable</u> nourishment for the spirit, for man does not live by bread alone, but by every word that proceeds from the mouth of God.

Meditation of some sort has been practiced throughout history by religious groups, including Christian, Muslim, Buddhist and Hindu. It is of first importance for our spiritual nurturing that we Christians understand the difference between Christian and other meditation. Buddhists and Hindus believe, through meditation focused on the inner man, the core of one's being, that they can receive enlightenment from God, or become one with the universe. For instance, in Buddhism, there is always a causal nexus between the universe and man. They believe that if all men die, the universe disappears.[104] Christian mystics have historically engaged in mental prayer similar to the others, but without restricting focus to the "inner man" or the universe. Christian mystics turn out from themselves in their mental prayers, addressing the immanent,[105] invisible God by their intention to do so. It is listening to, or "hearing" the still small voice of God Himself, rather than the voice of an "inner man" that is an earthshaking difference for us. For us, God IS, and His essence and composition are totally beyond our sensible understanding and comprehension.

How, then, do we direct actual worship to His presence or communicate directly with Him beyond the boundaries of the universe or the senses of man? Where do we direct our worship or adoration? For Christians, this difficulty is overcome when God

---

[104] Dictionary Of Philosophy, Dagobert Runes, 1982; cf Wikipedia, Buddhist Cosmology

[105] Immanence refers to philosophical and metaphysical theories of divine presence, in which the divine is seen to be manifested in or encompassing the material world. It is often contrasted with theories of transcendence, in which the divine is seen to be outside the material world. It is usually applied in monotheistic, pantheistic, or panentheistic faiths to suggest that the spiritual world permeates the non-spiritual. Wikipedia, "immanence"

sends the Holy Spirit to dwell within us at baptism. The Holy Spirit translates and transmits our worship and prayers for us.[106]

We have a scriptural example of the special communication we seek to initiate in 1 Kings. When praying on a mountain, the Word of the Lord came to the prophet Elijah in a friendly, two-way communication. The Lord chose this method to teach Elijah what He wanted him to know, saying, "'Go out and stand on the mountain before the LORD, for the LORD is about to pass by.' Now there was a great wind, so strong that it was splitting mountains and breaking rocks in pieces before the LORD, but the LORD was not in the wind; and after the wind an earthquake, but the LORD was not in the earthquake; and after the earthquake a fire, but the LORD was not in the fire; and after the fire a sound of sheer silence. When Elijah heard it, he wrapped his face in his mantle and went out and stood at the entrance of the cave. Then there came a voice to him that said, 'What are you doing here, Elijah?' He answered, 'I have been very zealous for the LORD, the God of hosts; for the Israelites have forsaken your covenant, thrown down your altars, and killed your prophets with the sword. I alone am left, and they are seeking my life, to take it away.' [...] (The Lord then corrects and relieves Elijah, saying that He has) 'seven thousand in Israel, all the knees that have not bowed to Baal, and every mouth that has not kissed him.'"[107]

The still small voice will be examined more closely below, but for now, realize that Elijah actually heard God speaking to him before he went out to witness God passing by. The mysterious sound of sheer silence as God passed by was demonstrating something different! It illustrated a two-way communication, spirit to spirit, a still small voice in a sound of sheer silence, which is humanly impossible. Spiritual communication is a sound of sheer silence. This difference is what *Lectio Divina* brings to us.

---

[106] See Rom 8:26-27
[107] 1 Kings 19:11-16

This still, small difference between Christian and other mental prayer was not clearly identified and defined as separate and distinct until a letter on the subject was published by Cardinal Ratzinger in 1989 pursuant to instructions of Pope John-Paul II.[108] Until then, it was thought by several writers that the Christian method of mental prayer could be merged with those of the Buddhists, Muslims, Hindus, etc. It was said that Christians merely needed to prayerfully focus on the Lord, who dwells within us. This concept grew popular in Christian circles.

However, it is now realized that seeking to focus on and locate God in one's core being, is totally beyond our capacity and power. Elijah taught us that we cannot physically locate God, only the powerful effects of his passing. A voice in a sound of sheer silence transcends physical reality. Physically, there is no sound in sheer silence. There cannot be a sound of sheer silence, except in a reality which transcends our senses.

How does one pray to God?

A movement to merge the great religions of the world, including the practice of mental prayer, was begun by a brilliant Trappist Monk, Fr. Thomas Merton, OCSO some time ago. He created quite a stir, but he died before his efforts gained traction. Since then, several attempts to incorporate elements of Eastern meditation into Christian mental prayer have been made. Early on, these attempts generated quite a considerable worldwide success among Christian laity, but more recently they have come under heavy criticism within the Church and among the laity. Eastern meditation focuses on the "inner man", the spirit that dwells inside, man being one with the universe. Christian meditation and mental prayer had traditionally "turned out" to present prayer to the emanant, invisible Lord. The basic attraction to merging Christian

---

[108] Cf. Appendix I, Congregation for the Doctrine of the Faith, October 15, 1989, document of the Letter to the Bishops of the Catholic Church on Some Aspects of Christian Meditation.

170

and Eastern meditation was bottomed upon the scriptural truth that the Holy Spirit dwells <u>within</u> every Christian.[109]

It seemed attractive and quite possible to merge the two methods into one. Indeed, many Christian contemplatives adopted the practice of Eastern mental prayer by focusing prayerful attention on the God who dwells within us at the very core of our being. However, it was eventually realized that directing prayer to the Holy Spirit who dwells within us at the core of our being is not directed to the Holy Spirit at all. Cardinal Ratzinger exposed this practice as impossible. At best, it is an ancillary and preliminary form of "psychological-corporate discipline" which can be helpful as <u>preparation</u> for prayer, but nothing more. A discipline that requires a "turning inward", as practiced in Eastern meditation, but fails to require a subsequent "turning outward," as taught by St. Augustine, a doctor of the Church, fails to direct our prayers to the Lord of the Universe.[110] [It is basically praying to our navel] The immanent God within us has no dimension or physical substance upon which we can focus. This is a critical insight for Christians to understand.

Eastern meditation is not the "infused contemplation" described by St. John of the Cross, St. Teresa of Avila or as described in the *Cloud of Unknowing*. However, as explained by Cardinal Ratzinger,[111] it can be a first step toward actual mental prayer, a preliminary of becoming "still" as described by St. John of the Cross in the "Stanzas of the Soul." After one comes to quiet, the spirit can <u>go out</u> to seek the immanent Lord in secret from his senses.[112] The practice of mental prayer in *Lectio Divina* unites our minds with the mind of Jesus Christ, thinking with the thought of Christ, praying in the spirit to the Father with the result "not my will, but thine, be done."[113] This unites us with transcendent reality.

---

[109] 2 Tim 1:14
[110] Cf Appendix II
[111] Cf Appendix I
[112] Ascent of Mount Carmel, Cf Appendix II

In sum, since God is pure spirit, we can neither focus on nor see either our own spirit or God. The Holy Spirit who dwells within us is immanent, as well as transcendent. He is everywhere and nowhere. The prayer of the spiritual man is focused solely by intention on unperceived, unseen reality, not experienced by the senses and not governed by or perceived as a location. An unspiritual mental prayer can undoubtedly be legitimate prayer, but it is couched in terms of the physical world. Unspiritual prayer is not that prayer and worship which the Father seeks.[114]

Spiritual Prayer.

The still small voice of God teaches us in a sound of silence which is understood clearly, purely and only by our spirit as we read, meditate, pray and contemplate upon the Word of God. As skill in the practice of *Lectio Divina* develops, we will recognize a residue of love within us as a sort of an afterglow of this prayer. It is like looking back and seeing "footprints in the sand or snow" from the Holy Spirit. This afterglow grows. In time, we perceive tremendous love, our hearts burning within us, as we exercise the great gift of spiritual prayer. "God is love, and he who abides in love abides in God, and God abides in him."[115]

To judge all things in the spirit and to be immune from judgment by anyone is indeed a divine gift worth pursuing! This is how our reading becomes divine. *Lectio Divina* not only allows us to pray in private, it actually enables us to hear His transcendent Spiritual voice with our own spirits, obey his commands, be judged by no one and be counted among his friends.

"You are my friends if you do what I command you. No longer do I call you servants, for the servant does not know what his master is doing; but I have called you friends, for all that I have heard from my Father I have made known to you. You did not choose me, but I chose you and appointed you that you should go

---

[113] Luke 22:42
[114] John 4:23
[115] 1 John 4:16

and bear fruit and that your fruit should abide; so that whatever you ask the Father in my name, he may give it to you. This I command you, to love one another."[116]

Divine Reading, well practiced.

Lectio Divina is the only sure and certain way for beginners to initiate and participate in actual spiritual dialog with the living God. This is impossible for man to accomplish by his own efforts. However, the Lord is faithful. He will not fail to empower one who approaches Him in this manner.

Oasis on the journey.

At this point, we have been introduced to *Lectio Divina* as something very worthwhile, highly recommended by Christian authority. It is a way to think with the thought of Christ and of being personally taught by the Holy Spirit. *Lectio Divina* has been preserved, for more than two thousand years in the cloistered religious communities for eventual use by all Christians. The time has now come for the lay Christian community to move, as it were, from milk to meat.[117] The Lord stands ready to teach each of us, both Catholic and Protestant. This will bring the entire Christian community to a Spiritual Springtime.

---

[116] John 15:12-17
[117] 1 Cor 3:2

174

Chapter 3. Virtues of the Holy Bible.

There is no reason to practice the *Lectio Divina* unless the Holy Bible is indeed the Word of God. Our goal is not to meditate upon whether the Bible is authentic, but to meditate because it is authentic. If the Holy Bible is the authentic Word of God, then *Lectio Divina* will have an authentic purpose in listening to what it says in secret. Therefore, this and the next Chapter are devoted to testing and recognizing the Holy Bible as the authentic and mystical written Word of the invisible God. If successful, we will know that our quest is legitimate. We will be able to affirm the written Word of God and listen to Jesus Christ as the living message within. If the test is not successful, we can abandon the practice as a waste of time.

Part of the proof of the test will be to preliminarily accept the Bible as authentic. This will allow it to be self-proving. A preliminary acceptance is critically important. It allows the words of the Holy Bible to be the solid platform from which the practice of *Lectio Divina* is performed and opens us to its power. Without interior proof, our test cannot be definitive. After all, we are testing for transcendent reality, for which there are no words, from within its written words. There is no real alternative to its self-proof.

Proposition: The Holy Bible is the authentic written Word of God.

Obviously, the Bible is written, but when we state that it is the Word of God we imply that it is true, without error, and that it was inspired by the Holy Spirit even though many men through a span of many years were authors of its various books.

The Bible invites self-testing because it states that it is true and inspired by God.[118] The Holy Spirit must inspire the reader as well as it did the writer. *Lectio Divina*, well-practiced, will allow us to hear that same truth which God wanted put into the sacred writings.[119] It is well and good to have the preface to the Constitution of Vatican II tell us that, but how do we confirm for ourselves that the Bible is the Word of God, and that it is true? In the search for an authentic means of encountering God in a personal encounter, that is a perfectly reasonable expectation.

To begin with, the Bible teaches that anyone can know that God exists. He is naturally manifest to all.[120] This is impossible to establish by human reason. The knowledge "comes to us" from the reality which we see every day. Christians struggle to explain to each other, or to strangers, that our knowledge that God exists is true, that He actually "IS".

Could our knowledge that God exists be instinctive? We know many things by instinct, but the conviction that God exists does not seem to be like that. We have no idea how we gained the instinctive knowledge that we must eat and grow; our hearts must be made to beat, etc. Although we recognize that instinctive knowledge of this sort is from a source unknown, we do not question that it dictates true requirements for continuing to live. We believe that we inherit instinctive knowledge in the womb. We also inherit imperatives that surface later, as we live and mature. For instance, we know and accept that we must mature, age and die. Our bodies know and obey these imperatives, even though we are not conscious of them. The most important of these is the imperative that we will die. Christians know that this imperative was somehow changed by what is called the "GOOD NEWS", brought by Jesus Christ.

The Holy Bible is true.

The Good News was proclaimed by Jesus Christ and it is set out in the Holy Bible. Therefore, believing the Bible is actually

---

[118] 2 Tim 3:16-17
[119] Vatican II Constitution Preface, 3
[120] Rom 1:20

176

true is extremely important if we are to learn how the Good News changes the imperative of death. That is, how we can know for certain that we are spiritual and immortal. Opinions about spiritual immortality are found in many religions. But, if the Bible is known to be true, it becomes our very source for certainty. The first Christians learned these truths directly from Jesus, who, in synagogue one day read a prophesy of Isaiah and then said:

> The Spirit of the Lord is upon me,
>
> because he has anointed me to preach good news to the poor.
>
> He has sent me to proclaim release to the captives
>
> and recovering of sight to the blind,
>
> to set at liberty those who are oppressed,
>
> to proclaim the acceptable year of the Lord.

And he closed the book, and gave it back to the attendant, and sat down; and the eyes of all in the synagogue were fixed on him.[121]

> At that time, differing opinions about spirituality abounded throughout the world. Even among the Jews with whom Jesus lived. The Jewish Pharisees believed in immortality, but the ruling Sadducees did not.

The Good News includes the possibility of being immortal and entering into the kingdom of heaven. But, it is necessary to be born anew and to live in a certain way:

"Now there was a Pharisee named Nicodemus, a leader of the Jews. He came to Jesus by night and said to him, 'Rabbi, we know that you are a teacher who has come from God; for no one can do these signs that you do apart from the presence of God.' Jesus answered him, 'Very truly, I tell you, no one can see the kingdom of God without being born from above. Nicodemus said to him, 'How can anyone be born after having grown old? Can one enter a second time into the mother's womb and be born?' Jesus answered,

---

[121] See Isaiah 61:1-3, Luke 4:18-19

177

'Very truly, I tell you, no one can enter the kingdom of God without being born of water and Spirit. What is born of the flesh is flesh, and what is born of the Spirit is spirit. Do not be astonished that I said to you, 'You must be born from above.' The wind blows where it chooses, and you hear the sound of it, but you do not know where it comes from or where it goes. So it is with everyone who is born of the Spirit.'"[122]

And: "And calling to him a child, he put him in the midst of them, and said, 'Truly, I say to you, unless you turn and become like children, you will never enter the kingdom of heaven. Whoever humbles himself like this child, he is the greatest in the kingdom of heaven.'"[123]

As for our test, we are Christians who began as spiritual infants, seeking to mature into spiritual adults. We are learners about spiritual things. We are learning about *Lectio Divina*, which totally relies on Sacred Scripture for meditation and contemplation. We provisionally accept that the things about which we meditate are authentic and true, so we can be open to receiving the promised benefits of practicing *Lectio Divina*. Even if final acceptance that the Bible is the authentic Word of God is tentative, final authentication will come in due course by obedience to what it teaches Because it will be confirmed to our total satisfaction. Scripture says:

"Now that you have purified your souls by your obedience to the truth so that you have genuine mutual love, love one another deeply from the heart. You have been born anew, not of perishable but of imperishable seed, through the living and enduring word of God. For 'All flesh is like grass and all its glory like the flower of grass. The grass withers, and the flower falls, but the word of the Lord endures forever.' That word is the good news that was announced to you."[124]

---

[122] John 3:1-9
[123] Matt 18:1-4
[124] 1 Peter 1:22-25

178

Scripture states that "Every word of God proves true."[125] Through the Word of the Bible, the Holy Spirit has promised to teach us.[126] The proof is in the pudding. We must take our time to let it cook. *Lectio Divina* is the oven for the cooking, the place for ruminating on the Word. If it is authentic, we need but to be patient until the proof appears.

Consider this: The Bible teaches that one is regenerated, reborn of water and the spirit through baptism.[127] Most of us, when baptized, do not report having sensed or felt a spiritual rebirth. We only feel water and hear baptismal words intoned over us. We also do not seem to feel spiritual growth.

But, all of us can know that these things are happening. Just as we hear the sound of the wind blowing and see the leaves moving from its force, we can know the spiritual rebirth has taken place by hearing new sounds and witnessing new movements within ourselves.[128]

We are able to know that we, of necessity, were reborn as the Bible teaches, if we recognize spiritual changes in ourselves and we see that we are maturing in spirit. Without doubt, we will also recognize that we are being transformed if a love that was not natural to us is growing within. We can tell when we relate to the world in a new, non-physical way and have a growing love for God. A growing love for God manifests as love for something other than fleshly, material things, or for money, or power. It is a spiritual love, unselfish, an *agape* love.[129] This way of loving

---

[125] Prov 30:5

[126] John 14:25-27 "I have said these things to you while I am still with you. But the Advocate, the Holy Spirit, whom the Father will send in my name, will teach you everything, and remind you of all that I have said to you. Peace I leave with you; my peace I give to you."

[127] Titus 3:5.

[128] John 3:1-9

[129] 1 John 4:7 "Beloved, let us love one another; for love is of God, and he who loves is born of God and knows God."

marks spiritual growth, a growth we do not control. It begins to infuse itself in us.

Like caterpillars who, without knowing how, turn into butterflies, we, without knowing how, turn into a new sort of lover. Amazingly, we begin to love each other in the same *agape* way that we began to love God, in a mysterious way! Even if this doesn't happen right away, we can afford to be patient, especially if we know that the Bible is authentic and true.

It is quite possible for us to believe that we were reborn simply by knowing that we have been baptized. But, when we experience the turning, the transformation, the spiritual growth and maturity, the *agape* peace and love, we are experiencing the proofs that make us know that we have been saved, that we have been reborn, that what the Bible tells us is true!

The Bible says: "We are of God. Whoever knows God listens to us, and he who is not of God does not listen to us. By this we know the spirit of truth and the spirit of error. Beloved, let us love one another; for love is of God, and he who loves is born of God and knows God. He who does not love does not know God; for God is love. In this the love of God was made manifest among us, that God sent his only Son into the world, so that we might live through him. In this is love, not that we loved God but that he loved us and sent his Son to be the expiation for our sins. [We are not the originators of love, He is!] Beloved, if God so loved us, we also ought to love one another. No man has ever seen God; but, if we love one another, God abides in us and his love is perfected in us."[130]

A butterfly-like metamorphosis from caterpillar to butterfly is like the change wrought by well-practiced *Lectio Divina*. The metamorphosis is normally subtle and takes place over time. It can be the proof in the pudding that the Bible is true. Much like caterpillars fattening in preparation for becoming butterflies, we

---

[130] 1 John 4:4-12

180

consume spiritual food for the purpose of salvation by practicing *Lectio Divina*. It teaches us individually, not only to a unity of faith with all others, but brings each of us to mature manhood, to the very measure and stature and fullness of Christ.[131] Our spiritual growth becomes manifest to us and to all the world because what is taking place in us is manifest.

We learn to digest spiritual food by meditation. Eventually, through the gush of reciprocal love, between God and ourselves, we begin to exercise our assent to spiritual maturity, pleasing to God, worshiping in spirit and truth. Once we realize that the transformations manifesting within us are in accordance with and as predicted by the Bible, our changed lives affirm that the teachings of the Bible are true.

The Holy Bible is inspired.

Orthodox Jewish Religion, the Catholic Church and main-stream Protestant Evangelicals all hold that the Holy Bible is divinely inspired and inerrant in content. We say it expresses the very Word of God. Others should not lightly dismiss out of hand or disregard and ignore these assertions. If, for no other reason than there are so many of us who assert the truth of it. Also, we hold that the entire Holy Bible, as originally written, asserts that it was divinely inspired by the Holy Spirit, according to its own content.[132] Such an internal claim to inerrancy invites attacks which would be devastating if successful. This assertion within the Holy Bible is solemnly and formally affirmed and continues to be solidly and formally asserted by the Roman Catholic Church[133] and by Orthodox Judaism.[134] This belief abounds throughout the world. This alone is a powerful testament. Of course, Muslims, Buddhists, Hindu's in general, and even Atheists might point out that they are also believers, but in other specifics. The question then becomes,

---

[131] Eph 4:13
[132] 2 Tim 3:16
[133] Cf. Vatican II Constitution 5:19, 20
[134] See Jewish Encyclopedia

181

what do their <u>lives</u> manifest? The Buddhists and Hindu believers might say that they have been "enlightened", or that they have become "one", but never that they have been reborn in the same body as before.[135] Additionally, the inspired nature of Holy Scripture becomes <u>manifest</u> to us during our practice of *Lectio Divina* as we experience that the Holy Spirit teaches us wisdom.

Others learn wisdom through meditation with their intellects. Muslims are included in this category, although they hold that the Koran is the Word of God *in hoc verba*. Yet, the Koran contains self-contradictions which must be rationalized and intellectualized by the mind in order to be accepted and believed. The Koran describes heavenly things as though they were of the world. For instance, one who expects to go to paradise can expect to be attended by a bevy of virgins. This implies the existence of physical sexual appetites, capacities and needs, ministered to by servants who are <u>physically</u> virgin. This necessitates a physical capacity for them to both be virgin and to lose their virginity, rather than to have no sexual capacity at all.

The wisdom of Muslims, Buddhists, Hindus and Atheists is always understood in terms of worldly reality, never transcendental reality. Even brilliant insights, such as that of Albert Einstein's theory of relativity, concern the relativity of matter, such as our world is made of. None of this, or any other human wisdom, penetrates to the purely spiritual, except the Bible.

On the other hand, Christians are taught by Jesus that there is no marriage or reproduction in the afterlife. When asked about the question of marriage in the afterlife, Jesus said, "Those who belong to this age marry and are given in marriage; but those who are considered worthy of a place in that age and in the resurrection from the dead neither marry nor are given in marriage, but are as angels in heaven."[136] They cannot die anymore, because they are

---

[135] Non-believing Jews, such as the Sadducees, also do not know this rebirth and would say that it is not possible.

[136] Matt 22:30; Mark 12:25, Luke 20:35

182

like angels and are children of God, being children of the resurrection. Again, the fact that the dead are raised was shown to Moses in the scripture about the burning bush. The voice speaks of the Lord as the God of Abraham, the God of Isaac, and the God of Jacob and he is God, not of the dead, but of the living; for all of them are alive, although they died. This implies resurrection. Only the Bible speaks of heavenly things from the <u>perspective</u> of <u>heaven</u>.

The Holy Bible teaches us.

We learn how to live in the world, even as we begin life in the spirit. As a result, we are enabled to be in the world, even though we are no longer of it. "Consider your own call, brothers and sisters: not many of you were wise by human standards, not many were powerful, not many were of noble birth. But God chose what is foolish in the world to shame the wise; God chose what is weak in the world to shame the strong; God chose what is low and despised in the world, things that are not, to reduce to nothing things that are, so that no one might boast in the presence of God. He is the source of your life in Christ Jesus, <u>who became for us wisdom from God</u>, and righteousness and sanctification and redemption, in order that, as it is written, 'Let the one who boasts, boast in the Lord.'"[137]

St. Paul said to St. Timothy, as he sent him on his way, "But as for you, continue in what you have learned and firmly believed, <u>knowing from whom you learned it</u>, and how from childhood you have known the sacred writings that are able to instruct you for salvation through faith in Christ Jesus. <u>All scripture is inspired by God</u> and is useful for teaching, for reproof, for correction, and for training in righteousness, so that everyone who belongs to God may be proficient, equipped for every good work."[138]

---

[137] 1 Cor 1:26-31
[138] 2 Tim 3:14-17

The Catholic Church in declaration pursuant to formal council, Vatican II (1962-1965), declared *Dei Verbum*, its Dogmatic Constitution on Divine Revelation, gave the following stirring words of belief, faith and assurance, which the sacred Synod proclaimed with reverence and faith, "[f]ollowing in the footsteps of the Council of Trent and of the First Vatican Council, authentic doctrine on divine revelation and how it is handed on, so that by hearing the message of salvation the whole world may believe, [...] (Drawing from paragraphs 5 and 6 of the Section on Revelation Itself, the Church holds that), 'The obedience of faith' (Rom 13, 26; cf. Rom 1, 5; 2 Cor 10, 5-6) 'is to be given to God who reveals, and obedience by which man commits his whole self freely to God, offering the full submission of intellect and will to God who reveals,' and freely assenting to the truth revealed by Him. To make this act of faith, the grace of God and the interior help of the Holy Spirit must precede and assist, moving the heart and turning it to God, opening the eyes of the mind and giving 'joy and ease to everyone in assenting to the truth and believing it.' To bring about an ever deeper understanding of revelation the same Holy Spirit constantly brings faith to completion by His gifts."

Again, "As a sacred Synod has affirmed, God, the beginning and end of all things, can be known with certainty from created reality by the light of human reason (see Rom 1, 20); but it teaches that it is through His revelation 'that those religious truths which are by their nature accessible to human reason can be known by all men with ease, with solid certitude and with no trace of error, even in this present state of the human race. [...] Those divinely revealed realities which are contained and presented in Sacred Scripture have been committed to writing under the inspiration of the Holy Spirit. For Holy Mother Church, relying on the belief of the Apostles, holds that the books of both the Old and New Testaments in their entirety, with all their parts, are sacred and canonical because, written under the inspiration of the Holy Spirit, they have God as their author and have been handed on as such to the Church herself. In composing the sacred books, God chose men and while employed by Him they made use of their powers and abilities, so that with Him action in them and through them, they, as true authors, consigned to writing everything and only those things which He wanted. Therefore, since everything asserted by the inspired authors or sacred writers must be held to be <u>asserted by the Holy Spirit</u>, it follows that the books of Scripture must be acknowledged as teaching solidly, faithfully and without error that truth which God wanted put into the sacred writings for the sake of our salvation [....] But since holy Scripture must be read and interpreted in the same spirit in which it was written, no less serious attention must be given to the content and unity of the whole of Scripture if the meaning of the sacred texts is to be correctly worked out..."[139]

If the foregoing is not enough, do not worry. Simply practice *Lectio Divina* and it will be taught directly to you by the Holy Spirit.

As St. Augustine reflected on the Mystery of Biblical Inspiration: "To explain all that was told to them, in their fullest sense, is beyond all human ability. Moreover, I do not doubt to affirm, my brothers, that perhaps not even Saint John himself was able; he spoke as he could, because he was a man who spoke on God's behalf – inspired, certainly, but always human. Thanks to the inspiration, he was able to say something: if he had not been inspired, he would have been unable to say anything. But although he was inspired he was unable to reveal the whole mystery; he said what a human being could say."[140]

These considerations, and many more which will manifest upon thoughtful reflection, establish that the Holy Bible is both inspired and true in its entirety.

---

[139] Vatican II (1962-1965), declared *Dei Verbum*.
[140] St. Augustine, Homilies on the Gospel of John 1:1

The Holy Bible is the Transcendent Word of God.

Transcendence refers to the aspect of spiritual nature and power which is wholly independent of, and different from the physical universe. God is Spirit and, therefore, transcendent.[141] The Bible is the work of many individuals, but it is, in its entirety, inspired by the Holy Spirit. Since God speaks in Sacred Scripture through men in human fashion, the interpreter of Sacred Scripture, in order to see clearly what God wanted to communicate to us, should carefully investigate what meaning the sacred writers really intended, and what God wanted to manifest by means of their words.[142]

WHAT A WONDER THIS IS! God, who is pure spirit,[143] communicates spiritual (invisible) realities to us. We, who have no perception of spiritual realities with our five senses communicate with the transcendent. This is done in the words of scripture, which we can understand and see physically, with our worldly eyes. When we believe that the Holy Bible is true, we will realize what a wondrous book this true, error free, inspired Word of God actually is. Vatican II guides us about a few things which necessarily follow:

Since God speaks in Sacred Scripture through men in human fashion, the interpreter of Sacred Scripture, in order to see clearly what God wanted to communicate to us, should carefully investigate what meaning the sacred writers really intended, and what God wanted to manifest by means of their words.[144] For the words of God, expressed in human language, have been made like human discourse, just as the word of the eternal Father, when he took to himself the flesh of human weakness, was in every way made like men.[145]

---

[141] John 4:24
[142] *Dei Verbum* 12a
[143] John 4:24
[144] Catechism of the Catholic Church, Part One, Section One, Chapter Two, Article 3 – Inspiration and Truth of Sacred Scripture 107

Jesus is the living word of God. He is the sword of the Spirit;[146] he, through whom God created all things.[147] In what other forms does the Bible teach us about the Word, Son of the eternal Father, besides that he is the only begotten Son of God? It teaches that the Word of God is a part of the Holy Trinity,[148] He is light and life to man,[149] He is a shepherd, the rock that provided water to the Israelites in the desert;[150] He is our savior in which our spirits rejoice;[151] our teacher;[152] He is the brother of those who do His will,[153] the savior of the world,[154] and much more.

The Holy Bible is Canonical.

The Holy Bible is declared by the Churches to be canonical. The Canon of the Bible refers to the definitive list of the books which are declared to be divine revelation. The word "canon" means "meter", "norm", "rule" or "pattern." Canonical Scripture constitutes our rule of faith, which leads us to God and allows us to live out the Gospel.

During the first three centuries of the Christian era, "the rule of faith" by which the Disciples of Christ were to live was not as easy to determine as it is now. From the fourth century, the books of the Biblical canon have been "normative" in that they are accepted by the Church and proposed to believers as the norm of faith and Christian life. The canon of books in the Bible was discerned by the Magisterium of the Holy Catholic Church, and applied to both the Old and New Testaments, but it took three centuries to clearly emerge. They were found by it to be of

---

145 *Dei Verbum* 13
146 Eph 6:17
147 John 1:3
148 Ps 2:7; Heb 1:5; 5:5
149 John 1:1-5
150 Gn 49:24; 1 Co 10:4
151 Luke 1:47
152 John 13:13
153 Matt 1:23-50
154 Luke 2:11

Apostolic origin, of extended use in liturgical and pastoral use within the Christian communities that developed as the faith spread throughout the known world; and in conformity with the rule of faith; that is, the text had to be clear of controversy and in conformity with the essential elements of the life of faith that had been established from the time of the Apostles in Christian communities.[155]

There is a clear relationship between Jesus Christ, the living Word of God, and the Holy Bible, the Written Word of God. In confronting the Jews, Jesus told them that the Scriptures (Old Testament) give testimony to him: "You study the Scriptures, because you think that in them you will find eternal life. And these very Scriptures speak about me! Yet you are not willing to come to me in order to have life."[156]

After his resurrection, Jesus said to his disciples: "These are the very things I told you about while I was still with you: everything written about me in the Law of Moses, the writings of the prophets, and the Psalms had to come true."[157]

Jesus is present in his Word, since it is he himself who speaks when the holy scriptures are read.[158] Then, after speaking in many and varied ways through the prophets, "now at last in these days God has spoken to us in his Son"[159] For He sent His Son, the eternal Word, who enlightens all men, so that he might dwell among men and tell them of the innermost being of God.[160] Jesus Christ, therefore, the Word made flesh was sent as "a man to men."[161] He "speaks the words of God,"[162] and completes the work of salvation which his Father gave him to do.[163] To see Jesus is to see

---

[155] Cf. Catholic Encyclopedia, "Canon"
[156] John 5:39-40
[157] Luke 24:44
[158] *Sacrosanctum Concilium*, (December 4, 1963)
[159] Hebrews 1:1-2
[160] cf. John 1:1-18
[161] Hebrews 1:1 and 4:7
[162] John 3:34

188

his Father.[164] For this reason Jesus perfected revelation by fulfilling it through his whole work of making himself present and manifesting himself: through his words and deeds, his signs and wonders, but especially through his death and glorious resurrection from the dead and final sending of the Spirit of truth. Moreover he confirmed with divine testimony what revelation proclaimed, that God is with us to free us from the darkness of sin and death, and to raise us up to life eternal.[165]

"The Word of God is an Unending Spring. Lord, who is able to understand all the richness of a single one of your words? We miss more than we perceive, just as those who are thirsty drink from a spring. The perspectives of the Word of God are so abundant, according to the possibilities of those who study them. The Lord has painted his word with different colors, so that each disciple might contemplate what pleases him. He enclosed in his Word many treasures, so that as each of us meditates, we might discover the riches. He that discovers a part of the treasure does not believe that Word contains only what he found, but understands that he simply found a part of all that is there enclosed. Enriched by the Word, he does not believe that the Word is thus poorer, but understanding that he was unable to perceive all of it, gives thanks because of its great richness. Rejoice because you have overcome, and do not be sad that others have gone farther. If you are thirsty, you are happy when you drink, and you are not saddened because you cannot deplete the spring, for if your thirst is satisfied before the spring runs dry, when you are thirsty again you can drink again from it; if, on the contrary, once your thirst is satisfied, the well runs dry, your victory becomes a loss. Give thanks for what you received, and do not be sad for what remains as abundance. What you received, what you enjoyed, is your part; but what remains is your inheritance. What you cannot receive now because of your own weakness, you will be able to

---

[163] See John 5:36; John 17:4
[164] John 14:9
[165] *Dei Verbum* 4a

189

receive, if you persevere, at another time. Do not try to drink with greed all at one time that which you cannot consume at one time, nor renounce by negligence what you are able to drink bit by bit."[166]

Since the Bible is actually a translation of transcendental spiritual truths, it cannot be understood by us unless we are Jesus' disciples, believers who open our hearts to the teachings of the Holy Spirit. For instance, Jesus always spoke in parables, but the unspoken, transcendental meaning is not understood by anyone who is not his disciple. Even Jesus' explanation of the parables is not understood by those who do not have "ears to hear":

Then the disciples came and asked him, "'Why do you speak to them in parables?' He answered, 'To you [His disciples] it has been given to know the secrets of the kingdom of heaven, but to them it has not been given. For to those who have, more will be given, and they will have abundance; but from those who have nothing, even what they have will be taken away. The reason I speak to them in parables is that seeing they do not perceive, and hearing they do not listen, nor do they understand. With them indeed is fulfilled the prophecy of Isaiah that says: 'You will indeed listen, but never understand, and you will indeed look, but never perceive. For this people's heart has grown dull, and their ears are hard of hearing, and they have shut their eyes; so that they might not look with their eyes, and listen with their ears, and understand with their heart and turn — and I would heal them.' But blessed are your eyes, for they see, and your ears, for they hear. Truly I tell you, many prophets and righteous people longed to see what you see, but did not see it, and to hear what you hear, but did not hear it.'"[167]

A clear understanding of parables is worth undertaking because the Holy Bible is Parabolic. The Bible is not an easy read under the best of circumstances, especially when attempting a

---

[166] Sidney H. Griffith, 'Faith Adoring the Mystery': Reading the Bible with St. Ephrem the Syrian, (Marquette University Press, Milwaukee, 1997), pp. iv.
[167] Matt 13:10-17

190

divine reading. The translation of transcendent reality into human language speaks to the heart. It is written in two senses, the literal sense and the spiritual sense. The literal sense of scripture is the platform from which the Holy Spirit teaches spiritual truth. It speaks to the brain and the heart. Transcendental reality is presented to our hearts, often in parables. It is nonsense to the brain.

Unless one believes, the literal sense is all one can receive from reading. It is clear that the Biblical writers employed their own skills, vocabularies and word usage in putting down what the Holy Spirit wanted to be taught spiritually. The spiritual teaching of the Bible is truly extraordinary and always mystical because there is absolutely no human vocabulary about the transcendental.[168] We have no human sensitivity to it. The spiritual transcends our sense capacities. Somehow, we become aware that we know what we know spiritually. Jesus taught spiritual truths by parables, which can be grasped mystically by believers, but which seem like utter nonsense to non-believers.[169]

The various ways of Biblical writing are called literary forms by scholars. But it is most important to read what the Bible says with a child-like attitude of faith, regardless of recognizing literary forms. The attitude of faith was recommended by Pope Benedict XVI in 1988, as a Hermeneutic to professional Biblical exegetes and interpreters. He was addressing a problem which had become apparent from scientific efforts embodied in the historical-critical methods of exegesis and interpretation.[170] The historical-critical methods do not penetrate into the spiritual. They clear away the

---

[168] 2 Cor 4:18

[169] Matt 13:13-14 "This is why I speak to them in parables, because seeing they do not see, and hearing they do not hear, nor do they understand. With them indeed is fulfilled the prophecy of Isaiah which says: 'You shall indeed hear but never understand, and you shall indeed see but never perceive.'"; Heb 5:14 "But solid food is for the mature, for those who have their faculties trained by practice to distinguish good from evil."

[170] 2 Tim 3:16-17

chaff, but do not expose the wheat. The problem is obviated by an attitude of child-like faith. Faith does not compromise the truth; it opens one to truth which is beyond our fleshly capacity to understand. Through faith, we eventually hear, understand and confirm; we can see and perceive the full and true spiritual message of the Holy Bible. It is guaranteed:

"I press on toward the goal for the prize of the upward call of God in Christ Jesus. Let those of us who are mature be thus minded; and if in anything you are otherwise minded, God will reveal that also to you. Only let us hold true to what we have attained."[171]

Although we may meditate with child-like innocence, we must always bear in mind that the Holy Bible was written in the individual styles of the inspired authors. They employed the idioms, genres and literary forms of their times. These things helped communicate with the immediate readership of the authors and they will help us too, if we bear them in mind. Three forms that should be remembered and identified during meditation are the parable, the allegory and the poem.[172]

Jesus Christ taught both pastoral and spiritual truths. Here, he prayed to his Father, "Sanctify them (the original apostles) in the truth; thy word is truth. As thou didst send me into the world, so I have sent them into the world. And for their sake I consecrate myself, that they also may be consecrated in truth. 'I do not pray for these only, but also for those who believe in me through their word, [their word survives in the scriptures and in the oral traditions of the Church] that they may all be one [The Bible is all one book, not an anthology of books by different authors.]; even as thou, Father, art in me, and I in thee, that they also may be in us, so that the world may believe that thou hast sent me.'"[173]

---

[171] Phil 3:13-16
[172] Cf. Vatican II Constitution, 6. Literary Genres Or Forms
[173] John 17:17-21

192

St. Paul, one of the apostles consecrated by Jesus Christ in truth, wrote: "All scripture is inspired by God and profitable for teaching, for reproof, for correction, and for training in righteousness, that the man of God may be complete, equipped for every good work."[174]

Although not directed toward *Lectio Divina*, much can be learned about the Bible by reading the introductory material at the beginning of the New American Bible.

Oasis on the journey.

At this stage, we have been presented with arguments that the Holy Bible is the written Word of God, that it is truly inspired, that it is intended to teach us in human terms the transcendent Word of God, that this inspiration and truth is formally recognized by the Canon of the Church and Christianity in general.

Also, we have learned that the Holy Bible teaches in parables. Parables are not "riddles" which can be understood and worked out by the intellect of man. Understanding is accomplished by disciples of Christ, who learn in a child-like (not childish) way because they believe that Christ is God and that the Holy Bible reflects His actual thoughts. The Holy Bible has mystical power which can be seen in the next Chapter by anyone, but it is only understood spiritually by His disciples. We can and will mature in our spiritual grasp of this mystical power, even as we learn to pray in spirit and in truth, as the Lord seeks for us to do. We will know that we know. We will see and hear with eyes and ears that cannot be seen or touched. This is a mystery. The Holy Bible is mysterious, as we undertake to demonstrate in the next Chapter.

---

[174] 2 Tim 3:16-17

Chapter 4. The Holy Bible Is Mysterious.

It is fashionable to believe that man can do anything. However, man has his limits. All of the motivational speakers, all of the self-help books, all of the architects, engineers, educators, philosophers, psychiatrists, and physicians in the world cannot make man into something he is not. Our egos, desire for self-determination, and an indomitable will, cannot drive us beyond our abilities. Our capacity for scnsual input is limited to five senses. Even our capacity to imagine or conceive are limited to material reality. Man's conception and imagination inevitably attempts to deal with transcendent reality, but it does so in physical, material ways. For instance, we cannot conceive of anything existing outside of or beyond the material universe. Try it.

As we observed earlier, we end up totally blank. We literally cannot conceive of something actually being outside the physical universe. Try it, and you'll see. The universe is our boundary. Indeed, even our imagination cannot penetrate to our creator. No wonder there are atheists! Unless we are called by the Lord, we cannot even imagine the possibility that He exists! Because even our imagination is limited to the perceptions of our senses, Renè Descartes, when trying to establish, philosophically that he exists, could do no more than say "*Cogitatio Ergo Sum*." (I think, therefore, I am.) He referred to himself as "somewhat" rather than "something" because of the philosophical difficulty in showing his own existence. In this way, Descartes retained the idea that man is not only physical, but also spiritual in that he "thinks". Because he thinks, he knows that he "is" something (somewhat). Note, thinking is not physical. Therefore, the only proof of existence available to him was non-physical. He is somewhat. We have no way of knowing that someone else senses things the same as we do. For instance, no one can know or demonstrate that anyone else senses "red" the same as he.

Be that as it may, whatever the process of thinking may be, we only do so concerning <u>material</u> things. We think of heaven as a <u>place</u>. We think of God in human, physical ways. We even think of ghosts in terms of smoke or wind. If we actually focus on what God looks like, we either conceive of a physical thing or we are absolutely blank. But we somehow do perceive that God is "out there". Those who can do so have been called.[175] Yet, like Descartes, we who are called can only say that He is "somewhat."

Restated, our perceptions of reality are solely and only of material things. We have no natural ability to <u>sense</u> spiritual reality, but we <u>know</u> God is "real". We know He exists. God is a mystery for all of us. We cannot imagine or reason his essence, what he looks like, because he does not look like anything in our experience. He IS. No one has seen God and lived to tell the story.[176] This is not because seeing God is deadly. It is because to see God, we must first die. In short, we <u>instinctively</u> know that reality is more than we can sense. Our eyes, ears, nose, touch and taste and our imaginations are not enough to perceive all that we know, of necessity, exists. Much better than Descartes, the Lord told Moses in human words what he is in transcendental reality: God said to Moses, "I AM WHO I AM." And he said, "Say this to the people of Israel, 'I AM has sent me to you.'"[177] In other words, we can speak to and hear from God, but we cannot perceive or "see" him. It is beyond our capacity, even though we know that he IS.

St. Paul tells us that our knowledge that God exists is from God Himself. He shows himself to us in mysterious ways. "For the invisible things of him since the creation of the world are clearly seen, being perceived through the things that are made, (even) his everlasting power and divinity; [...]"[178] This is the key. God shows

---

[175] See John 6:44 *et seq*
[176] John 1:18
[177] Ex 3:14

196

us aspects of reality that are invisible to us, things we cannot see, or in any direct way, sense or imagine. <u>There is a reality that is beyond our perception</u>. God shows it to us.

One of the ways God reveals hidden reality is through his written word, the Holy Bible. It is the Word of God in human language. His Word is permanent. The written Word of God is the narration of God's revelation. In other words, the Bible is not only the authentic Word of God; it reveals knowledge about reality <u>which we cannot know by ourselves</u>. That is why it is so important that we truly recognize and accept that the Bible is the authentic Word of God. Once we recognize this, to question whether or not it "really means" what it says or if there is some sort of a mistake in the text is the worst sort of folly. We must simply accept the text and be in unquestioning peace when we meditate and contemplate in *Lectio Divina*, allowing ourselves to be taught by the Holy Spirit.

Striving for Fruitful Meditation on Scripture is its very purpose. We are now focused on an extremely important point. *Lectio Divina*, through meditation and contemplation on the Scriptures, is actually an ongoing human response to the call of the Lord, an effort to nurture spiritual growth, to "equip [us] for the work of ministry, for building up the body of Christ, until all of us come to the unity of the faith and of the knowledge of the Son of God, to maturity, to the measure of the full stature of Christ."[179]

"The grass withers, the flower fades; but the word of our God will stand forever."[180] "Heaven and earth will pass away, but my words will not pass away."[181] "Indeed, the word of God is living and active, sharper than any two-edged sword, piercing until it divides soul from spirit, joints from marrow; it is able to judge the thoughts and intentions of the heart.[182]

---

[178] Rom 1:20
[179] Eph 4:12-13
[180] Isa 40:8
[181] Mark 13:31

Unless and until we affirmatively accept that the Holy Bible is the authentic Word of God, our meditation and contemplation can only be a relatively unfruitful personal introspection, no better than Eastern mysticism. Think about it! Mental prayer about the words of a mere book cannot possibly open one to hearing the full Word of God, who speaks in the most subtle whispers.

If we must evaluate for ourselves the meaning of the words of text, we filter them through our own experiences. In this way, we torture the text by squeezing the transcendent spirituality out of it. This is absolutely self-defeating. Spiritual truths are invisible to us. So far as we can tell, spiritual things are simply not there. We are not capable of receiving the spiritual teachings of the Holy Spirit on our own.

True, the Holy Spirit can penetrate the barriers which we erect to his teaching, but He honors our free will. A non-accepting attitude on our part is, of necessity, a rejection of spiritual teaching because the Word of God is not errant. Disciples, believers in the Word of God, are given ears to hear and eyes to see transcendental truths because they were believers first.

Then the disciples came and asked him, 'Why do you speak to them in parables?' He answered, "To you it has been given to know the secrets of the kingdom of heaven, but to them it has not been given".[183] Those who do not believe, do not hear. Believing that the Bible is the authentic inspired Word of God is the very test which Jesus gives to everyone! The correct attitude in our mental prayers is that of little children in the presence of their Farther. Then, we will be given spiritual "ears" to hear and "eyes" to see. Jesus said, "Let the little children come to me; do not stop them; for it is to such as these that the kingdom of God belongs."[184] Truly I tell you, whoever does not receive the kingdom of God as a little child will never enter it.[185]

---

[182] Heb 4:12-13
[183] Matt 13:10-11
[184] Luke 18:16

Again, "Truly I tell you, unless you change and become like children, you will never enter the kingdom of heaven. Whoever becomes humble like this child is the greatest in the kingdom of heaven."[186]

A child-like attitude of faith, hope and love gives an opportunity to grow and mature in the Spirit. Eventually, like Paul, we will look back on our early mental prayer as immature, loving adults. Once we are mature, we will no longer need milk and will consume solid food.[187] We will know fully, as we are now fully known: "Love never ends. But as for prophecies, they will come to an end; as for tongues, they will cease; as for knowledge, it will come to an end. For we know only in part, and we prophesy only in part; but when the complete comes, the partial will come to an end. When I was a child, I spoke like a child, I thought like a child, I reasoned like a child; when I became an adult, I put an end to childish ways. For now we see in a mirror, dimly, but then we will see face to face. Now I know only in part; then I will know fully, even as I have been fully known. And now faith, hope, and love abide, these three; and the greatest of these is love."[188]

When we become mature, we will know as St John of the Cross knew when he wrote in his poem, "I went out from myself, leaving my cares forgotten among the lilies."[189] Until then, we rely on faith, hope and love, fully sufficient for our current needs.[190] In His communication to mankind, God made the Bible as a permanent record, through the efforts of men, which would be translated into many languages and discerned by members of many cultures through the passage of many years. Something is virtually always lost from or added to the original text in any translation.

---

[185] Mark 10:14-16
[186] Matt 18:3-4
[187] 1 Col 3:2
[188] 1 Cor 13:8-13
[189] Dark Night Of The Soul, Stanza 8, St John of the Cross, Barcelona, 1619; Cf. Appendix II
[190] 1 Cor 8:13-18

Therefore, reversion to the original word is always necessary when scholarly inquiry is being made. This is in order to discern the communication the scrivener intended to communicate about his enlightenment from the Holy Spirit. Likewise, references to his culture at the time must be examined for clarity. The Word of God is normative and these inquiries are sometimes necessary in order to retain the norm. Although the Torah, the first five books of the Old Testament, was gathered into written form about the sixth century B.C. it had been proclaimed around Israelite camp fires for thousands of years before. The entire Old Testament was accumulated over several centuries. The New Testament was written within about sixty years of Jesus' crucifixion.

The Second Vatican Council observed that the Word of God is in fully human words, and much more, just as Jesus was fully human flesh, and much more: "[F]or the words of God, expressed in human language, have been made like human discourse, just as the word of the eternal Father, when he took to himself the flesh of human weakness, was in every way made like men.[191]

Having affirmed that the Holy Bible is the Word of God in human language, we must seriously and continually bear in mind that it is fully both of these things, just as we must continually bear in mind that Jesus was of two distinct natures, fully human and fully divine. We must continually maintain intrinsic equilibrium between these affirmations. For, by emphasizing one and de-emphasizing the other, we will fail to grasp the full spiritual or the full human meaning of scripture. We will favor one over the other, and that is not the attitude of a little child.

---

[191] IBID

Chapter 5. Ruminations On Ephesians.

The foregoing should be sufficient to allow one to practice *Lectio Divina* well. Even so, beginning to practice requires a level of confidence and care which may be daunting at first. To help the reader develop familiarity and confidence in the actual practice, I have concluded this book as a set of suggested ruminations on Paul's First Letter to the Ephesians. Although they may seem like a Bible study, they are not. However, if the reader familiarizes himself with all ten ruminations by reading the scriptures and actually undertaking *Lectio Divina* during the reading, they are life changing.

For the serious practitioner of *Lectio Divina*, they are much too long and much too complex. However, for the novice, they are a beginning. Just try. Remember, whether in community or alone, the practitioner,

1. Comes to quiet.

2. Carefully and attentively reads (or listens to) a scripture passage.

3. Peacefully meditates upon the scripture.

4. Re-reads (or listens to) the scripture.

5. Prays to the Lord "in the flesh." One important prayer could be for the health or well-being of your loved ones. Another important prayer is that the Lord allow you to serve him, in any particular that occurs to you. A third could be to pray to receive one or more of the known charisms.

6. Reads the scripture a third time.

7. Prays to the Lord in truth and in spirit by spiritually contemplating him and allowing the holy spirit to speak on your

behalf. Do this in as purely a contemplative and spiritual manner as possible. Do not sub-vocalize or otherwise engage fleshly activity.

Don't neglect to revert to the techniques set out in Chapter 1 in order to deepen the attained quiet of the senses. Do not be in a hurry and do not "re-write" anything the scripture says. Do not think.

It does not matter what particular translation of the Bible is used. The Bible text is only used in meditation. The imagination will make the text "fit" your particular preferences and desires. Allow it to do so. The idea is that one seriously undertakes to "emote" with the various characters and subjects being read.

The contemplative phase is where serious learning takes place. The Word of God Himself is the teacher of your spirit. Do not try to "know", in a fleshly sense, what you are being taught. What the spirit learns will tend to reform and transform what the flesh believes.

It is not a conscious process, unless the Lord determines to speak to you in words. In that event, do not be anxious or excited. If what is heard with the ears or in the brain is truly from the Lord, it will either already be true or will be confirmed as true in the passage of time. Be patient. The peace and joy one experiences during the encounter is its own reward.

In our Lectio Divina of Ephesians, we will not come to the end of the story of how we should live in order to safeguard our salvation, but we will definitely turn a corner. Ephesians is Paul's final, and profound, word about what it means to be a Christian and how to live a Christian life. Paul teaches that we must mature spiritually from the time we are sealed with the Holy Spirit until we die. He shows us many things which can serve as check points of progress during the passage of time, as we mature along the way. We simply let the Holy Spirit teach us.

As we travel this journey, this WAY, things will begin to fall into place. We know that the Bible really is one Book, written by

202

many, but always inspired by the Holy Spirit. The impact of every word in it reverberates throughout the entire volume, from beginning to the end. The Book is all one and it lights the path for our feet. In this sense, the Bible is the path which we must tread and we see clearly that the teachings of Paul are actually food for our journey. The longer we study, the more it feeds us. We need never go hungry again.

Having responded with our "yes" to the call of God and having determined to mature from milk to meat, let us carefully chew upon the words of Paul: "When I was a child, I spoke like a child, I thought like a child, I reasoned like a child; when I became a man, I gave up childish ways. For now, we see in a mirror dimly, but then face to face. Now I know in part; then I shall understand fully, even as I have been fully understood. So, faith, hope, love abide, these three; but the greatest of these is love." Yes, let us give up childish thoughts, our "personal" versions of truth. Let us begin to perceive the inspired truth, as in a mirror dimly. The Holy Spirit leads us toward understanding fully, even as we have been fully understood. Let us choose to take life seriously.

Remembering the words of Paul, we accept that we have been sealed with the Holy Spirit in baptism: "In him you also, who have heard the word of truth, the gospel of your salvation, and have believed in him, were sealed with the promised Holy Spirit, which is the guarantee of our inheritance until we acquire possession of it, to the praise of his glory. NOW we can see what Jesus meant when he said, "Nevertheless I tell you the truth: it is to your advantage that I go away, for if I do not go away, the Counselor will not come to you; but if I go, I will send him to you. And when he comes, he will convince the world concerning sin and righteousness and judgment..." Jesus is the savior and the redeemer. It would have been futile for the Holy Spirit to teach the truth about sin, righteousness and judgment until we were redeemed! The teaching of the Holy Spirit is what Ephesians is all about. Learning about Jesus' coming and His salvific work is basic, the milk of our salvation. But, our growth toward maturity is what the Holy Spirit is about.

Paul was constrained to speak to the Corinthians in this manner: "Now I would remind you, brethren, in what terms I preached to you the gospel, which you received, in which you stand, by which you are saved, if you hold it fast - unless you believed in vain. For I delivered to you as of first importance what I also received, that Christ died for our sins in accordance with the scriptures, that he was buried, that he was raised on the third day in accordance with the scriptures, and that he appeared to Cephas, then to the twelve. Then he appeared to more than five hundred brethren at one time, most of whom are still alive, though some have fallen asleep. Then he appeared to James, then to all the apostles. Last of all, as to one untimely born, he appeared also to me." "But I, brethren, could not address you as spiritual men, but as men of the flesh, as babes in Christ. I fed you with milk, not solid food; for you were not ready for it; and even yet you are not ready, for you are still of the flesh. For while there is jealousy and strife among you, are you not of the flesh, and behaving like ordinary men?"

And he wrote to the Hebrews, "For though by this time you ought to be teachers, you need someone to teach you again the first principles of God's word. You need milk, not solid food; for everyone who lives on milk is unskilled in the word of righteousness, for he is a child. But solid food is for the mature, for those who have their faculties trained by practice to distinguish good from evil. "Therefore let us leave the elementary doctrine of Christ and go on to maturity, not laying again a foundation of repentance from dead works and of faith toward God, with instruction about ablutions, the laying on of hands, the resurrection of the dead, and eternal judgment." "[d]o not throw away your confidence, which has a great reward. For you have need of endurance, so that you may do the will of God and receive what is promised. For yet a little while, and the coming one shall come and shall not tarry; but my righteous one shall live by faith, and if he shrinks back, my soul has no pleasure in him. But we are not of those who shrink back and are destroyed, but of those who have faith and keep their souls."

Now, full of hope, which is born of our faith and belief; sealed with the Holy Spirit, which is the guarantee of our inheritance, let us turn away from the milk of repentance and faith and encouraged by He who dwells within us, let us build endurance by eating flesh. "[s]ince we are surrounded by so great a cloud of witnesses, let us also lay aside every weight, and sin which clings so closely, and let us run with perseverance the race that is set before us, looking to Jesus the pioneer and perfecter of our faith, who for the joy that was set before him endured the cross, despising the shame, and is seated at the right hand of the throne of God. With the end in view, let us strive to adopt the words Paul said to his disciple Timothy, "[I] am already on the point of being sacrificed; the time of my departure has come. have fought the good fight, I have finished the race, I have kept the faith. Henceforth there is laid up for me the crown of righteousness, which the Lord, the righteous judge, will award to me on that Day, and not only to me but also to all who have loved his appearing."

Rumination 1. Ephesians 1:1-14.

Turning to Ephesians, the last of the Captivity Epistles, we readily perceive that Paul ran far beyond mere belief in the first things of salvation. He starts by affirming that he is an apostle of Christ Jesus, meaning that he, who did not know Jesus personally, had "been sent" by Jesus, after his physical death. The Lord Jesus confirmed to Ananias that Paul was "[a] chosen instrument of mine to carry my name before the Gentiles and kings and the sons of Israel;" and the other apostles also affirmed Paul as an apostle, Doing miracles in Jesus' name, and exhibiting an unshakable faith, Paul's credentials to speak for the Lord are of the highest possible kind.

Paul proclaimed "Grace to you and peace from God our Father and the Lord Jesus Christ." He then launched into what is often called a hymn of praise to the Lord. (A hymn is a type of song, specifically for the purpose of praise, adoration or prayer, addressed to a deity.) However, it immediately transforms into a witness of how we have been blessed with every spiritual blessing in the heavenly places. As we shall see, this blessing includes that we believers were "sealed with the promised Holy Spirit, who is the guarantee of our inheritance." Perhaps this was more of a teaching to the reader, than a hymn to the Lord, but I get ahead of myself. This encouraging hymn continues through verse 14 of Ephesians.

Back to verse 3, Paul affirms that we are predestined to holiness, ourselves eventually to be made into gods, constituent parts of the Lord Jesus: "even as he chose us in him before the foundation of the world, that we should be holy and blameless before him. He destined us in love to be his sons through Jesus Christ, according to the purpose of his will, to the praise of his glorious grace which he freely bestowed on us in the Beloved." Of course, we know that freely means we will not earn anything. We see that we are given this gift to the praise of his glorious grace bestowed on us "in the Beloved". What could this mean?

According to Navarre, this gift of divine filiation (making us brothers of the Lord Jesus) is the greatest expression of the glory of God, because it reveals the full extent of God's love for man. The purpose of this eternal divine, predestined, plan is to promote "the praise of his glorious grace." In this light, we can see that God's love for us is merciful in the truest sense. This love is like an ocean cascading down upon us in a never ceasing bath of grace and goodness so we can share in Jesus' life and glory. Our creator offers an opportunity to everyone to have everything, simultaneously to assuring praise to his glorious grace, he assures our happiness "In the Beloved":

The Old Testament stresses again and again that God loves his people and that Israel is the cherished people. In the New Testament Christians are called "beloved of God." However, there is only one "Beloved", strictly speaking, Jesus Christ our Lord – as God revealed from the bright cloud at the Transfiguration: "This is my beloved Son, with whom I am well pleased" The Son of his love has obtained man's redemption and brought forgiveness of sins, and it is through his grace that we become pleasing to God, lovable by him with the same love with which he loves his Son. At the Last Supper, Jesus asked his Father for this very thing – "So that the world may know that thou hast sent me and hast loved them even as thou hast love me"

NOTE: This precise, profound explication demonstrates in the strongest possible terms that Paul was in no sense confused or tentative about these things. They defy human intelligence, logic or imagination. Yet they mesh seamlessly with the entirety of the Bible. Paul is demonstrating, once again, that he is merely teaching us what has been taught him by the Lord.

At this point, verse 7, Paul began to describe the redemptive work of Jesus Christ in continuing the predestined plan described above; i. e., redemption by his blood, the forgiveness of our trespasses, according to the riches of his grace which he lavished upon us. The redemption wrought by Christ frees us from the worst

208

of all slaveries – that of sin – even though, in our imperfection, we must grow away from the predisposition to sin. His is a plan for the fullness of time, to unite all things in him and we, individually, are each part of the complete process. God will unite all things in heaven and things on earth in Him. Remember, God created both the heavens and the earth. He begat the Word, his Son, the incarnated Jesus, destined to be a brother to us, and the Holy Spirit emanates from both of them. In awe, fear and trembling we contemplate these mysteries and, even though we are assured that we have been sealed with the promised Holy Spirit, who is the guarantee of our inheritance, we know that we cannot merit these wonders. Praise God, this knowledge is the first step toward maturity and perfection. It brings crushing humility. But we can have hope. God tells us so in many places and in many ways. It does not matter that we have no worth. Our creator will mature, nurture, preserve and love us into perfection. All anguish and fear within us will disappear, as we grow. Our chains are broken. Our sorrows have fled. Jesus is with us, as he was with the Apostles. Have faith: "I will not leave you desolate; I will come to you. Yet a little while, and the world will see me no more, but you will see me; because I live, you will live also. In that day you will know that I am in my Father, and you in me, and I in you. He who has my commandments and keeps them, he it is who loves me; and he who loves me will be loved by my Father, and I will love him and manifest myself to him." Amen. Come Lord Jesus.

Rumination 2. Ephesians 1:15-23.

Thus far, Paul has presented his credentials to speak on behalf of the Lord Jesus Christ and has sung his hymn of praise to God's glory. Now, at verse 15, he launches into thanksgiving for the faith in Jesus Christ of those to whom he was writing and because of their love for all of those who form the church of God, the saints. This telegraphs the message to whoever reads this Epistle, throughout history, that it was written for the benefit of practicing Christians who are already filled with faith in Jesus and love for their brothers. Paul says he is praying for them, not that they respond to the call of the Lord, they are already doing that! He prays that the God of Jesus, the Father of glory, may give them a spirit of wisdom and of revelation in the knowledge of him. He asks that the eyes of their hearts may be enlightened; that they may know what is the hope to which they have been called; what are the riches of their inheritance; and what is the immeasurable power in us who believe, the same as He accomplished in Christ when He raised him from the dead, and placed him far above all "rule, authority, power and dominion – above every name that is named or will be named in time to come." God has placed all things under Jesus' feet and we, the church, are participants in Jesus. We are his body!

WOW!! That is a mouth full! Thank God that we already have faith and love within us. If we did not believe, if we did not have some sense of the awesome majesty and power of God within us, we might walk away from this, deeming it foolish nonsense. Now we can begin to see what Paul was driving home to the Corinthians in the two Epistles. Here is a sample:

"Where is the wise man? Where is the scribe? Where is the debater of this age? Has not God made foolish the wisdom of the world? For since, in the wisdom of God, the world did not know God through wisdom, it pleased God through the folly of what we preach to save those who believe. [...] For the foolishness of God is wiser than men, and the weakness of God is stronger than men."

211

"Let no one deceive himself. If any one among you thinks that he is wise in this age, let him become a fool that he may become wise. For the wisdom of this world is folly with God." "You foolish man! What you sow does not come to life unless it dies. And what you sow is not the body which is to be, but a bare kernel, perhaps of wheat or of some other grain. But God gives it a body as he has chosen, and to each kind of seed its own body. For not all flesh is alike, ..." Christ is the wisdom and power of God. "The spiritual man judges all things, but is himself to be judged by no one. "For [...] we have the mind of Christ."

A few years later, Paul wrote consistently with this to the Galatians: "O foolish Galatians! Who has bewitched you, before whose eyes Jesus Christ was publicly portrayed as crucified? Let me ask you only this: Did you receive the Spirit by works of the law, or by hearing with faith? Are you so foolish ? Having begun with the Spirit, are you now ending with the flesh?"

In other words, the spiritual mind can be lost, as well as gained. "Therefore, do not be foolish, but understand what the will of the Lord is."

We have a natural tendency to incredulity about things which we cannot touch, feel, smell, taste or hear. Without being called to a spirit of wisdom and a revelation in the knowledge of God, this teaching would be more than we could take in. But, thanks be to God, our acceptance of the gospels, including the teachings of Paul, proves than we have been called by Him! Therefore, since we can be confident in the call of the Lord, let us remember that God is trustworthy and true. He is where there is peace, hope and rest for our souls: "At that time Jesus declared, 'I thank thee, Father, Lord of heaven and earth, that thou hast hidden these things from the wise and understanding and revealed them to babes; yea, Father, for such was thy gracious will. All things have been delivered to me by my Father; and no one knows the Son except the Father, and no one knows the Father except the Son and any one to whom the Son chooses to reveal him. Come to me, all who labor and are heavy laden, and I will give you rest. Take my yoke upon you, and learn from me; for I am gentle and lowly in heart, and you will find rest for your souls. For my yoke is easy, and my burden is light."

The hope that delights us so is a gift from God, an infused virtue. "Hope is a supernatural virtue, infused by God into our soul, by which we desire and expect eternal life, promised by God to his servants, and the means necessary to obtain it." This is a part of what Paul was praying about when he prayed for the readers of Ephesians that God may give "a spirit of wisdom and of revelation in the knowledge of him, having the eyes of your hearts enlightened, that you may know what is the hope to which he has called you, ...". Paul also prayed that the Father of glory grant us supernatural wisdom to recognize the greatness of the blessings he has given us through his son.

These special gifts from the spirit of wisdom, were known of old and reflected in the scriptures of the Old Testament: "Who has learned thy counsel, unless thou hast given wisdom and sent thy holy Spirit from on high? And thus, the paths of those on earth were set right, and men were taught what pleases thee, and were saved by wisdom."

As part of the wisdom and supernatural knowledge of Him, Paul prays that we shall see what are the riches of his glorious inheritance in us and the immeasurable greatness of his power in raising Jesus from the dead. What is this inheritance? It is, stated in Paul's prayer for the Colossians, written shortly before he wrote Ephesians: "May you be strengthened with all power, according to his glorious might, for all endurance and patience with joy, giving thanks to the Father, who has qualified us to share in the inheritance of the saints in light. He has delivered us from the dominion of darkness and transferred us to the kingdom of his beloved Son, in whom we have redemption, the forgiveness of sins."

Mind you, as Paul says in Eph 1:19, this immeasurable power is in us! It is the power with which he first raised Jesus Christ from the dead and made him sit at the right hand in the heavenly places. This same power, at work in us, does not sit placidly, waiting until we die to whirl into action. No, it fights a battle with that which is of the flesh, within us, moving us toward perfection. The battle will last until the day we die and sometimes we can feel its violent force. The clashes, hopefully in the form of what are actually small, transforming victories, may be manifested by sorrowful memories of our own past errors and sins. But we do not despair. We are being united more closely to the Lord by these transformations and He will not abandon us. According to Saint Escriva, He allows these trials to befall us so as to have us love him the more and discover even more clearly his constant protection and Love.

When we are resurrected through the transforming power of God, we will not be born again. Although rebirth, is absolutely necessary, "Jesus answered him, 'Truly, truly, I say to you, unless one is born anew, he cannot see the kingdom of God.'" "Therefore, if any one is in Christ, he is a new creation; the old has passed away, behold, the new has come. Rebirth was the basis of our justification. At the resurrection, already justified, we shall be raised from the dead. Our bodies shall be rejoined to our spirits and we shall be changed. "Lo! I tell you a mystery. We shall not all sleep, but we shall all be changed, in a moment, in the twinkling of an eye, at the last trumpet. For the trumpet will sound, and the dead will be raised imperishable, and we shall be changed. For this perishable nature must put on the imperishable, and this mortal nature must put on immortality. When the perishable puts on the imperishable, and the mortal puts on immortality, then shall come to pass the saying that is written: "Death is swallowed up in victory. O death, where is thy victory? O death, where is thy sting?" Remember, there is nothing intrinsically unique about our bodies. They are mere ashes and dust. Our spirits animate us. "[t]hen the Lord God formed man of dust from the ground, and

214

breathed into his nostrils the breath of life; and man became a living being." "In the sweat of your face you shall eat bread till you return to the ground, for out of it you were taken; you are dust, and to dust you shall return." "And many of those who sleep in the dust of the earth shall awake, some to everlasting life," The spirits of the dead are rejoined to their bodies.

"So I prophesied as I was commanded; and as I prophesied, there was a noise, and behold, a rattling; and the bones came together, bone to its bone. And as I looked, there were sinews on them, and flesh had come upon them, and skin had covered them; but there was no breath in them. Then he said to me, 'Prophesy to the breath, prophesy, son of man, and say to the breath, Thus says the Lord God: Come from the four winds, O breath, and breathe upon these slain, that they may live.' So I prophesied as he commanded me, and the breath came into them, and they lived, and stood upon their feet, an exceedingly great host." "Bear fruit that befits repentance, and do not presume to say to yourselves, 'We have Abraham as our father'; for I tell you, God is able from these stones to raise up children to Abraham."

"As he (Jesus) was now drawing near, at the descent of the Mount of Olives, the whole multitude of the disciples began to rejoice and praise God with a loud voice for all the mighty works that they had seen, saying, 'Blessed is the King who comes in the name of the Lord! Peace in heaven and glory in the highest!' And some of the Pharisees in the multitude said to him, 'Teacher, rebuke your disciples.' He answered, 'I tell you, if these were silent, the very stones would cry out.'"

And, although we, as dirt, have no intrinsic worth or special merit, we are precious in God's eyes, He loves us. "For God so loved the world that he gave his only Son, that whoever believes in him should not perish but have eternal life. For God sent the Son into the world, not to condemn the world, but that the world might be saved through him."

But, in our conceit, we feel so important, to the exclusion of all else. How can it possibly be that we are nevertheless precious, loved, by God and redeemed by Jesus? This is a mystery. However, God has given us some penetration into the mystery in the scriptures: "[G]od is love . In this the love of God was made manifest among us, that God sent his only Son into the world, so that we might live through him. In this is love, not that we loved God but that he loved us and sent his Son to be the expiation for our sins. Beloved, if God so loved us, we also ought to love one another. No man has ever seen God; if we love one another, God abides in us and his love is perfected in us. God has [p]ut all things under his (Jesus') feet and has made him the head over all things for the church, which is his body, the fulness of him who fills all in all. According to Navarre, what this means is that, "[t]hrough the Church, Christ becomes present in and fills the entire universe and extends to it the fruits of his redemptive activity. [...] that is why St. Paul calls the Church the 'body' of Christ; [...] not because it in any way fills out or completes Christ but because it is filled with Christ ..." "For the creation waits with eager longing for the revealing of the sons of God; for the creation was subjected to futility, not of its own will but by the will of him who subjected it (God) in hope; because the creation itself will be set free from its bondage to decay and obtain the glorious liberty of the children of God. We know that the whole creation has been groaning in travail together until now;..." Amen. Come Lord Jesus.

Rumination 3. Ephesians 2:1-10.

In Rumination 2 we learned that Paul prays that God may give us a spirit of wisdom and of revelation in the knowledge of him. He asks that the eyes of our hearts may be enlightened; that we may know what is the hope to which we have been called; what are the riches of our inheritance; and what is the immeasurable power in us who believe, the same as He accomplished in Christ when He raised him from the dead, and placed him far above all "rule, authority, power and dominion – above every name that is named or will be named in time to come." Along the way, we learned about the great importance of Jesus' resurrection, conquering death, and that we have the power within us to do the same. This is not a rebirth, it is a perfecting of what we are. We will be changed forever, in the twinkling of an eye. We, who are merely dirt, into which God has breathed life. Without Him, we are helpless, but He LOVES us. We are being changed into something that is beautiful and perfect. Much like a diamond, dug out of the earth, we have no intrinsic value; but, we are precious in his eyes. We, like all of creation, have been subjected to futility, but in hope, by the will of God, so that all creation will be set free from this bondage to decay and obtain the glorious liberty of the children of God. All creation has been groaning in travail together until now; in anticipation of our perfection.

By looking closely, we see that something of the "mystery" of our creation and salvation is being explained to us. For instance, "For he has made known to us in all wisdom and insight the mystery of his will, according to his purpose which he set forth in Christ as a plan for the fulness of time, to unite all things in him, things in heaven and things on earth. We are taught that God has "[m]ade him (Jesus) the head over all things for the church, (us) which is his body, the fulness of him who fills all in all. This sounds like He is blood, flowing in our veins, filling our entire bodies. According to Navarre, this means Christ is present in and fills the entire universe [...] not because the universe in any way fills out or completes Christ but because it is filled with Christ ..."

Is this describing how God developed Jesus' body as part of the kingdom of heaven? Jesus taught about the kingdom in parables: "Another parable he put before them, saying, 'The kingdom of heaven may be compared to a man who sowed good seed in his field;...'" "Another parable he put before them, saying, The kingdom of heaven is like a grain of mustard seed which a man took and sowed in his field; ...'" "He told them another parable. 'The kingdom of heaven is like leaven which a woman took and hid in three measures of flour, till it was all leavened.'" And many more. They all describe some sort of growing, flourishing. In private, Jesus explained the parables to his disciples, but the explanations themselves are still mere metaphors. We are given no description of heaven in concrete terms, only that it does exist. Apologists refer to this kingdom as "transcendental" or, outside of, something other than, the material universe. Yet, since our conversion, we know in our heart of hearts that we very seriously want to go there. We want to be with, to worship, God in the Kingdom. We know from scripture that "God is spirit and those who worship him must worship in spirit and truth." "I appeal to you therefore, brethren, by the mercies of God, to present your bodies as a living sacrifice, holy and acceptable to God, which is your spiritual worship. Do not be conformed to this world but be transformed by the renewal of your mind, that you may prove what is the will of God, what is good and acceptable and perfect." "[w]e who first hoped in Christ have been destined and appointed to live for the praise of his glory." And it says late in the Book of Revelation that, after the end of this age, in the new age, "There shall no more be anything accursed, but the throne of God and of the Lamb (Jesus) shall be in it, and his servants shall worship him; they shall see his face, ..." With only hope, helpless to do this ourselves, we must leave sin behind, "For the wages of sin is death, but the free gift of God is eternal life in Christ Jesus our Lord."

But, what is eternal life? "And this is eternal life, that they know thee the only true God, and Jesus Christ whom thou hast sent." How can knowing God possibly be eternal life? This is

218

another mystery, but Paul gives us our answer, if we can grasp it! He prayed that the God of Jesus, the Father of glory, may give us a spirit of wisdom and of revelation in the knowledge of him. The words of revelation are set forth in the Bible. We must trust - be at peace about this:

"Then Moses said to God, "If I come to the people of Israel and say to them, 'The God of your fathers has sent me to you,' and they ask me, 'What is his name?' what shall I say to them? God said to Moses, 'I AM WHO I AM' And he said, 'Say this to the people of Israel, 'I AM has sent me to you.' [...] this is my name for ever, and thus I am to be remembered throughout all generations. Again, "In the beginning God created the heavens and the earth." In other words, God was existing before creation. Also, "In the beginning was the Word, and the Word was with God, and the Word was God. He was in the beginning with God; all things were made through him, and without him was not anything made that was made. In him was life, and the life was the light of men." Further, "And the Word became flesh and dwelt among us, full of grace and truth; we have beheld his glory, glory as of the only Son from the Father." From this we know that Jesus, the Son of God, existed and was with the Father before creation, before he was incarnated as Jesus! Remember, God created both the heavens and the earth in the beginning, before time began. God and Jesus are spirit. They ARE outside of any of the "things" which make up the universe. Neither God nor Jesus "occupy" time or space. It is as though time and the universe, all of creation, is a sphere and the Holy Trinity is "present" to all points of the sphere, inside and out, as their own created "place". They are not trapped in the flow of time, as we experience it. That is why the name of God, to us, is I AM! He is always "present" to all points in time. Time is measured by motion within the universe. As St Thomas Aquinas explains it, God is the unmoved mover.

Now, what Paul says in Eph 2:4-7 makes more sense: "But God, who is rich in mercy, out of the great love with which he loved us, even when we were dead through our trespasses, made us alive together with Christ (by grace you have been saved), and raised (past tense) us up with him, and made (past tense) us sit with him in the heavenly places in Christ Jesus, [We were made alive with Christ and we are currently sitting with him in heaven?]" Whether the Holy Trinity, spirits, actually "sit" and where the "heavenly places" are, (outside of the created universe?), remain mysteries about which we are not specifically told. But, the foregoing does give us some guidance about how eternal life means to "know" God and Jesus Christ. And how we could have been crucified with Jesus, died with Him and sit with Him in the heavenly places in Christ Jesus because, to him, all time is "now" and, we are now His body. In that sense, we are with him now and throughout all time and in eternity: This could mean that since God "IS", then we "ARE" and being with him is eternal life! Unfortunately, we are only conscious of the flow of time in which we live. Therefore, we cannot "see" if we are individually sitting "in" Jesus or "with" the Father on his throne, currently present to all points in time, as is God. "For now we see in a mirror dimly, but then face to face. Now I know in part; then I shall understand fully, even as I have been fully understood. Assuming the foregoing perception is accurate, the question remains, who are the weeds and who is the wheat? Look around.

Now, it is obvious that Paul was not confused and he was not using words carelessly. It is us who simply had no understanding! For instance, in the foregoing view, it makes sense for Paul to say, "For we are his workmanship, created in Christ Jesus for good works, which God prepared beforehand, that we should walk in them." God knew what we should do, in the stream of time, to best move us toward perfection, before time began. Of course, he also knew what of those good works, which he created for us, we would not do. But they are available to us in his love and mercy.

This brings into play the doctrine of free will. Clearly, man has the freedom of will. We see this early on, in the Garden of Eden. There, both Adam and Eve exercised their wills contrary to the commands of God. This is another mystery.

220

How can man have free will if everything is predestined? St Thomas Aquinas grappled with this issue several times in the Summa Theologica. To roughly paraphrase his thoughts, St Thomas held that man exercises his will freely within a sphere of predestination. That is, man has every option of action at his command, but God infallibly knows what he will do before he does it. God refrains from dictating to man how he must act. He only tells man how he should act, leaving man to take whatever actions his will decides for him to do. This freedom allows man to truly grow and mature toward perfection. Anything else and man's love and adoration would not be freely and truly created by himself. And what about those who do not eventually believe in God? He allows them to grow as freely as those who do. He will separate us later. "Then he left the crowds and went into the house. And his disciples came to him, saying, 'Explain to us the parable of the weeds of the field.' He answered, 'He who sows the good seed is the Son of man; the field is the world, and the good seed means the sons of the kingdom; the weeds are the sons of the evil one, and the enemy who sowed them is the devil; the harvest is the close of the age, and the reapers are angels. Just as the weeds are gathered and burned with fire, so will it be at the close of the age. The Son of man will send his angels, and they will gather out of his kingdom all causes of sin and all evildoers, and throw them into the furnace of fire; there men will weep and gnash their teeth. Then the righteous will shine like the sun in the kingdom of their Father. He who has ears, let him hear.

And how are we to "work out" our salvation in this sphere of predestination? Paul taught the Philippians: "Therefore, my beloved, as you have always obeyed, so now, not only as in my presence but much more in my absence, work out your own salvation with fear and trembling; for God is at work in you, both to will and to work for his good pleasure."

According to Navarre, salvation acts in man by means of faith, that is, by man's acceptance of the salvation offered him in Jesus Christ. But even faith is a divine gift. St Paul tells us, "For by grace

221

you have been saved through faith; and this is not your own doing, it is the gift of God - not because of works, lest any man should boast. For we are his workmanship, created in Christ Jesus for good works, which God prepared beforehand, that we should walk in them." We cannot merit salvation. It is never exclusively the outcome of our exercise of free will. Always, God's grace is at work to help us.

This is well supported by scripture: "For it has been granted to you that for the sake of Christ you should not only believe in him but also suffer for his sake," "And I am sure that he who began a good work in you will bring it to completion at the day of Jesus Christ. Therefore, we can see that we have no free, predestined ride into heaven. Indeed, we must grope forward in good faith, with fear and trembling. Although we know that we are not able to surprise God, we are able to please Him.

The good works were prepared beforehand, but we must choose to do them. When we do so, it is pleasing to God. "[w]e have not ceased to pray for you, asking that you may be filled with the knowledge of his will in all spiritual wisdom and understanding, to lead a life worthy of the Lord, fully pleasing to him, bearing fruit in every good work and increasing in the knowledge of God. May you be strengthened with all power, according to his glorious might, for all endurance and patience with joy, giving thanks to the Father, who has qualified us to share in the inheritance of the saints in light." Oh, joyful night. He is the light. Amen. Come, Lord Jesus.

Rumination 4. Ephesians 2:11-22.

In Eph 2:11-22, St Paul explains that, through the death and resurrection of Jesus Christ, God removed all barriers, everything that separates, Jews from Gentiles. According to the Old Covenant between God and Abraham, all of Abrahams descendants, who would be more numerous that the sands on the shore of the sea, must be circumcised. Everyone else was called the uncircumcision, outsiders, Gentiles. The barrier between the circumcision and the uncircumcision was removed by Jesus' conquering death through resurrection. For thus, Jesus established a New Covenant of salvation through belief in Him.

What does this mean, that circumcision was no longer to be performed as a sign of the covenant? YES, and much more! First, a Jew who did not accept, with certainty, that Jesus is Lord, would not dare withhold circumcision from his children. This would alienate them from the entire Jewish community. The covenant with Abraham was established by the very word of God Himself! Paul admits this. However, he says, circumcision of the flesh is not true circumcision. Spiritual circumcision of the heart is true circumcision! Clearly, this requires that one totally accept the teachings of Jesus, Paul, and the other Apostles, as true God, prophets and Apostles of God before he could dare to withhold circumcision from his children.

Think about it. Truly devout Jews would be required, not only to accept Christ, but to turn away from the very thing that undeniably affirms their Jewishness. Circumcision permanently identified them as Jews! Even if they accepted Christ, they would still have the identifying mark of the Jew. They could maintain that Christianity was a fulfillment of the prophesies of their religion. But, to withhold circumcision from one's children, would be to identify them as rebels. This would cast their children adrift. It would be considered the most serious insult imaginable.

Yet, this is what Paul taught, not only must the Jews accept Christ, but they must deny the physical requirements of the old covenant. The impossibility of this dilemma served the will of God. He blinded the eyes and hearts of all Jews but a few. Paul and the other Christians were among the exceptions. Their eyes and hearts were opened by the Lord. The others could not see the truth. The Bible is very clear about this being God's will: "Lest you (Gentiles) be wise in your own conceits, I want you to understand this mystery, brethren: a hardening has come upon part of Israel, until the full number of the Gentiles come in, and so all Israel will be saved; as it is written, 'The Deliverer will come from Zion, he will banish ungodliness from Jacob; (the Jews) and this will be my covenant with them when I take away their sins.' As regards the gospel they are enemies of God, for your sake; but as regards election they are beloved for the sake of their forefathers. For the gifts and the call of God are irrevocable. Just as you were once disobedient to God but now have received mercy because of their disobedience, (crucifixion of Jesus) so they have now been disobedient in order that by the mercy shown to you they also may receive mercy. For God has consigned all men to disobedience, that he may have mercy upon all."

WOW!! The Jews are a chosen people! They were not chosen because they were especially lovable or good. They were chosen to be the instrument of God in the process of salvation. They were the instruments of suffering which God himself underwent in atonement for the sins of the entire world! Paul says in Romans that the Jews did no conscious wrong by crucifying Jesus, they served God's purpose in doing so! They are an important part of the process of salvation from sinfulness (falling short) because of our own pride. This pride comes from the same source as the very thing that in mankind is precious to God, his free will to love. Since original sin, we choose to love ourselves! Once the sinful part is corrected through the process of salvation, man will have been perfected – he will love perfectly, as God loves him. Gaining the power to love without reservation must come from the free will of man in order to actually create love for God. Without man's free will, his love would be merely reciprocal, it would be a reflection,

224

a mirror, a mere return, of the love unreservedly given him by God.

Thus, it is that the salvation of mankind is a totally loving act of God that mankind can become able to return, not merely reflect, love. When perfected, man's love of God is freely created from within man, by his own choice and will.

This delicate process of perfection requires the sequential movement of time. It takes the motion of time for man to be perfected into a truly creating lover. Is this is the way God creates and begets His children? We are becoming his progeny, his children by the process disclosed to us in the Bible? Are we being drawn into Him and held together by a magnetic-like force of love, which both He and we create? Is mankind, in the passage of time, becoming the body of Christ, God's only begotten Son? We were created as man, but were born into original sin.

The process of salvation which mankind is undergoing could be viewed as a begetting into a perfection which dwells eternally, in the present tense, outside of time. Remember scripture, "For a thousand years in thy sight are but as yesterday when it is past, or as a watch in the night;" "But do not ignore this one fact, beloved, that with the Lord one day is as a thousand years, and a thousand years as one day."

It seems as though the universe may be a hot house in which man is created, born and perfected, begotten into brothers of Jesus and children of God. To us, much happens in the process. Time passes. But to God, it all occurs in an instant. God is timeless. We, and all creation, shall be freed from bondage to sin and death, locked in the passage of time, when the saved ones are identified: "Let it be known to you therefore, brethren, that through this man (Jesus) forgiveness of sins is proclaimed to you, and by him every one that believes is freed from everything from which you could not be freed by the law of Moses. Beware, therefore, lest there come upon you what is said in the prophets: 'Behold, you scoffers, and wonder, and perish; (in time, not being released to eternity) for

I do a deed in your days (time), a deed you will never believe, if one declares it to you.'" "For he who has died is freed from sin. But if we have died with Christ, we believe that we shall also live (present tense) with him. For we know that Christ being raised from the dead will never (refers to the flow of time) die again; death no longer has dominion over him. The death he died he died to sin, once for all, but the life he lives he lives to God (in eternity). So you also must consider yourselves (present tense) dead to sin and alive to God in Christ Jesus" (outside of time?).

In this view, God will surely not punish the Jews for being mere instruments of His will. On the contrary, when the purpose of this chosen race is fully accomplished, the blinders on their eyes will be removed and they will see the Lord for who he is. One can only imagine the joy and rejoicing that will fill all hearts at that time, when we all have been freed from our sins: "To him who loves us and has freed us from our sins by his blood and made us a kingdom, priests to his God and Father, to him be glory and dominion for ever and ever. Amen. Behold, he is coming with the clouds, and every eye will see him, every one who pierced him; and all tribes of the earth (not just the Jews?) will wail on account of him. Even so. Amen. 'I am the Alpha and the Omega,' (the beginning and the end) says the Lord God, who is and who was and who is to come, the Almighty."

Paul put these truths straight to anyone, whether Jew or Gentile: "We have renounced disgraceful, underhanded ways; we refuse to practice cunning or to tamper with God's word, but by the open statement of the truth we would commend ourselves to every man's conscience in the sight of God. And even if our gospel is veiled, it is veiled only to those who are perishing. In their case the god of this world (Satan) has blinded the minds of the unbelievers, to keep them from seeing the light of the gospel of the glory of Christ, who is the likeness of God. For what we preach is not ourselves, but Jesus Christ as Lord, with ourselves as your servants for Jesus' sake. For it is the God who said, 'Let light shine out of darkness,' who has shone in our hearts to give the light of the knowledge of the glory of God in the face of Christ. But we have this treasure in earthen vessels, to show that the transcendent power belongs to God and not to us."

In other words, no one can believe in Jesus unless God calls him by name. "Jesus said to them, 'If you were blind, you would have no guilt; but now that you say, 'We see,' your guilt remains." 'To him the gatekeeper (Jesus) opens; the sheep hear his voice, and he calls his own sheep by name and leads them out. When he has brought out all his own, (the end of the age) he goes before them, and the sheep follow him, for they know his voice. A stranger they will not follow, but they will flee from him, for they do not know the voice of strangers.' This figure Jesus used with them, but they did not understand what he was saying to them."

These comments on the scriptures are not definitive. They are only offered in the hope that all our hearts will open further to the teaching of the Holy Spirit. Our hearts will know what is true. We must allow the Holy Spirit to bring us to peace about His teachings. He teaches the truth, perfects us in understanding and allows us to grow. It is extremely important to remember that the Evil One is ever vigilant, "Humble yourselves therefore under the mighty hand of God, that in due time he may exalt you. Cast all your anxieties on him, for he cares about you. Be sober, be watchful. Your adversary the devil prowls around like a roaring lion, seeking someone to devour. Resist him, firm in your faith, knowing that the same experience of suffering is required of your brotherhood throughout the world. And after you have suffered a little while, the God of all grace, who has called you to his eternal glory in Christ, will himself restore, establish, and strengthen you. To him be the dominion for ever and ever. Amen."

We are being weaned, and are learning to eat meat. From this, we gain strength for the journey as we follow THE WAY. The Lord, lights our paths. But, we are all sinners and can easily stray. We help each other to be patient, to mature and to take life seriously. As St Thomas More said, "Lets all get to heaven together." Biblical truth brings peace to our hearts and, as meat which we savor, chew and digest, wisdom begins to emerge.

Returning to Eph 2:11-22, our entire rumination this week, we see that Paul is specifically writing to Gentiles who have already become Christians. Therefore, it can have special application to us. His thrust was to remove the wall between Jews and Gentiles. However, scripture demonstrates that the wall must remain to those Jews whom God has blinded, until the full number of Gentiles come in (Rom 11:25).

But, as we progress toward perfection, all hostility in our own hearts comes to an end.: "But now in Christ Jesus you who once were far off have been brought near in the blood of Christ. For he is our peace, who has made us both one, and has broken down the dividing wall of hostility, by abolishing in his flesh (and only there) the law of commandments and ordinances (the law of Moses), that he might create in himself one new man in place of the two, so making peace, and might reconcile us both to God in one body through the cross, thereby bringing the hostility to an end. And he came and preached peace to you who were far off and peace to those who were near; (the Jews) for through him we both have access in one Spirit to the Father. So then you are no longer strangers and sojourners, but you are fellow citizens with the saints and members of the household of God, built upon the foundation of the apostles and prophets, Christ Jesus himself being the cornerstone, in whom the whole structure is joined together and grows into a holy temple in the Lord; in whom you also are built into it for a dwelling place of God in the Spirit."

What more can we want than to grow into this magnificent service of Jesus to all? Remember Jesus' descriptions of heaven as growing, flourishing. (Matt 13:24-33) These revelations identify a place for us, in service to all, as He served, that we may know the love of Christ. (Mt 20:25-28). This revelation helps us grasp the one remaining doctrinal mystery touched on by Paul in Ephesians.

Paul's insights into the mystery of Jesus Christ Himself are next. Amen. Come, Lord Jesus.

Rumination 5. Ephesians 3:1-13.

The Book of Ephesians is a proclamation of the mystery of Christ, revealed, not guessed at, by his minister and apostle, St. Paul. The mystery of Christ may be the most difficult possible subject to grasp; however, Paul says that this scripture displays his insight into the mystery and, that we can perceive that he knows what he is talking about. If we read this explanation with anything less than a firm determination to purely and simply grasp what it says, we may lose an opportunity to be fed the meat of the teaching by the Holy Spirit!!

Solid food does not simply jump on the plate: "When you read this you can perceive my insight into the mystery of Christ, which was not made known to the sons of men in other generations as it has now been revealed to his holy apostles and prophets by the Spirit; that is, how the Gentiles are fellow heirs, members of the same body, and partakers of the promise in Christ Jesus through the gospel."

Technically, the original Greek is in the form of a present infinitive. That is, a present tense verb form functioning as a substantive while retaining certain verbal characteristics, as modified by adverbs. The translators appropriately used the word "how the Gentiles are fellow heirs". To say "That" the Gentiles are fellow heirs would merely refer to an accomplished fact, but "how" the heirship is being accomplished, thrusts us into accepting the unfathomable mystery of Jesus Christ. As Paul says, penetration into this mystery had never occurred before. He is telling it to us, in scripture, as revealed truth. Indeed, we can perceive that he has insight into how the mystery of Christ functions to make Gentiles fellow heirs. Our perception affirms the scripture!

Paul prays that, "[y]ou, being rooted and grounded in love, may have power to comprehend with all the saints what is the breadth and length and height and depth, and to know the love of Christ which surpasses knowledge, that you may be filled with all the fulness of God." To know this love surpasses knowledge?!! These verses are substantive meat.

We can feel comfortable and serene in examining scripture with extreme attention to detail, but we must be extremely cautious not to read into them our own preferences and prejudices. We seek to learn what the writer intended and what God wanted to manifest. Scripture says what it says. It is divinely inspired in its entirety and it is true.

The Church has always said so, and so do the Apostles Paul, John and Peter: "And we have the prophetic word made more sure. You will do well to pay attention to this as to a lamp shining in a dark place, until the day dawns and the morning star rises in your hearts. First of all you must understand this, that no prophecy of scripture is a matter of one's own interpretation, because no prophecy ever came by the impulse of man, but men moved by the Holy Spirit spoke from God."

The Church has also always assured us, "[t]hat the books of both the Old and New Testaments in their entirety, […] have God as their author and […] Therefore, since everything asserted by the inspired authors or sacred writers must be held to be asserted by the Holy Spirit, it follows that the books of Scripture must be acknowledged as teaching solidly, faithfully and without error that truth which God wanted put into the sacred writings for the sake of our salvation. […] However, since God speaks in Sacred Scripture through men in human fashion, the interpreter of sacred scripture, in order to see clearly what God wanted to communicate to us, should carefully investigate what meaning the sacred writers really intended, and what God wanted to manifest by means of their words."

Paul begins by telling we Gentiles that what he has to say to us is important. He is in prison for Jesus Christ on our behalf and assumes that we know that he was given responsibility, as a steward of God's grace that was given to him for us, to tell about the mystery that was made known to him by revelation.

232

In other words, he is not guessing and he is not thinking or philosophizing. He is revealing to us what has been made known to him by the revelation of God Almighty Himself, and it is important! We recall that Paul had been in prison for 4 years, in Caesarea and in Rome, when he wrote Ephesians. He had not tried to obtain his own release in his several defenses of criminal charges that were urged against him, but had instead, witnessed about the Lord and the Gospel. He actually engineered a trip to Rome in response to revelations from God that he go there, by appealing to Caesar as a citizen entitled to trial in a higher court. Toward the end of his third missionary journey, "[P]aul resolved in the Spirit to pass through Macedonia and Achaia and go to Jerusalem, saying, 'After I have been there, I must also see Rome.'" Then, one night, after witnessing in Jerusalem, Paul had this vision," The following night the Lord stood by him and said, "Take courage, for as you have testified about me at Jerusalem, so you must bear witness also at Rome ."

Thus, we can begin to see that Paul was not only a prisoner on our behalf, but that he was simply performing a service, as a minister, for the Lord. In this light, verses 7 – 12 take on special significance: "Of this gospel I was made a minister according to the gift of God's grace which was given me by the working of his power. To me, though I am the very least of all the saints, this grace was given, to preach to the Gentiles the unsearchable riches of Christ, and to make all men see what is the plan of the mystery hidden for ages in God who created all things; that through the church the manifold wisdom of God might now be made known to the principalities and powers in the heavenly places. This was according to the eternal purpose which he has realized in Christ Jesus our Lord, in whom we have boldness and confidence of access through our faith in him.

Paul recognized that he had been given special grace by the Lord's power to minister (serve) the gospel by preaching to us the unsearchable riches of Christ. In other words, if we are not told, we cannot reason, but can know these things about Christ. Paul's duty was to make all men "see" the plan of the mystery (hidden thing), hidden up to this time in God, who created all things. That through the church (the believers in God), God's manifold (many kinds, having many forms) wisdom might now be known to the principalities and powers (various angels) in the heavenly places.

WAIT A MINUTE! This is saying that Paul's preaching to us will demonstrate the wisdom of God to the angels in heaven? YES! WHY? We can be sure that this is what Paul means in verses 11 and 12. Well then, in all humility, why is that important to us? God's power could certainly work his plan in us without our knowledge. It is the angels he wants to inform. Why does Paul tell us about this? How, from this knowledge, will we benefit from the changes the Lord will be working in us?

Verse 11 says that the church's demonstration of the wisdom of God to the angels is according to the eternal purpose (in contradistinction to "plan") which God realized in Jesus. Of course, this calls to mind the scripture, "For God so loved the world that he gave his only Son, that whoever believes in him should not perish but have eternal life. For God sent the Son into the world, not to condemn the world, but that the world might be saved through him." God's eternal purpose, realized in Jesus was that we should not perish but have eternal life.

Verse 12 says that we have confidence of access (to God) through our faith in him. Is it possible that this confidence of access through faith refers to mere prayer and belief? NO! It must be something more because Hebrews teaches that, from the times of Abraham, we are justified by faith and we know that from the time of Adam, God has granted access to Him as He wills. Well then, we may well ask, what else is there? There is knowledge of God, from actual access, about the unsearchable riches of Christ (verse 8).

Could it be that we are being told about this revelation to the powers and principalities by God through His church because we will gain knowledge about the Lord which had always been hidden from both heaven and earth? YES! This new insight into the mystery of Christ, which was first revealed to God's holy apostles and prophets by the Spirit (verse 5) and was not made known to the sons of men in other generations, is being revealed to us? YES!! ACCESS, "that is, how the Gentiles are fellow heirs, members of the same body, and partakers of the promise in Christ Jesus through the gospel."

All of this is well and good. We can indeed, "[p]erceive (Paul's) insight into the mystery of Christ, ..." (Eph 3:4), but haven't we come full circle? What are these insights? Why is Paul beating around the bush? Answer: He is not beating around the bush. His insights are not ours to know. He is preparing us for the same experiences. NOTE, Paul is not just trying to communicate. We can assume he is communicating precisely what the Lord wanted communicated to us. That being the case, why do we not understand? BECAUSE IT IS BEYOND UNDERSTANDING!

Remember what Paul said: "To me, though I am the very least of all the saints, this grace was given to preach to the Gentiles the unsearchable riches of Christ, and to make all men see what is the plan of the mystery hidden for ages in God who created all things; that through the church the manifold wisdom of God might now be made known to the principalities and powers in the heavenly places." Our job is to see what Paul is talking about! How? Clearly, the changes (maturing) that take place in us, will manifest the manifold wisdom of God to the principalities and powers in the heavenly places and, through that access to God, we will see.

Otherwise, how could the exhibition of the manifold wisdom of God in the heavenly places be important? The angels are the ones who will separate the weeds from the wheat (the evil from the righteous) (Mt 13:49). They minister to the Lord (Mt 4:11). They will gather the Lord's elect from the four winds (Mt 24:31). The angels are not fully informed in the mind or will of God: "But of that day and hour no one knows, not even the angels of heaven,..." (Matt 24:36). Of course!!

Principalities are ordinary servants of God in what pertains to the visible world. Powers have special efficacy in restraining the Devil. Our progress toward perfection brings them joy in demonstrating the success of their battles: "[f]or they cannot die any more, because they are equal to angels and are sons of God, being sons of the resurrection." "Just so, I tell you, there is joy before the angels of God over one sinner who repents."

So, up to this point in Chapter 3, Paul is telling us how the mystery was made known to him by revelation, which we can perceive from reading his words; that we may see what is the plan of the mystery; that through the church, the manifold wisdom of God might be made known to the principalities and powers in the heavenly places; according to God's eternal purpose; realized in Christ Jesus; in whom we have boldness and confidence of access through our faith. WOW! We are not just potted plants! We perform this purpose while we grow! We sustain, bring joy to, angels in heaven! Amen. Come, Lord Jesus.

Rumination 6. Ephesians 3:14-21.

Verses 14 – 21 are a prayer of St. Paul by which he asks that the Father may grant that His Spirit in us will strengthen with might, our "inner man"; that Christ may dwell in our hearts through faith; that we, being rooted and grounded in love, may have power to comprehend with all the saints what is the breadth and length and height and depth, (A description of? - Like Jesus, Paul used metaphors, because – there are no words?) and to know the love of Christ which surpasses knowledge; that we may be filled with all the fullness of God.

In other words, Paul is asking God to give us what we need to comprehend what is the breadth and length and height and depth and to have the supernatural love of Christ. Clearly, Paul intends this to empower us to gain and experience insight into the mystery of Christ! (verse 4). As flimsy as his words seem, they are the absolute most that he, or anyone else but God, can say or do. We are truly helpless. We simply are not able, on our own, to penetrate, to any extent, the mystery of Christ. Is he giving us enough? Yes, that is enough.

If we Gentiles hear and learn the word of God, we will find Jesus in all his mysterious glory: "It is written in the prophets, 'And they shall all be taught by God.' Every one who has heard and learned from the Father comes to me". There are many who have heard and learned from the Father and have come to Jesus and have seen the mystery of Christ. They are called mystics.

However, mystics who have written about the experience are few. To accurately write about the experience itself is impossible because there are no words to describe it. For instance, if we "see" such glory, it cannot be with the eyes.

St. John of the Cross calls this phenomenon the "dark night." He speculates that the glory of God is so dazzling and bright that one's eyes are rendered useless. The unknown author of The Cloud of Unknowing describes the experience as involving a rejection of conceptualization. All thoughts, all concepts, all images are buried beneath a cloud of forgetting, while our love rises, divested of thought, upward toward God, hidden in the cloud of unknowing.

There is an unlimited variety of mystical experiences, all of them being different in one particular or another. (cf. William James, The varieties of Religious Experience). But what I am referring to here, is the experience in which one comprehends what is the breadth and length and height and depth, in addition to experiencing the supernatural love of Christ described by Paul. This is the central experience which is the eventual fruit of contemplative prayer and is very different from Paul's experience on the road to Damascus. Contemplative prayer normally requires both skill and practice.

In practice, the contemplative first brings himself to "quiet". This is measured by the relaxation of Beta and Theta waves in the mind. For the experienced and blessed contemplative, coming to quiet causes his spirit to "come out of his body." The contemplative can then proceed out of the world, in spirit, and into the presence of the Lord. (heaven?).There is no light in this place. The eyes see absolutely nothing. Yet, there is some sort of sense sensation by which one knows the breadth and length and height and depth.

The Lord is sensed to be filling the entirety. One feels as though he is basking in love in the darkness, similar to basking in the sun on the beach. One must exercise effort to stay in this place, in this expansive, quiet darkness, feeling very alert, not drugged or sedated in any sense. If one relaxes in the quiet, or begins thinking or is distracted by outside noise, he immediately returns to his body. Energy is expended to stay in the place, not to exit from it.

Therefore, one needs to be strengthened in his inner man in order to maintain presence and comprehend the breadth and length and height and depth and to know the love of Christ which surpasses knowledge and to be filled with all the fullness of God. This feels like, and I suppose it is, true worship in the spirit. At least that is what it seems to be. It is not forced upon one. One can sense the love reciprocating between oneself and the other.

These experiences are very refreshing and enjoyable. They give the body and soul rest at a much greater rate than sleep. They also tend to purge the soul of the effects of sin and mature it. (cf. St Teresa of Avila, *The Way Of Perfection*, St. John of the Cross, *The Ascent of Mount Carmel*, and *The Cloud Of Unknowing*, author unknown. The unknown author wrote in the 14th century. From his works, we know that he was an Englishman, a mystic, a theologian and a spiritual director).

These three teach the discipline of contemplative prayer. All three of their books are classics. Excellent English translations are available. All three of these authors would say that they wrote books about the way to perfection and purgation of the soul from sin, and so they are.

Be that as it may, the best contemporaneous book on contemplative prayer, in the opinion of the writer, is that written by Fr. Thomas H. Green, S.J., entitled *When The Well Runs Dry*. Fr. Green is a spiritual director and a Professor of Philosophy and Theology. His book surveys the writings of the above authors, and others, and he teaches the basics of contemplative prayer. It is easy to read and an outstanding first, or second, book in this discipline. Highly recommended.

Fr. Green recommends first reading his book for beginners, *Opening To God*, for learning the first stages of meditation and/or contemplation, along with the related techniques for coming to quiet and for purifying the soul of all that blocks love. He says this stage may last for several years once we begin a serious life of prayer, but it can also be much more brief. (Do not be discouraged).

Fr. Green assures us that, regardless of how long the first stages may last, they will come to an end. The first stages are thought of as simply getting to know the Lord and, he says, no one is "meant to spend his entire life getting to know the Lord, any more than human lovers would spend their whole lives just seeking to know each other better. Thus, sooner or later, the one who prays faithfully moves into an advanced stage of prayer." He characterizes this as the move from knowing to loving, and it is the topic of the first part of *When The Well Runs Dry*. Contemplative prayer is thought by many to be the highest and best form of worship in which the Christian can engage.

Now, let us turn to the Bible to see if it supports a position that Paul was praying that the readers of Ephesians be blessed with the experiences of contemplative prayer, regardless of whether or not it was called such in his day: First, from Chapter 1 of Ephesians, Paul was writing to an established church, saints who are faithful in Christ Jesus; who are blessed with every spiritual blessing in the heavenly places; chosen before the foundation of the world, that we should be holy and blameless before him; destined, in love, to be his sons through Jesus Christ. Because Paul had heard of our faith in the Lord Jesus and our love for one another, he prays that the Lord gives us a spirit of wisdom and of revelation in the knowledge of him, having the eyes of our hearts enlightened that we may know hope and know the riches of his inheritance and the immeasurable greatness of his power in us.

Then, in Chapter 2, we learned that God, in great love, raised us up with Jesus and made (past tense) us sit with God in the heavenly places in Jesus Christ. Through Jesus, we have access in one Spirit to the Father. So we are fellow citizens with the saints and members of the household of God, built upon Jesus as the cornerstone, joined together growing into a holy temple in the Lord, in whom we also are built into it for a dwelling place of God in the spirit. What does this mean?

In Chapter 3, the mystery of Jesus Christ was made known to Paul for us to have insight into that mystery, not known to men in prior generations; Paul's ministry is to make all men "see" what is the plan of the mystery hidden for all ages in God. Paul prays that God may grant us strength, with might through his Spirit in the inner man, that Christ may dwell in our hearts through faith, rooted and grounded in love, have power to comprehend what is the breadth and length and height and depth and to know the love of Christ, which surpasses knowledge and that we be filled with all the fullness of God. "…That is how the Gentiles are fellow heirs, members of the same body, and partakers of the promise in Christ Jesus through the gospel."

Paul prayed that we all have a power in prayer, through faith, and in love, to comprehend something indescribable, and to know the love of Christ. "But the hour is coming, and now is, when the true worshipers will worship the Father in spirit and truth, for such the Father seeks to worship him. God is spirit, and those who worship him must worship in spirit and truth." Can anyone "know" without knowledge? YES!! The mystics above attest that contemplative prayer results in spiritual worship and that the prayer knows a mystical love that is beyond reason or knowledge.

This is a new and great legacy Paul has prayed for us. It allows a simple and true spiritual worship, an exchange, a transformation, a joining of the beloved with the lover. Exquisite beyond description, once the relationship is joined, nothing can separate us from it. "No, in all these things we are more than conquerors through him who loved us. For I am sure that neither death, nor life, nor angels, nor principalities, nor things present, nor things to come, nor powers, nor height, nor depth, nor anything else in all creation, will be able to separate us from the love of God in Christ Jesus our Lord.

St John of the Cross composed what is considered the greatest mystical poem ever written, entitled "Stanzas of the Soul". It is here set out in the narrative, rather than in verse form, to conserve space: "On a dark night, Kindled in love with yearnings-oh, happy chance!-I went forth without being observed, My house being now at rest. In darkness and secure, By the secret ladder, disguised-oh, happy chance!-In darkness and in concealment, My house being now at rest. In the happy night, In secret, when none saw me, Nor I

241

beheld aught, Without light or guide, save that which burned in my heart. This light guided me More surely than the light of noonday To the place where he (well I knew who!) was awaiting me-A place where none appeared. Oh, night that guided me, Oh, night more lovely than the dawn, Oh, night that joined Beloved with lover, Lover transformed in the Beloved! Upon my flowery breast, Kept wholly for himself alone, There he stayed sleeping, and I caressed him, And the fanning of the cedars made a breeze. The breeze blew from the turret As I Parted his locks; With his gentle hand he wounded my neck And caused all my senses to be suspended. I remained, lost in oblivion; My face I reclined on the Beloved. All ceased and I abandoned myself, Leaving my cares forgotten among the lilies." This poem summarizes, exquisitely, the mystical experience of the contemplative. It rightly sounds effeminate because our souls are female.

Fr. Green describes contemplative prayer as "prayer beyond the beginnings." The "Stanzas of the Soul" describes the experiences in the most beautiful verse ever written. The prayer is in secret; the prayer comes to quiet; without light or guide, except that which burns in the heart, guiding more surely than the light of noon day; One loses oneself in darkness, Beloved with lover, lover transformed in the Beloved! He caused all senses to be suspended. And there, we "comprehend with all the saints what is the breadth and length and height and depth, and "know the love of Christ which surpasses knowledge, that you may be filled with all the fulness of God."

The experiences described by St. John of the Cross are called "consolations". There seems to come a time when God wants us to walk the path of love by ourselves, to love him for His own sake, and not the consolations. The experience of walking on our own and loving God for His own sake is called "dryness" or the "desert experience". It always comes. Eventually, we learn to prefer the desert. Aridity becomes beautiful. Amen. Come, Lord Jesus.

Rumination 7. Ephesians 4:1-16.

With the close of Chapter 3, Paul has finished his highest, most difficult and arcane (hidden) teaching about prayer and worship. Now, in Chapter 4, he begins his final guidance about how to live in the world while the power works within us. From the four corners of the Bible, we can see that Paul is teaching in Ephesians about the most vulnerable stage in man's legacy of growth, maturation and fruition - into the body of Christ. From the time of his writing the Epistle until the end of the age, man can become better equipped to move toward perfection because of this teaching. But, at the same time, we will also become more vulnerable to persecution, and even death, at the hands of the prince of this earth.

Why? Because, in giving ourselves over to Him, we lose our propensity, our drive, for self-protection. Therefore, he gives us spiritual armor at the end. When we think of ourselves as partaking in this process, we realize that by entering into the process, we give ourselves over to it. The growth will lead to an attitude of self-sacrifice for our brothers, not to seeking salvation. (We already have that gift.) These chapters are Paul's guidance on how the Lord wants us to live life on earth, to mature us toward perfection. He will make us joyful and personally strong, not comfortable. Paul seeks to assist us to attain the greatest common good as we race toward our personal destinies, at the end times.

Remember, we will be persecuted, and that is as it must be. Persecution goads us into striving for improvement. Striving, under the guidance of the Holy Spirit, is what matures us. Temptations are many. Each one seems as enticing as the apple was to Adam and Eve. These are the thoughts of the writer, suggested by Chapters 4, 5, and 6. What Paul said was, "For the grace of God has appeared for the salvation of all men, training us to renounce irreligion and worldly passions, and to live sober, upright, and godly lives in this world, awaiting our blessed hope, the appearing of the glory of our great God and Savior Jesus Christ, who gave

243

himself for us to redeem us from all iniquity and to purify for himself a people of his own who are zealous for good deeds."

Paul had already declared to the Corinthians how we must live and why he troubles himself about us, "Therefore, having this ministry by the mercy of God, we do not lose heart. We have renounced disgraceful, underhanded ways; we refuse to practice cunning or to tamper with God's word, but by the open statement of the truth we would commend ourselves to every man's conscience in the sight of God. And even if our gospel is veiled, it is veiled only to those who are perishing. In their case the god of this world has blinded the minds of the unbelievers, to keep them from seeing the light of the gospel of the glory of Christ, who is the likeness of God. For what we preach is not ourselves, but Jesus Christ as Lord, with ourselves as your servants for Jesus' sake. For it is the God who said, 'Let light shine out of darkness,' who has shone in our hearts to give the light of the knowledge of the glory of God in the face of Christ."

Earlier in Ephesians, Paul joyfully exhorted us that God knows what we should do in our own best interests, the good works that he prepared beforehand, that we should walk in them: "And you he made alive, when you were dead through the trespasses and sins in which you once walked, following the course of this world, following the prince of the power of the air, the spirit that is now at work in the sons of disobedience. Among these we all once lived in the passions of our flesh, following the desires of body and mind, and so we were by nature children of wrath, like the rest of mankind. But God, who is rich in mercy, out of the great love with which he loved us, even when we were dead through our trespasses, made us alive together with Christ (by grace you have been saved), and raised us up with him, and made us sit with him in the heavenly places in Christ Jesus, that in the coming ages he might show the immeasurable riches of his grace in kindness toward us in Christ Jesus. For by grace you have been saved through faith; and this is not your own doing, it is the gift of God - not because of works, lest any man should boast. For we are his workmanship, created in Christ Jesus for good works, which God prepared beforehand, that we should walk in them." This is what God wants us to do!!

Beginning in Chapter 4, Paul begs us "[t]o lead a life worthy of the calling to which you have been called, with all lowliness and meekness, with patience, forbearing one another in love, eager to maintain the unity of the Spirit in the bond of peace. (Eph 4:1-3). But, our flesh argues, "Since salvation is a gift, are we really required to do something more than truly believe?" YES, for the rest of our lives! We must cooperate. We must try. We will sin, fall short, fail in perfection, but we must try. We must try to govern our unmanageable egos, seek to be meek, have patience, forbear one another in love and eagerly maintain the unity of the spirit in the bond of peace. (Eph 4:3).

WAIT!! This means we are not like a butterfly in a cocoon, a bird in an egg or a baby in the womb! This means we are each like one cell in the body of Christ, cooperating and growing – TOGETHER! YES! We are to practice being meek, having patience, forbearing one another in love so we can maintain the unity of the spirit in the bond of peace. How many times must Paul say it, for us to hear? It is like he is taking us by our lapels, shaking us and saying, begging us, to "do something". Paul is like a honey bee, scampering about in the hive, hovering over each egg in each cell saying, hey, you OK? When we give our soft, childish yes, he says, "Then get busy, try to grow, practice". In all honesty, practicing is the least we can do.

First, we start to crawl, then to stand and walk, then to run. All we have to do, is try. Our shortcomings will be forgiven. Paul assures us that we are all one body. We were called to one hope, by one Spirit, one Lord, to one faith, one baptism, by one God and Father of us all. This God is above all and through all and in all. (cf. Eph 4:4-7). He has given each of us grace appropriate to that part of Christ's body for which we are destined. We are willing captives and our captor has given us gifts. (cf. Eph 4:8).

"He who came upon the earth has ascended far above all the heavens, that He might fill all things!" Oh, happy day! He is in us and fills us, as He is in all things. We need have no fear. If we simply surrender our death grip on controlling our lives, we will proceed toward our destiny. To this end, the gifts that Jesus sends us are to provide leadership, to empower us to build up the body of Christ, to grow, and work, until we all attain to the unity of the faith: "And his gifts were that some should be apostles, some prophets, some evangelists, some pastors and teachers, [these are the servants] to equip the saints for the work of ministry, for building up the body of Christ, until we all attain to the unity of the faith and of the knowledge of the Son of God, to mature manhood, to the measure of the stature of the fulness of Christ;…"

WOW!! This is indeed solid meat. Paul is telling us that we will all attain the unity of faith and the knowledge of Jesus, into mature manhood, to the size and fullness of Christ! WOW!! Why didn't someone point this out before? This is a virtual road map! It is a light unto our feet! But, let's go slow. If it were really very simple, it wouldn't have been necessary for Paul to explain it to us in so many different ways.

First, we should be aware of the next paragraph. It says what will happen if we cooperate: "[s]peaking the truth in love, we are to grow up in every way into him who is the head, into Christ, from whom the whole body, joined and knit together by every joint with which it is supplied, when each part is working properly, makes bodily growth and upbuilds itself in love."

Note: These verses say that the growth will, in every way, be into Jesus. We will form, become the whole body, joined and knitted together, upbuilding itself in love. Isn't this clear? Is it some sort of metaphor? Is it figurative or literal? Dare we believe that we will actually grow into being someone's body, albeit the body of the Glorified Jesus Christ himself? Why not? Is this too fantastic for us to accept, to focus on, as an actual possibility? Why not? Is this what Paul is actually saying? Apparently, but are these

246

mere metaphors? Undoubtedly, to some extent. Remember, there are no words that explain and we cannot comprehend. But, are these things beyond all revealing? No, "In that same hour he rejoiced in the Holy Spirit and said, 'I thank thee, Father, Lord of heaven and earth, that thou hast hidden these things from the wise and understanding and revealed them to babes; yea, Father, for such was thy gracious will. All things have been delivered to me by my Father; and no one knows who the Son is except the Father, or who the Father is except the Son and any one to whom the Son chooses to reveal him.'"

And to whom is this revelation made? Obviously, understanding was revealed to Paul by the Lord. Just as obviously, Paul has prayed for us, "For I want you to know how greatly I strive for you, [...] and for all who have not seen my face, that their hearts may be encouraged as they are knit together in love, to have all the riches of assured understanding and the knowledge of God's mystery, of Christ, in whom are hid all the treasures of wisdom and knowledge. I say this in order that no one may delude you with beguiling speech."

What more can we ask? If we are to "[a]ttain to the unity of the faith and of the knowledge of the Son of God, to mature manhood, to the measure of the stature of the fulness of Christ; so that we may no longer be children, tossed to and fro and carried about with every wind of doctrine, by the cunning of men, by their craftiness in deceitful wiles" then we are counted among those to whom the revelation is made. Nevertheless, we must continually give our assent to growth. Only in maturity will we modify our way of living.

God has granted us the ability to speak the truth in love, to grow up in every way into him, who is the head, into Christ. If we are blessed with the Dark Night of the Soul, as was St. John of the Cross, then we will "know" God from direct encounter. But to love is also to know God. There is no excuse. But, horror of horrors, what if we must die, for love of God, like Apostles? They die martyrs' deaths. Is that maturity? What if we must choose to be humiliated, publicly embarrassed and scorned, scourged, or crucified for love of the Lord?

Why not? After all, that is what he did for us, even while we wallowed in our self-indulgent sins. Isn't it only fair that we be willing to do the same for him, who was perfect and without sin? Our wills and our freedom to choose, to love, will also mature and grow, nurtured by the Holy Spirit. Remember, we are powerless to create love if we are powerless to choose not to love. Nevertheless, we should not be surprised when we find ourselves unable to equal the measure of Jesus. After all, we are not mature. But, what does that mean? Does it mean that we have an excuse? No, we are without excuse. It means that we literally require mercy until we are fully mature. Without God's constant forgiveness, in response to our repentance and resolution to sin no more, we have no chance. We are helpless. We will never see the kingdom of God, much less enter it. (Jn 3:3-5).

Therefore, let those who seek and willingly receive mercy, be at peace. Let us love, as best we can, at this time in our growth. Let us be patient to attain unity, work in our ministry, building up the body of Christ, "[u]ntil we all attain to the unity of the faith and of the knowledge of the Son of God, to mature manhood, to the measure of the stature of the fulness of Christ;". That is what the Lord created for us to work toward, in His mercy and in the hope that we are wheat, not tares. That is also what St. Paul prayed for us to have.

Let us be faithful and true, continuing as though members of the army of heaven until we attain it, in the grace of God. Then, St. John will say of us, "Then I saw heaven opened, and behold, a white horse! He who sat upon it is called Faithful and True, and in righteousness he judges [...] And the armies of heaven, arrayed in fine linen, white and pure, followed him on white horses. From his mouth issues a sharp sword with which to smite the nations, and he will rule them with a rod of iron;..." Lord, have mercy on us, mere sinners who try to do your will. Amen. Come Lord Jesus.

Rumination 8. Ephesians 4:17-5:21.

In Ephesians 4:17 – 5:21, Paul brings to a close that section of the Epistle dealing with how to live in the world while we grow. Then, he begins the last segment negatively, telling us what we must not do. "[y]ou must no longer live as the Gentiles do, in the futility of their minds; they are darkened in their understanding, alienated from the life of God because of the ignorance that is in them, due to their hardness of heart;" This is serious!

Paul does not call for a mere radical change, he calls for a complete and total change. Of course, he has already recognized that we cannot extinguish the dictates of the flesh. We must mature with them. However, Paul is serving notice that the change which we seek is no less than a complete rejection of worldly living. He says that a worldly life is futile, with darkened understanding, alienated from the life of God because of ignorance and hardness of heart. Such life is callous, greedy to practice uncleanness and licentiousness. If we take Paul seriously, and we know we must, we are undone! Although we will be in the world, we are not to enjoy its pleasures. We must actually turn away from the world, the things that seem good, not just integrate Christianity into our lives? YES!!

How can we do this? We cannot. We can envision Paul, standing at our sides, holding up a new nature for us to put on, like an overcoat. He says, "Put off your old nature which belongs to your former manner of life and is corrupt through deceitful lusts, and be renewed in the spirit of your minds, and put on the new nature, created after the likeness of God in true righteousness and holiness.

Oh, terror of terrors!! He wants us to put it on, of our own free will. This is not an ecstatic conversion experience, it is a measured, willful act. We know, in our heart of hearts that we will fail. We will besmirch and dirty this nature of righteousness and holiness over and over again, so many times that it will seem absolutely shameful, even to us. God, not just Paul, expects us to hold

251

ourselves to a standard that we know is absolutely impossible, doomed to failure. We cannot truly do so! We hardly dare to "put on" this new nature.

We cannot "be" righteous and holy of our own free will. To be consistent, we must then condemn our acts from our own mouths. WAIT! Neither God nor Paul is telling us to perform to new standards of righteousness and holiness. They are offering us a gift, a new nature. It is not conditioned upon our future performance. The gift of a new nature is final, absolute, unconditional. We merely have to <u>accept</u> it and put it on.

It is love we thirst for. We seek it from God. We seek it from others. We seek, are desperate to, return the same love, in all its purity, to God and to others. How can we refuse this new nature, even though we know we are unworthy of it? God knows we will dishonor it, yet He asks us to wear it anyway! He made it Himself, for us.

WOW, such a gift, this new nature of righteousness and holiness is of necessity made in love, since it is unconditionally made to sinners like us. We, who are governed by our own rebellious concupiscence.

Perhaps we can become good if we allow this new nature some time to take over? Perhaps we can eventually stop doing what we do not want to do? YES! This is life in the spirit. This love, this burning fire, is not quenched by our failures under the law. We now live our lives aside from the law. We regret our failures, but they do not condemn us, so long as we remain in good faith, repent when we fall, admit we were wrong, rise again in hope, and try again. If we do this, nothing in all creation can separate us from the love of God.

Paul wrote about this very issue to the Romans: "Did that which is good, then, bring death to me? By no means! It was sin, working death in me through what is good, in order that sin might be shown to be sin, and through the commandment might become sinful beyond measure. We know that the law is spiritual; but I am

252

carnal, sold under sin. I do not understand my own actions. For I [my spirit, my will] do not do what I want, but I [my flesh] do the very thing I hate. Now if I do what I do not want, I agree that the law is good. So then it is no longer I that do it, but sin which dwells within me. For I know that nothing good dwells within me, that is, in my flesh. I can will what is right, [with my spirit] but I cannot do it. [with my flesh] For I do not do the good I want, but the evil I do not want is what I do. Now if I do what I do not want, it is no longer I that do it, but sin which dwells within me."

What, then, is the problem? This is a piece of cake! God is a safety net, to catch us whenever we fall. We love to love. We can leave this vale of tears, do our best, and live life worry free. Ah, but there is a problem, a big one. It is known as concupiscence, "[a]n inclination to sin. Metaphorically, it is a demon, hidden and lurking within us, trying always to drag us back to our old nature. It "is left for us to wrestle with, it cannot harm those who do not consent but manfully resist it by the grace of Jesus Christ." (CCC 1264).

For a dictionary definition, "concupiscence, an insubordination of man's desires to the dictates of reason, and the propensity of human nature to sin as a result of original sin. More commonly, it refers to the spontaneous movement of the sensitive appetites toward whatever the imagination portrays as pleasant and away from whatever it portrays as painful. However, concupiscence also includes the unruly desires of the will, such as pride, ambition, and envy." Paul teaches that we must try to reject what is fueled by concupiscence, regardless of whether it feels painful or pleasant. Satan fuels concupiscence, but the Holy Spirit matures us if we try be faithful.

Paul gives practical, down to earth instruction and advice about warfare with Satan. Since Paul, others have tried to illustrate this. For instance, St Anastasius of Sinai said, "Entering the church and venerating sacred images and crosses is not sufficient for pleasing God, just as washing one's hands does not make one clean all over. What truly pleases God is that a person flees from sin and gets rid of his stains by means of confession and penance. Let him break the chains of his faults by being humble of heart." (Sermon on the holy Synaxis).

Putting on a new nature of righteousness and holiness is something which we should not undertake, unless we are willing to accept God's help. It is futile. The futility of our minds so darkens understanding that we are doomed to failure. For instance, who would have thought that going to church and venerating sacred images is not enough to please God, but that we must confess our short comings and do penance in order to break the chains of concupiscence? This is more than worship. This clarifies our vision through committed, reasoned, work for the good of our souls.

Paul said, "Be angry but do not sin; do not let the sun go down on your anger, and give no opportunity to the devil. This involves the will. This is conscious work. We know that being angry is not necessarily sinful. Jesus, who knew no sin, was said to be angry just once in scripture. However, Jesus also said, "But I say to you that every one who is angry with his brother shall be liable to (enochos, in danger of) judgment.

In other words, anger is not necessarily a sin, but it gives rise to duties of the will, to forgiveness. With this, it is clear that St Anastasius was saying that sins give rise to duties of confession and forgiveness. Although attending church in worship is not enough to totally cleanse us, we note that St Anastasius does not say that receiving Holy Communion in church is not enough, but that we must be sensitive to our duties. Receiving communion cleanses us of venial, but not mortal, sins. Therefore, receiving communion either cleanses us or, if we are in mortal sin, compounds our problems.

Again, what Paul said in Eph 4:26-27 about being angry does not give us permission to be angry nor does he contradict Jesus. Paul is merely repeating Ps 4:4 ("Be angry, but sin not; commune with your own hearts on your beds, and be silent."). Additionally,

Paul is teaching us to "give no opportunity to the devil." That is, repent, confess and do penance. This is healing activity. It is the way we fight, and eventually overcome, concupiscence.

Paul gives much more divinely inspired advice; i.e.: Let the thief work. God created man to work. "The Lord God took the man and put him in the Garden of Eden to till it and keep it." (Gen 2:15). And, "let him (the thief) labor, doing honest work with his hands, so that he may be able to give to those in need. Let no evil talk come out of your mouths, but only such as is good for edifying, as fits the occasion, that it may impart grace to those who hear. And do not grieve the Holy Spirit of God, in whom you were sealed for the day of redemption. Let all bitterness and wrath and anger and clamor and slander be put away from you, with all malice, and be kind to one another, tenderhearted, forgiving one another, as God in Christ forgave you.

Then, Paul begins Chapter 5 with instructions about how to live life in Christian Holiness: Imitate God, walking in love as Christ loved us and gave himself up as a fragrant offering and sacrifice to God. WAIT A MINUTE!! Does that mean we should be willing to lay down our lives for each other, even people we do not personally know? Yes, that is what John says in scripture, and scripture cannot be broken.

"Do not wonder, brethren, that the world hates you. We <u>know</u> that we have passed out of death into life, <u>because we love the brethren</u>. He who does not love abides in death. Any one who hates his brother is a murderer, and you know that no murderer has eternal life abiding in him. By this we know love, that he laid down his life for us; and we ought to lay down our lives for the brethren. But if any one has the world's goods and sees his brother in need, yet closes his heart against him, how does God's love abide in him? Little children, let us not love in word or speech but in deed and in truth." Mother of mercy! John wants us to go the whole hog! This is very serious business indeed!

Some old prayer warriors among us, who have been trying to be good for years, fighting Satan, feel they are not truly making progress. Yet hope, nevertheless, remains in them. They should be at peace and they are. They can simply look back down the road or back at their wake, if they go by sea, and they are surprised at the things they no longer desire or the things they no longer do. It is merely their hearts that condemn. Their hearts know their failures well. And we should all be encouraged, for John, just after telling us to be ready to lay down our lives for our brothers, gives us God's love as our measure, for assurance: "By this we shall know that we are of the truth, and reassure our hearts before him whenever our hearts condemn us; for God is greater than our hearts, and he knows everything. And then, "Beloved, if our hearts do not condemn us, we have confidence before God; and we receive from him whatever we ask, because we keep his commandments and do what pleases him. And this is his commandment, that we should believe in the name of his Son Jesus Christ and love one another, just as he has commanded us. All who keep his commandments abide in him, and he in them. And by this we know that he abides in us, by the Spirit which he has given us.

We do not live the old life, we are running a race! It is not a picnic or a lark. It is serious work. We follow the path God provided for us "Do not be deceived; God is not mocked, for whatever a man sows, that he will also reap. [...] And let us not grow weary in well-doing, for in due season we shall reap, if we do not lose heart. "Consider him who endured from sinners such hostility against himself, so that you may not grow weary or fainthearted. In your struggle against sin you have not yet resisted to the point of shedding your blood. And have you forgotten the exhortation which addresses you as sons? 'My son, do not regard lightly the discipline of the Lord, nor lose courage when you are punished by him. For the Lord disciplines him whom he loves, and chastises every son whom he receives.'" Amen. Come, Lord Jesus.

Rumination 9 Ephesians 5:22-33; 6:1-9.

Paul, at this point in Ephesians, is rapidly bringing us to the very apex, the pinnacle, of his legacy, his final guidance, to the great mass of humanity who must live in the world after we are no longer of the world. Let us bear in mind our new natures as we struggle to grasp his teaching. By conscious exercise of our wills, we can cooperate with the Holy Spirit as we become love, in the same way that Jesus Christ is love. That means that we use our fleshly ability "for building up the body of Christ, until we all attain to the unity of the faith and of the knowledge of the Son of God, to mature manhood, to the measure of the stature of the fulness of Christ; so that we may no longer be children, tossed to and fro and carried about with every wind of doctrine, by the cunning of men, by their craftiness in deceitful wiles."

We must consciously resist, as best we can, the influence of the world, while we grow. Our own rebellious concupiscence, not our new nature, is our greatest burden. Concupiscence, not sin itself, causes our flesh to be insubordinate, rebellious, to our wills. This is the tendency within us which makes us seek only to receive love, rather than to be love. Paul uses family relationships between, husband, wife and children, to guide us in the exercise of our wills in cooperation with the Holy Spirit. Gradually, the new nature will become a joy. The yoke of Christ should become our wings of flight and concupiscence should become a mere word, hardly remembered.

This is all well and good for us individually and, undoubtedly, it is taking place in each of us at a different pace. But Paul wrote his Epistles almost two thousand years ago. The thrust of his teaching in Ephesians is that "[t]he grace of God has appeared for the salvation of all men, training us to renounce irreligion and worldly passions, and to live sober, upright, and godly lives in this world, […] to redeem us from all iniquity and to purify for himself a people of his own who are zealous for good deeds."

Why have we not seen a corporate progress in holiness in mankind? Why are we not becoming more holy, as a people, as a body? Our studies have satisfied our hearts that scripture truly is the Word of God. The Church affirms that the Bible teaches us solidly, truthfully and without error the Word of God. Paul assures us of the same thing; i.e.: "All scripture is inspired by God and profitable for teaching, for reproof, for correction, and for training in righteousness, that the man of God may be complete, equipped for every good work. Jesus himself asserts that "scripture cannot be broken." (John 10:35).

Although God grants us gifts of salvation individually, why have we failed so miserably to grow into one holy, catholic (universal) and apostolic people, as He wants? Paul advises us to be subject to one another out of reverence for Christ. This has absolutely nothing to do with admiring merit, or the lack of it, in others.

We, who have begun to love the Lord, begin to see that we have no individual merit. No, not one. As the Psalmist said, "They have all gone astray, they are all alike corrupt; there is none that does good, no, not one. In Romans, Paul affirms that this sorry lot includes Gentiles, and Jews alike, "What then? Are we Jews any better off? No, not at all; for I have already charged that all men, both Jews and Greeks, are under the power of sin, as it is written: 'None is righteous, no, not one; no one understands, no one seeks for God. All have turned aside, together they have gone wrong; no one does good, not even one. Their throat is an open grave, they use their tongues to deceive. The venom of asps is under their lips. Their mouth is full of curses and bitterness. Their feet are swift to shed blood, in their paths are ruin and misery, and the way of peace they do not know. There is no fear of God before their eyes.'"

Indeed, Paul could be describing the world in which we live this very day. Focusing on marriage, he has advice for us, we who are no longer of the world but remain in it, constantly battling our own concupiscence with love. He said, "Be subject to one another out of reverence for Christ.

Subjecting ourselves to our spouses has to do with respect for Jesus, not the spouse. When we fail to be subject to one another, we fail Jesus. Husbands are to serve and love their wives the same as Jesus does the Church. We are to love our wives fully, the same as we love ourselves. If one's rib becomes broken, bruised, or one even suffers discomfort, the entire body endures pain or discomfort. The entire body also dedicates itself to healing and protecting the rib. In the same sense, husbands are to sacrifice themselves for the benefit and sanctification of their wives, even at the cost of their own lives. (See 1 John 3:16). The burden and responsibility of protecting and leading the family to perfect maturity is upon the husband. This burden, this yoke, is borne out of reverence for Jesus Christ. Shouldering this burden, for this reason, brings great joy to our new natures, a gift from God which we have accepted.

The burden is light but concupiscence makes it seem to be a drudgery. Bearing it down the path is extremely difficult, especially for beginners. In marriage, men become responsible for the sanctification of another soul, as Christ is for the entire church, whether we know it or not. It does not matter whether or not we accept responsibility or whether or not our wives recognize us, or honor us, as head of the family. We are responsible and we are the heads of the family. "For the husband is the head of the wife as Christ is the head of the church, his body, and is himself its Savior."

What, then, are husbands to do in this day and age, this vale of tears, meekly go to hell? Are husbands doomed to failure? Shall we just "go with the flow"? No, success requires that we are to stop lording it over our wives as masters of the house and begin to love them as Jesus loves the church.

Precisely as Jesus demonstrated at the Last Supper, we are their servants, even though it is true that we are their lords: "Then he poured water into a basin, and began to wash the disciples' feet, and to wipe them with the towel with which he was girded. [...] When he had washed their feet, and taken his garments, and resumed his place, he said to them, 'Do you know what I have done to you? You call me Teacher and Lord; and you are right, for so I am. If I then, your Lord and Teacher, have washed your feet, you also ought to wash one another's feet. For I have given you an example, that you also should do as I have done to you. [...] If you know these things, blessed are you if you do them.'"

WAIT, husbands simply cannot do this! Wives do not respect husbands as the apostles did Jesus! So?? "They have all gone astray, [even wives] they are all alike corrupt; there is none that does good, no, not one. (Ps 14:3). So, what's new?

Remember, all men have to do is to be faithful, to try to do the will of God and repent of failures. The Holy Spirit will do the rest. Men are what we are. Men are the servant-lords. Men are the teachers. Men are responsible for the sanctification and protection of the wives, even at the cost of their own lives. So far as position and rights and duties and salvation are concerned, it does not matter whether or not wives grant love or respect. Men's positions, rights and duties are not theirs to grant or decide whether or not to honor!! But, if men lord it over wives, they offend both God and wife! "Even so husbands should love their wives as their own bodies. He who loves his wife loves himself. For no man ever hates his own flesh, but nourishes and cherishes it, as Christ does the church, because we are members of his body."

Men must sacrifice their very selves in nourishing and cherishing their wives. As unalterably as they are head of the family, they are unalterably servants to it. This, with total disregard of whether or not wives deserve their love or care. This is done out of reverence for Christ. There is no getting around it, that is their God given duty and their job to do.

Wives are likewise subject to their husbands out of reverence for Christ. "To the woman he [God] said, (...) 'your desire shall be for your husband and he shall rule over you.'" Despite their desire for a husband, women tend to develop frustrations with their husbands and to judge them. With the passage of time, they see short comings and inabilities which they seek to remedy. Often, children are born to the union and this tends to make wives more dependent on the same husbands with whom they have grown frustrated.

Paul gave very specific advice for both husbands and wives, "Even so husbands should love their wives as their own bodies. He who loves his wife loves himself. For no man ever hates his own flesh, but nourishes and cherishes it, as Christ does the church, because we are members of his body. 'For this reason a man shall leave his father and mother and be joined to his wife, and the two shall become one flesh.' This mystery is a profound one, and I am saying that it refers to Christ and the church; however, let each one of you love his wife as himself, and let the wife see that she respects her husband."

What?, we ask indignantly!! Are husbands not entitled to love, in addition to respect? No, they are not. Nowhere does God, through any of the scriptures, instruct wives to love their husbands! Think about it. A man must have respect from the family if he is to function as the head. Also, a wife must have love from her husband if she is to be protected, safe from others, his own arrogance and from our heavy handedness. God joins husband and wife together as one flesh. Therefore, marriage is a sacrament.

God defines the relationship between spouses and their duties insofar as one is entitled to love and the other is entitled to respect. They are not the same. Husbands dare not fail in their duties and wives dare not fail in theirs. The original Greek word in scripture for respect is phobeo (fob-eh'-o); to be in awe of, i.e. revere. The original scriptural Greek for love is agapao (ag-ap-ah'-o); to love (in a social or moral sense), affection or benevolence.

Paul, preparing his disciple Titus for a pastoral ministry, taught him to, "Bid the older women [...] to teach what is good,

261

and so train the young women to love their husbands and children, to be sensible, chaste, domestic, kind, and submissive to their husbands, that the word of God may not be discredited." Therefore, it is good for wives to love their husbands, but never is a marriage to be without love, because it is always up to the husband to make sure he provides it to the wife. Love on the one hand and respect on the other, this is the very basis of a happy marriage. All else flows from this.

The last formal word of the Church on the relationship of husband and wife appears in The Pastoral Constitution on the Church in the Modern World, *Gaudium Et Spes*, promulgated by His Holiness, Pope Paul VI on December 7, 1965. Part II, "Some Problems Of Special Urgency," Chapter 1, "Fostering The Nobility Of Marriage And The Family." This Pastoral Constitution did not focus on the minimum scriptural requirement that husbands love their wives and that wives respect their husbands. Apparently, that is presumed. The Bible already established these rules. Man, the stronger, more aggressive, dominant and arrogant of the sexes is required to do things as the head, such as love and sacrifice himself as husband. Woman, the less strong and aggressive, is required to respect and submit to the head as wife. Both requirements are acts of the will in reverence for the Lord, not the spouse. There is no nobility in discrediting the word of God. Amen. Come, Lord Jesus.

Rumination 10 Ephesians 6:1-24.

In the first half of Ephesians, St. Paul taught us the meaty things of worship and prayer. In the second half, he led us through the meaty things of how to live life during our remaining time on earth. First, Paul showed us that we were created to work, to do the things he had prepared for us to do, before time began. This draws us together, into one body, to unity of faith and of the knowledge of the Son of God, to mature manhood, to the measure of the stature of the fulness of Christ. We merely have to make the effort and He will accomplish the goal.

Second, Paul taught us that we must battle concupiscence during the entire journey. This disciplines us, purifies us and allows us to grow. Satan fuels concupiscence, but the Holy Spirit matures us as we try be faithful. We learned that love is not in word or speech but in deed and in truth and we ought to be willing to lay down our lives for our brethren. Frightening though the road may appear, we cannot fail if we have confidence before God and do what pleases him. This is his commandment, that we should believe in the name of his Son Jesus Christ and love one another, just as he has commanded us. God is not mocked, for whatever a man sows, that he will also reap. In due season we shall reap, if we do not lose heart.

Third, Paul gave us the very key to a happy and enduring family life. He observed that no man ever hates members of his own flesh, but nourishes and cherishes them, just as Christ does us, the church, because we are members of his body. God sets the standard for both husbands and wives. Husbands must sacrifice their very selves in nourishing and cherishing each their wives. Husbands must love their wives, and serve them, the same as Christ served the Apostles at the Last Supper. Wives must respect their husbands, subjecting themselves, the same as the Apostles subjected themselves to being served by Christ at the Last Supper. These are the minimums, the imperative instructions given to us. We must do this with total disregard of what, in our opinions, the spouse deserves or what we deserve. We do it out of reverence for Christ. (Eph 5:21).

Finally, Paul ends Ephesians by exhorting us to put on the whole armor of God, making us strong in the strength of the Lord's might, so that we are able to stand against the wiles of the devil. This armor is a metaphor to us, just as it was in Paul's day. We cannot use our hands to "put on" armor such as this, any more than we could use them to "put on" our new nature. We use our wills to love our wives and respect our husbands, but we cannot even exercise our wills to keep this armor on. Our own concupiscence wars against our wills constantly. Satan, our adversary, roams about like a roaring lion, seeking to devour us. (1 Peter 5:8). We need to perceive this armor realistically. We need the protection. Now that the Lord has called us beyond the beginnings and we have begun to eat meat, we have a sense of direction. Our spirits are willing, but the flesh is still weak. What, then, must we do?

Paul advises us to be strong in the strength of his might. We are to "Put on the whole armour of God, that you may be able to stand against the wiles of the devil. For we are not contending against flesh and blood, but against the principalities, against the powers, against the world rulers of this present darkness, against the spiritual hosts of wickedness in the heavenly places." Clearly, this is a mysterious defense against mysterious forces! Now that we are maturing, a little, we can chew on this and "see" what we can see. We are lost without proceeding in faith.

Earlier in Ephesians, Paul had said, "Of this gospel (truth) I was made a minister according to the gift of God's grace which was given me by the working of his power. To me, though I am the very least of all the saints, this grace was given, to preach to the Gentiles the unsearchable riches of Christ, and to make all men see what is the plan of the mystery hidden for ages in God who created all things; that through the church the manifold wisdom of God might now be made known to the principalities and powers in the heavenly places. This was according to the eternal purpose which he has realized in Christ Jesus our Lord, in whom we have boldness and confidence of access through our faith in him.

NOW we are getting somewhere! Through faith, we have access to Jesus Christ our Lord. Of course, the Lord is the source of our protection, our armor. Paul has made known to us that the principalities and powers in the heavenly places know that we have access, through faith, to the Lord. We learned earlier that Principalities are ordinary servants of God in what pertains to the visible world. Powers have special efficacy in restraining the Devil. Here, Paul is teaching us that there are good and evil Principalities and Powers. The good ones are joyful at the prospect of our success and the bad ones are placed on notice that the Lord himself is our protector, in faith. The Lord told us that He has already overcome those angels who rebelled against God. When we rely on faith for our defense, they are undone! The flaming darts of the evil one are quenched by the "shield of faith, with which you can quench all the flaming darts of the evil one." Of course, we cannot rely on the Lord to take away our concupiscence. He will take away the actual power of evil, but our struggle with concupiscence is the thorn in our side which goads us and overcoming evil causes us to mature. It seems that what the Lord does is protect us from everything but ourselves and each other, allowing us to grow in the midst of the battle with evil. He shields us from spiritual harm, through faith.

Additionally, Paul tells us that when we put on the whole armor of God, we will be able to persevere against the devil, the principalities, the powers, the world rulers of this present darkness, and against the spiritual hosts of wickedness in the heavenly places. By taking the whole armor of God, we will be able to withstand [evil] in the evil day and having done all, to stand.

It seems that the angels are similar to us in that some of us are tares [weeds] among the wheat. We know Satan was shown to be among the Sons of God who presented themselves to the Lord from of old. (Job 1:6). That he came "From going to and fro on the earth, and from walking up and down on it." Scripture tells us that the Lord allowed Satan to do many evil things to Job's possessions, but he was prohibited from harming Job himself. (Job 1:7). The remainder of the Book of Job describes the process of growth and maturation to which we are all subjected. So that, in the end, Job had learned humility, respect, peace and love:

"Then Job answered the Lord: 'I know that thou canst do all things, and that no purpose of thine can be thwarted. Who is this that hides counsel without knowledge? [makes us know the unknowable] Therefore I have uttered what I did not understand, things too wonderful for me, which I did not know. Hear, and I will speak; I will question you, and you declare to me. I had heard of thee by the hearing of the ear, but now my eye sees thee; therefore I despise myself, and repent in dust and ashes." [humility]

"Eliphaz the Temanite: 'My wrath is kindled against you and against your two friends; for you have not spoken of me what is right, as my servant Job has. Now therefore take seven bulls and seven rams, and go to my servant Job, and offer up for yourselves a burnt offering; and my servant Job shall pray for you, for I will accept his prayer [here is access!] not to deal with you according to your folly; [intercession] for you have not spoken of me what is right, as my servant Job has.' So Eliphaz the Temanite and Bildad the Shuhite and Zophar the Naamathite went and did what the Lord had told them; and the Lord accepted Job's prayer. [Job became a priest to God] And the Lord restored the fortunes of Job, when he had prayed for his friends; [charity] and the Lord gave Job twice as much as he had before. [mercy]

"Then came to him all his brothers and sisters and all who had known him before, and ate bread with him in his house; [community] and they showed him sympathy and comforted him for all the evil that the Lord had brought upon him; [testing- "For the Lord disciplines him whom he loves, and chastises every son whom he receives." (Heb 12:6).] and each of them gave him a piece of money and a ring of gold. [Job inspired charity.] And the Lord blessed the latter days of Job more than his beginning; and he had fourteen thousand sheep, six thousand camels, a thousand yoke of oxen, and a thousand she-asses. He had also seven sons and three daughters. And he called the name of the first Jemimah; and the name of the second Keziah; and the name of the third Keren-happuch. And in all the land there were no women so fair as Job's daughters; and their father gave them inheritance among their brothers. [restoration] And after this Job lived a hundred and forty years, and saw his sons, and his sons' sons, four generations. And Job died, an old man, and full of days."

In short, Paul gives us the tools (armor) with which to protect ourselves from the sufferings of Job, while we are undergoing the discipline and chastisement of the Lord which is necessary for our maturity and purification! If we avail ourselves of this armor, we can receive our reward with only the sufferings, disciplines and chastisements, personally and in community, which we require for an ever increasing maturity in ourselves and in community.

These are precious tools indeed! Of course, the shield is faith. The other armor consists of truth, righteousness, the gospel peace, salvation and the word of God. We are to espouse truth. It is objective, the same for everyone; guard the righteousness which the Lord has bestowed upon us, by totally avoiding mortal sin and receiving forgiveness through confession and communion; live our lives in the peace we receive from study of the gospel and thank God for the salvation of our souls by his own crucifixion, death and resurrection. Finally, we rely on the word of God. "All scripture is inspired by God and profitable for teaching, for reproof, for correction, and for training in righteousness, that the man of God may be complete, equipped for every good work." This is the entire armor of God, good for both defense and offense.

Once we have "put on" the entire armor of God, what are we to do? We are to stand against the wiles of the devil. With this additional strength and protection, we will be able to withstand the evil day and to stand, praying at all times in the Spirit, with supplication for ourselves and for all the saints.

And what will we therefore be doing in the evil day? Why, we will be laborers.in the field of the Lord as we ourselves mature. Remember, God created us to labor and to till his field. We will till the fields (evangelize) until the harvest fully ripens and the end of the age arrives. "The harvest is plentiful, but the laborers, (those who actually do something) are few; pray therefore the Lord of the harvest to send out laborers into his harvest."

Then, when the end time comes, we will be reaped, taken into eternal life. "And his disciples came to him (Jesus), saying, "Explain to us the parable of the weeds of the field." He answered, "He who sows the good seed is the Son of man; the field is the world, and the good seed means the sons of the kingdom; the weeds are the sons of the evil one, and the enemy who sowed them is the devil; the harvest is the close of the age, and the reapers are angels. Just as the weeds are gathered and burned with fire, so will it be at the close of the age. The Son of man will send his angels, and they will gather out of his kingdom all causes of sin and all evildoers, and throw them into the furnace of fire; there men will weep and gnash their teeth.

Then the righteous will shine like the sun in the kingdom of their Father. As instructed by Paul, "[s]peaking the truth in love, we are to grow up in every way into him who is the head, into Christ, from whom the whole body, joined and knit together by every joint with which it is supplied, when each part is working properly, makes bodily growth and upbuilds itself in love." We are all one body. Amen. Come, Lord Jesus.

Appendix I. Stanzas Of The Soul.

This poem is considered by many to be the most beautiful poem in history. It was written by the saint designated "Doctor of Mystic Theology" of the Catholic Church. St John of the Cross comments on his poem, explaining that in the dark night of the senses, his spirit "goes out" without the knowledge of his senses and that, his "house" being at rest, his soul, fired with love's urgent longings, is concealed by the darkness of his senses than the Holy Spirit that guides him and burns in his heart, to where his Holy Master awaits him. Upon encountering the Lord, his soul (always expressed in the feminine) states in the last stanza that it abandons and forgets itself, laying its face on his Beloved; all things ceased; it went out from itself, leaving its cares forgotten among the lilies.

With these considerations, one can appreciate why the writer is anxious that the reader learn how to "come to quiet" (or "rest") preliminarily to practicing *Lectio Divina*. I pray that *Lectio Divina*, well practiced, leads the reader into the "Dark Night", expressed below:

1. One dark night,

fired with love's urgent longings

- ah, the sheer grace! -

I went out unseen,

my house being now all stilled.

2. In darkness, and secure,

by the secret ladder, disguised,

- ah, the sheer grace! -

in darkness and concealment,

my house being now all stilled.

3. On that glad night,

in secret, for no one saw me,

nor did I look at anything,

with no other light or guide

than the one that burned in my heart.

4. This guided me

more surely than the light of noon

to where he was awaiting me

- him I knew so well -

there in a place where no one appeared.

5. O guiding night!

O night more lovely than the dawn!

O night that has united

the Lover with his beloved,

transforming the beloved in her Lover.

6. Upon my flowering breast

which I kept wholly for him alone,

there he lay sleeping,

and I caressing him

there in a breeze from the fanning cedars.

7. When the breeze blew from the turret,

as I parted his hair,

it wounded my neck

with its gentle hand,

suspending all my senses.

270

8. I abandoned and forgot myself,

laying my face on my Beloved;

all things ceased; I went out from myself,

leaving my cares

forgotten among the lilies.

The following is excerpted from an explanation by Padre Fray John of the Cross concerning his poem about the way a soul must conduct itself along the road leading to union with God through love:

Before embarking on an explanation of these stanzas, we should remember that the soul recites them when it has already reached the state of perfection - that is, union with God through love - and has now passed through severe trials and conflicts by means of the spiritual exercise (Contemplation during *Lectio Divina*) that leads one along the constricted way to eternal life, of which our Savior speaks in the Gospel [Mt. 7:14]. The soul must ordinarily walk this path to reach that sublime and joyous union with God. Recognizing the narrowness of the path and the fact that so very few tread it - as the Lord himself says [Mt. 7:14] - the soul's song in this first stanza is one of happiness in having advanced along it to this perfection of love. Appropriately, this constricted road is called a dark night, as we shall explain in later verses of this stanza. The soul, therefore, happy at having trod this narrow road from which it derived so much good, speaks in this manner.

Appendix II. Letter On Meditation.

I. Introduction

1. Many Christians today have a keen desire to learn how to experience a deeper and authentic prayer life despite the not inconsiderable difficulties which modern culture places in the way of the need for silence, recollection and meditation. The interest which in recent years has been awakened also among some Christians by forms of meditation associated with some eastern religions and their particular methods of prayer is a significant sign of this need for spiritual recollection and a deep contact with the divine mystery. Nevertheless, faced with this phenomenon, many feel the need for sure criteria of a doctrinal and pastoral character which might allow them to instruct others in prayer, in its numerous manifestations, while remaining faithful to the truth revealed in Jesus, by means of the genuine Tradition of the Church. This present letter seeks to reply to this urgent need, so that in the various particular Churches the many different forms of prayer, including new ones, may never lose their correct personal and communitarian nature.

These indications are addressed in the first place to the Bishops, to be considered in that spirit of pastoral solicitude for the Churches entrusted to them, so that the entire people of God—priests, religious and laity—may again be called to pray, with renewed vigor, to the Father through the Spirit of Christ our Lord.

2. The ever more frequent contact with other religions and with their different styles and methods of prayer has, in recent decades, led many of the faithful to ask themselves what value non-Christian forms of meditation might have for Christians. Above all, the question concerns eastern methods.1 Some people

273

today turn to these methods for therapeutic reasons. The spiritual restlessness arising from a life subjected to the driving pace of a technologically advanced society also brings a certain number of Christians to seek in these methods of prayer a path to interior peace and psychic balance. This psychological aspect is not dealt with in the present letter, which instead emphasizes the theological and spiritual implications of the question. Other Christians, caught up in the movement towards openness and exchanges between various religions and cultures, are of the opinion that their prayer has much to gain from these methods. Observing that in recent times many traditional methods of meditation, especially Christian ones, have fallen into disuse, they wonder whether it might not now be possible, by a new training in prayer, to enrich our heritage by incorporating what has until now been foreign to it.

3. To answer this question7 one must first of all consider, even if only in a general way, in what does the intimate nature of Christian prayer consist. Then one can see if and how it might be enriched by meditation methods which have been developed in other religions and cultures. However, in order to achieve this, one needs to start with a certain clear premise. Christian prayer is always determined by the structure of the Christian faith, in which the very truth of God and creature shines forth. For this reason, it is defined, properly speaking, as a personal, intimate and profound dialogue between man and God. It expresses therefore the communion of redeemed creatures with the intimate life of the Persons of the Trinity. This communion, based on Baptism and the Eucharist, source and summit of the life of the Church, implies an attitude of conversion, a flight from "self" to the "You" of God. Thus Christian prayer is at the same time always authentically personal and communitarian. It flees from impersonal techniques or from concentrating on oneself, which can create a kind of rut, imprisoning the person praying in a spiritual privatism which is incapable of a free openness to the transcendental God. Within the Church, in the legitimate search for new methods of meditation it must always be borne in mind that the essential element of

274

authentic Christian prayer is the meeting of two freedoms, the infinite freedom of God with the finite freedom of man.

II. **Christian Prayer In The Light Of Revelation**

4. The Bible itself teaches how the man who welcomes biblical revelation should pray. In the Old Testament there is a marvelous collection of prayers which have continued to live through the centuries, even within the Church of Jesus Christ, where they have become the basis of its official prayer: The Book of Praises or of Psalms.2 Prayers similar to the Psalms may also be found in earlier Old Testament texts or re-echoed in later ones.3 The prayers of the book of Psalms tell in the first place of God's great works on behalf of the Chosen People. Israel meditates, contemplates and makes the marvels of God present again, recalling them in prayer.

In biblical revelation Israel came to acknowledge and praise God present in all creation and in the destiny of every man. Thus he is invoked, for example, as rescuer in time of danger, in sickness, in persecution, in tribulation. Finally, and always in the light of his salvific works, he is exalted in his divine power and goodness, in his justice and mercy, in his royal grandeur.

5. Thanks to the words, deeds, passion and resurrection of Jesus Christ, in the "New Testament" the faith acknowledges in him the definitive self-revelation of God, the Incarnate Word who reveals the most intimate depth of his love. It is the Holy Spirit, he who was sent into the hearts of the faithful, he who "searches everything, even the depths of God" (1 Cor 2:10), who makes it possible to enter into these divine depths. According to the promise Jesus made to the disciples, the Spirit will explain all that he had not yet been able to tell them. However, this Spirit "will not speak on his own authority," but "he will glorify me, for he will take what is mine and declare it to you" (Jn 16:13f.). What Jesus calls "his" is, as he explains immediately, also God the Father's because

"all that the Father has is mine; therefore I said that he will take what is mine and declare it to you" (Jn 16:15).

The authors of the New Testament, with full cognizance, always spoke of the revelation of God in Christ within the context of a vision illuminated by the Holy Spirit. The Synoptic Gospels narrate Jesus' deeds and words on the basis of a deeper understanding, acquired after Easter, of what the disciples had seen and heard. The entire Gospel of St. John is taken up with the contemplation of him who from the beginning is the Word of God made flesh. Paul, to whom Jesus appeared in his divine majesty on the road to Damascus, instructs the faithful so that they "may have power to comprehend with all the saints what is the breadth and length and height and depth [of the mystery of Christ], and to know the love of Christ which surpasses all knowledge, that you may be filled with all the fullness of God" (Eph 3:18 ff.). For Paul the mystery of God is Christ, "in whom are hidden all the treasures of wisdom and knowledge" (Col 2:3) and, the Apostle clarifies, "I say this in order that no one may delude you with beguiling speech" (v. 4).

6. There exists, then, a strict relationship between revelation and prayer. The Dogmatic Constitution "*Dei Verbum*" teaches that by means of his revelation the invisible God, "from the fullness of his love, addresses men as his friends (cf. Ex 33:11; Jn 15:14-15), and moves among them (cf. Bar 3:38), in order to invite and receive them into his own company."4 This revelation takes place through words and actions which have a constant mutual reference, one to the other; from the beginning everything proceeds to converge on Christ, the fullness of revelation and of grace, and on the gift of the Holy Spirit. These make man capable of welcoming and contemplating the words and works of God and of thanking him and adoring him, both in the assembly of the faithful and in the intimacy of his own heart illuminated by grace.

This is why the Church recommends the reading of the Word of God as a source of Christian prayer, and at the same time exhorts all to discover the deep meaning of Sacred Scripture through prayer "so that a dialogue takes place between God and man. For, 'we speak to him when we pray; we listen to him when we read the divine oracles.'"5

7. Some consequences derive immediately from what has been called to mind. If the prayer of a Christian has to be inserted in the Trinitarian movement of God, then its essential content must also necessarily be determined by the twofold direction of such movement. It is in the Holy Spirit that the Son comes into the world to reconcile it to the Father through his works and sufferings. On the other hand, in this same movement and in the very same Spirit, the Son Incarnate returns to the Father, fulfilling his will through his passion and resurrection. The "Our Father," Jesus' own prayer, clearly indicates the unity of this movement: the will of the Father must be done on earth as it is in heaven (the petitions for bread, forgiveness and protection make explicit the fundamental dimensions of God's will for us), so that there may be a new earth in the heavenly Jerusalem.

The prayer of Jesus6 has been entrusted to the Church ("Pray then like this"—Lk 11:2). This is why when a Christian prays, even if he is alone, his prayer is in fact always within the framework of the "communion of saints" in which and with which he prays, whether in a public and liturgical way or in a private manner. Consequently, it must always be offered within the authentic spirit of the Church at prayer, and therefore under its guidance, which can sometimes take a concrete form in terms of a proven spiritual direction. The Christian, even when he is alone and prays in secret, is conscious that he always prays for the good of the Church in union with Christ, in the Holy Spirit and together with all the saints.7

III. **Erroneous Ways Of Praying**

8. Even in the first centuries of the Church some incorrect forms of prayer crept in. Some New Testament texts (cf. 1 Jn 4:3;

277

1 Tim 1:3-7 and 4:3-4) already give hints of their existence. Subsequently, two fundamental deviations came to be identified: Pseudognosticism and Messalianism, both of concern to the Fathers of the Church. There is much to be learned from that experience of primitive Christianity and the reaction of the Fathers which can help in tackling the current problem.

In combating the errors of "pseudognosticism"[8] the Fathers affirmed that matter is created by God and as such is not evil. Moreover, they maintained that grace, which always has the Holy Spirit as its source is not a good proper to the soul, but must be sought from God as a gift. Consequently, the illumination or superior knowledge of the Spirit ("gnosis") does not make Christian faith something superfluous. Finally, for the Fathers, the authentic sign of a superior knowledge, the fruit of prayer, is always Christian love.

9. If the perfection of Christian prayer cannot be evaluated using the sublimity of gnostic knowledge as a basis, neither can it be judged by referring to the experience of the divine, as "Messalianism" proposed.[9] These false fourth-century charismatics identified the grace of the Holy Spirit with the psychological experience of his presence in the soul. In opposing them, the Fathers insisted on the fact that the soul's union with God in prayer is realized in a mysterious way, and in particular through the sacraments of the Church. Moreover, it can even be achieved through experiences of affliction or desolation. Contrary to the view of the Messalians, these are not necessarily a sign that the Spirit has abandoned a soul. Rather, as masters of spirituality have always clearly acknowledged, they may be an authentic participation in the state of abandonment experienced on the cross by our Lord, who always remains the model and mediator of prayer.

10. Both of these forms of error continue to be a "temptation for man the sinner." They incite him to try and overcome the distance separating creature from Creator, as though there ought

not to be such a distance; to consider the way of Christ on earth, by which he wishes to lead us to the Father, as something now surpassed; to bring down to the level of natural psychology what has been regarded as pure grace, considering it instead as "superior knowledge" or as "experience."

Such erroneous forms, having reappeared in history from time to time on the fringes of the Church's prayer, seem once more to impress many Christians, appealing to them as a kind of remedy, be it psychological or spiritual, or as a quick way of finding God.11

11. However, these forms of error, wherever they arise, "can be diagnosed" very simply. The meditation of the Christian in prayer seeks to grasp the depths of the divine in the salvific works of God in Christ, the Incarnate Word, and in the gift of his Spirit. These divine depths are always revealed to him through the human-earthly dimension. Similar methods of meditation, on the other hand, including those which have their starting-point in the words and deeds of Jesus, try as far as possible to put aside everything that is worldly, sense perceptible or conceptually limited. It is thus an attempt to ascend to or immerse oneself in the sphere of the divine, which, as such, is neither terrestrial, sense-perceptible nor capable of conceptualization.12 This tendency, already present in the religious sentiments of the later Greek period (especially in "Neoplatonism"), is found deep in the religious inspiration of many peoples, no sooner than they become aware of the precarious character of their representations of the divine and of their attempts to draw close to it.

12. With the present diffusion of eastern methods of meditation in the Christian world and in ecclesial communities, we find ourselves faced with a pointed renewal of an attempt, which is not free from dangers and errors, "to fuse Christian meditation with that which is non-Christian." Proposals in this direction are numerous and radical to a greater or lesser extent. Some use eastern methods solely as a psycho-physical preparation for a truly

Christian contemplation; others go further and, using different techniques, try to generate spiritual experiences similar to those described in the writings of certain Catholic mystics.13 Still others do not hesitate to place that absolute without image or concepts, which is proper to Buddhist theory, 14 on the same level as the majesty of God revealed in Christ, which towers above finite reality. To this end, they make use of a "negative theology," which transcends every affirmation seeking to express what God is, and denies that the things of this world can offer traces of the infinity of God. Thus they propose abandoning not only meditation on the salvific works accomplished in history by the God of the Old and New Covenant, but also the very idea of the One and Triune God, who is Love, in favor of an immersion "in the indeterminate abyss of the divinity."15 These and similar proposals to harmonize Christian meditation with eastern techniques need to have their contents and methods ever subjected to a thorough-going examination so as to avoid the danger of falling into syncretism.

IV. **The Christian Way To Union With God**

13. To find the right "way" of prayer, the Christian should consider what has been said earlier regarding the prominent features of the "way of Christ," whose "food is to do the will of him who sent [him], and to accomplish his work" (Jn 4:34). Jesus lives no more intimate or closer a union with the Father than this, which for him is continually translated into deep prayer. By the will of the Father he is sent to mankind, to sinners. to his very executioners, and he could not be more intimately united to the Father than by obeying his will. This did not in any way prevent him, however, from also retiring to a solitary place during his earthly sojourn to unite himself to the Father and receive from him new strength for his mission in this world. On Mount Tabor, where his union with the Father was manifest, there was called to mind his passion (cf. Lk 9:31), and there was not even a consideration of the possibility of remaining in "three booths" on the Mount of the

Transfiguration. Contemplative Christian prayer always leads to love of neighbor, to action and to the acceptance of trials, and precisely because of this it draws one close to God.

14. In order to draw near to that mystery of union with God, which the Greek Fathers called the "divinization" of man, and to grasp accurately the manner in which this is realized, it is necessary in the first place to bear in mind that man is essentially a creature, 16 and remains such for eternity, so that an absorbing of the human self into the divine self is never possible, not even in the highest states of grace. However, one must recognize that the human person is created in the "image and likeness" of God, and that the archetype of this image is the Son of God, in whom and through whom we have been created (cf. Col 1:16). This archetype reveals the greatest and most beautiful Christian mystery: from eternity the Son is "other" with respect to the Father and yet, in the Holy Spirit, he is "of the same substance." Consequently this otherness, far from being an ill, is rather the greatest of goods. There is otherness in God himself, who is one single nature in three Persons, and there is also otherness between God and creatures, who are by nature different. Finally, in the Holy Eucharist, as in the rest of the sacraments—and analogically in his works and in his words—Christ gives himself to us and makes us participate in his divine nature,17 without nevertheless suppressing our created nature, in which he himself shares through his Incarnation.

15. A consideration of these truths together brings the wonderful discovery that all the aspirations which the prayer of other religions expresses are fulfilled in the reality of Christianity beyond all measure, without the personal self or the nature of a creature being dissolved or disappearing into the sea of the Absolute. "God is love" (1 Jn 4:8). This profoundly Christian affirmation can reconcile perfect "union" with the "otherness" existing between lover and loved, with eternal exchange and eternal dialogue. God is himself this eternal exchange and we can truly become sharers of Christ, as "adoptive sons" who cry out

with the Son in the Holy Spirit, Abba, Father." In this sense, the Fathers are perfectly correct in speaking of the divinization of man who, having been incorporated into Christ, the Son of God by nature, may by his grace share in the divine nature and become a "son in the Son." Receiving the Holy Spirit, the Christian glorifies the Father and really shares in the Trinitarian life of God.

V. **Questions Of Method**

16. The majority of the "great religions" which have sought union with God in prayer have also pointed out ways to achieve it. Just as "the Catholic Church rejects nothing of what is true and holy in these religions,"18 neither should these ways be rejected out of hand simply because they are not Christian. On the contrary, one can take from them what is useful so long as the Christian conception of prayer, its logic and requirements are never obscured. It is within the context of all of this that these bits and pieces should be taken up and expressed anew. Among these one might mention first of all that of the humble acceptance of a master who is an expert in the life of prayer, and of the counsels he gives. Christian experience has known of this practice from earliest times, from the epoch of the desert Fathers. Such a master, being an expert in "*sentire cum ecclesia*," must not only direct and warn of certain dangers; as a "spiritual father," he has to also lead his pupil in a dynamic way, heart to heart, into the life of prayer, which is the gift of the Holy Spirit.

17. In the later non-Christian classical period, there was a convenient distinction made between three stages in the life of perfection: the purgative way, the illuminative way and the unitive way. This teaching has served as a model for many schools of Christian spirituality. While in itself valid, this analysis nevertheless requires several clarifications so as to be interpreted in a correct Christian manner which avoids dangerous misunderstandings.

18. The seeking of God through prayer has to be preceded and accompanied by an ascetical struggle and a purification from one's

own sins and errors, since Jesus has said that only "the pure of heart shall see God" (Mt 5:8). The Gospel aims above all at a moral purification from the lack of truth and love and, on a deeper level, from all the selfish instincts which impede man from recognizing and accepting the will of God in its purity. The passions are not negative in themselves (as the Stoics and Neoplatonists thought), but their tendency is to selfishness. It is from this that the Christian has to free himself in order to arrive at that state of positive freedom which in classical Christian times was called "apatheia," in the Middle Ages "*Impassibilitas*" and in the Ignatian Spiritual Exercises "*indiferencia.*"19

This is impossible without a radical self-denial, as can also be seen in St. Paul who openly uses the word "mortification" (of sinful tendencies).20 Only this self-denial renders man free to carry out the will of God and to share in the freedom of the Holy Spirit.

19. Therefore, one has to interpret correctly the teaching of those masters who recommend "emptying" the spirit of all sensible representations and of every concept, while remaining lovingly attentive to God. In this way, the person praying creates an empty space which can then be filled by the richness of God. However, the emptiness which God requires is that of the renunciation of personal selfishness, not necessarily that of the renunciation of those created things which he has given us and among which he has placed us. There is no doubt that in prayer one should concentrate entirely on God and as far as possible exclude the things of this world which bind us to our selfishness. On this topic St. Augustine is an excellent teacher: if you want to find God, he says, abandon the exterior world and re-enter into yourself. However, he continues, do not remain in yourself, but go beyond yourself because you are not God; he is deeper and greater than you. "I look for his substance in my soul and I do not find it; I have however meditated on the search for God and, reaching out to him, through created things, I have sought to know 'the invisible perfections of God' (Rom 1:20)."2 "To remain in oneself": this is

the real danger. The great Doctor of the Church recommends concentrating on oneself, but also transcending the self which is not God, but only a creature. God is "deeper than my inmost being and higher than my greatest height."22 In fact God is in us and with us, but he transcends us in his mystery.23

20. "From the dogmatic point of view," it is impossible to arrive at a perfect love of God if one ignores his giving of himself to us through his Incarnate Son, who was crucified and rose from the dead. In him, under the action of the Holy Spirit, we participate, through pure grace, in the interior life of God. When Jesus says, "He who has seen me has seen the Father" (Jn 14:9), he does not mean just the sight and exterior knowledge of his human figure (in the flesh is of no avail"—Jn 6:63). What he means is rather a vision made possible by the grace of faith: to see, through the manifestation of Jesus perceptible by the senses, just what he, as the Word of the Father, truly wants to reveal to us of God ("It is the Spirit that gives life [...]; the words that I have spoken to you are spirit and life"—ibid.). This "seeing" is not a matter of a purely human abstraction ("*abstractio*") from the figure in which God has revealed himself; it is rather the grasping of the divine reality in the human figure of Jesus, his eternal divine dimension in its temporal form. As St. Ignatius says in the "Spiritual Exercises," we should try to capture "the infinite perfume and the infinite sweetness of the divinity" (n. 124), going forward from that finite revealed truth from which we have begun. While he raises us up, God is free to "empty" us of all that holds us back in this world, to draw us completely into the Trinitarian life of his eternal love. However, this gift can only be granted "in Christ through the Holy Spirit," and not through our own efforts, withdrawing ourselves from his revelation.

21. On the path of the Christian life, illumination follows on from purification, through the love which the Father bestows on us in the Son and the anointing which we receive from him in the Holy Spirit (cf. 1 Jn 2:20). Ever since the early Christian period, writers have referred to the "illumination" received in Baptism.

After their initiation into the divine mysteries, this illumination brings the faithful to know Christ by means of the faith which works through love. Some ecclesiastical writers even speak explicitly of the illumination received in Baptism as the basis of that sublime knowledge of Christ Jesus (cf. Phil 3:8), which is defined as "*theoria*" or contemplation.24 The faithful, with the grace of Baptism, are called to progress in the knowledge and witness of the mysteries of the faith by "the intimate sense of spiritual realities which they experience."25 No light from God can render the truths of the faith redundant. Any subsequent graces of illumination which God may grant rather help to make clearer the depth of the mysteries confessed and celebrated by the Church, as we wait for the day when the Christian can contemplate God as he is in glory (cf. 1 Jn 3:2).

22. Finally, the Christian who prays can, if God so wishes, come to a particular experience of "union." The Sacraments, especially Baptism and the Eucharist,26 are the objective beginning of the union of the Christian with God. Upon this foundation, the person who prays can be called, by a special grace of the Spirit, to that specific type of union with God which in Christian terms is called "mystical."

*23. Without doubt, a Christian needs certain periods of retreat into solitude to be recollected and, in God's presence, rediscover his path. Nevertheless, given his character as a creature, and as a creature who knows that only in grace is he secure, his method of getting closer to God is not based on any "technique" in the strict sense of the word. That would contradict the spirit of childhood called for by the Gospel. Genuine Christian mysticism has nothing to do with technique: it is always a gift of God, and the one who benefits from it knows himself to be unworthy.27

24. There are certain "mystical graces," conferred on the founders of ecclesial institutes to benefit their foundation, and on other saints, too, which characterize their personal experience of prayer and which cannot, as such, be the object of imitation and

aspiration for other members of the faithful, even those who belong to the same institutes and those who seek an ever more perfect way of prayer.28 There can be different levels and different ways of sharing in a founder's experience of prayer, without everything having to be exactly the same. Besides, the prayer experience that is given a privileged position in all genuinely ecclesial institutes, ancient and modern, is always in the last analysis something personal. And it is to the individual person that God gives his graces for prayer.

25. With regard to mysticism, one has to distinguish between "the gifts of the Holy Spirit and the charisms" granted by God in a totally gratuitous way. The former are something which every Christian can quicken in himself by his zeal for the life of faith, hope and charity; and thus, by means of a serious ascetical struggle, he can reach a certain experience of God and of the contents of the faith. As for charisms, St. Paul says that these are, above all, for the benefit of the Church, of the other members of the Mystical Body of Christ (cf. 1 Cor 12:17). With this in mind, it should be remembered that charisms are not the same things as extraordinary ("mystical") gifts (cf. Rom 12:3-21), and that the distinction between the "gifts of the Holy Spirit" and "charisms" can be flexible. It is certain that a charism which bears fruit for the Church, cannot, in the context of the New Testament, be exercised without a certain degree of personal perfection, and that, on the other hand, every "living" Christian has a specific task (and in this sense a "charism") "for the building up of the body of Christ" (cf. Eph 4:15-16),29 in communion with the hierarchy whose job it is "not indeed to extinguish the Spirit, but to test all things and hold fast to what is good" (LG, n. 12).

VI. **Psychological-Corporal Methods**

26. Human experience shows that the "position and demeanor of the body" also have their influence on the recollection and

dispositions of the spirit. This is a fact to which some eastern and western Christian spiritual writers have directed their attention.

Their reflections, while presenting points in common with eastern non-Christian methods of meditation, avoid the exaggerations and partiality of the latter, which, however, are often recommended to people today who are not sufficiently prepared.

The spiritual authors have adopted those elements which make recollection in prayer easier, at the same time recognizing their relative value: they are useful if reformulated in accordance with the aim of Christian prayer.30 For example, the Christian fast signifies, above all, an exercise of penitence and sacrifice; but, already for the Fathers, it also had the aim of rendering man more open to the encounter with God and making a Christian more capable of self-dominion and at the same time more attentive to those in need.

In prayer it is the whole man who must enter into relation with God, and so his body should also take up the position most suited to recollection.31 Such a position can in a symbolic way express the prayer itself, depending on cultures and personal sensibilities. In some aspects, Christians are today becoming more conscious of how one's bodily posture can aid prayer.

27. Eastern Christian meditation32 has valued "psychophysical symbolism," often absent in western forms of prayer. It can range from a specific bodily posture to the basic life functions, such as breathing or the beating of the heart. The exercise of the "Jesus Prayer," for example, which adapts itself to the natural rhythm of breathing can, at least for a certain time, be of real help to many people.33 On the other hand, the eastern masters themselves have also noted that not everyone is equally suited to making use of this symbolism, since not everybody is able to pass from the material sign to the spiritual reality that is being sought.

Understood in an inadequate and incorrect way, the symbolism can even become an idol and thus an obstacle to the raising up of the spirit to God. To live out in one's prayer the full awareness of one's body as a symbol is even more difficult: it can degenerate into a cult of the body and can lead surreptitiously to considering all bodily sensations as spiritual experiences.

28. Some physical exercises automatically produce a feeling of quiet and relaxation, pleasing sensations, perhaps even phenomena of light and of warmth, which resemble spiritual well-being. To take such feelings for the authentic consolations of the Holy Spirit would be a totally erroneous way of conceiving the spiritual life. Giving them a symbolic significance typical of the mystical experience, when the moral condition of the person concerned does not correspond to such an experience, would represent a kind of mental schizophrenia which could also lead to psychic disturbance and, at times, to moral deviations.

That does not mean that genuine practices of meditation which come from the Christian East and from the great non-Christian religions, which prove attractive to the man of today who is divided and disoriented, cannot constitute a suitable means of helping the person who prays to come before God with an interior peace, even in the midst of external pressures.

It should, however, be remembered that habitual union with God, namely that attitude of interior vigilance and appeal to the divine assistance which in the New Testament is called "continuous prayer,"34 is not necessarily interrupted when one devotes oneself also, according to the will of God, to work and to the care of one's neighbor. "So, whether you eat or drink, or whatever you do, do all to the glory of God," the Apostle tells us (1 Cor 10:31). In fact, genuine prayer, as the great spiritual masters teach, stirs up in the person who prays an ardent charity which moves him to collaborate in the mission of the Church and to serve his brothers for the greater glory of God.35

VII. **"I Am The Way"**

288

29. From the rich variety of Christian prayer as proposed by the Church, each member of the faithful should seek and find his own way, his own form of prayer. But all of these personal ways, in the end, flow into the way to the Father, which is how Jesus Christ has described himself. In the search for his own way, each person will, therefore, let himself be led not so much by his personal tastes as by the Holy Spirit, who guides him, through Christ, to the Father.

30. For the person who makes a serious effort there will, however, be moments in which he seems to be wandering in a desert and, in spite of all his efforts, he "feels" nothing of God. He should know that these trials are not spared anyone who takes prayer seriously. However, he should not immediately see this experience, common to all Christians who pray, as the "dark night" in the mystical sense. In any case in these moments, his prayer, which he will resolutely strive to keep to, could give him the impression of a certain "artificiality," although really it is something totally different: in fact it is at that very moment an expression of his fidelity to God, in whose presence he wishes to remain even when he receives no subjective consolation in return.

In these apparently negative moments, it becomes clear what the person who is praying really seeks: is he indeed looking for God who, in his infinite freedom. always surpasses him; or is he only seeking himself, without managing to go beyond his own "experiences," whether they be positive "experiences" of union with God or negative "experiences" of mystical "emptiness ."

31. The love of God, the sole object of Christian contemplation, is a reality which cannot be "mastered" by any method or technique. On the contrary, we must always have our sights fixed on Jesus Christ, in whom God's love went to the cross for us and there assumed even the condition of estrangement from the Father (cf. Mk 13:34). We therefore should allow God to decide the way he wishes to have us participate in his love. But we can never, in any way, seek to place ourselves on the same level as

the object of our contemplation. the free love of God; not even when, through the mercy of God the Father and the Holy Spirit sent into our hearts, we receive in Christ the gracious gift of a sensible reflection of that divine love and we feel drawn by the truth and beauty and goodness of the Lord.

The more a creature is permitted to draw near to God, the greater his reverence before the thrice-holy God. One then understands those words of St. Augustine: "You can call me friend; I recognize myself a servant."36 Or the words which are even more familiar to us, spoken by her who was rewarded with the highest degree of intimacy with God: "He has looked upon his servant in her lowliness" (Lk 1:48).

The Supreme Pontiff, John Paul II, in an audience granted to the undersigned Cardinal Prefect, gave his approval to this letter, drawn up in a plenary session of this Congregation, and ordered its publication.

At Rome, from the offices of the Congregation for the Doctrine of the Faith, October 15, 1989, the Feast of Saint Teresa of Jesus.

Joseph Card. Ratzinger Prefect

Alberto Bovone Titular Archbishop of Caesarea in Numidia

Secretary

Endnotes

1. The expression "eastern methods" is used to refer to methods which are inspired by Hinduism and Buddhism, such as "Zen," "Transcendental Meditation" or "Yoga." Thus it indicates methods of meditation of the non-Christian Far East which today are not infrequently adopted by some Christians also in their meditation. The orientation of the principles and methods contained in this present document is intended to serve as a reference point not just for this problem, but also, in a more

general way. for the different forms of prayer practiced nowadays in ecclesial organizations, particularly in associations, movements and groups.

2. Regarding the Book of Psalms in the prayer of the Church, cf. "*Institutio generalis de Liturgia Horarum*," nn. 100-109.

3. Cf. for example, Ex 15, Deut 32, 1 Sam 2, 2 Sam 22 and some prophetic texts, 1 Chron 16.

4. Dogmatic Constitution "*Dei Verbum*," n. 2. This document offers other substantial indications for a theological and spiritual understanding of Christian prayer; see also, for example, nn. 3, 5, 8, 21.

5. Dogmatic Constitution "*Dei Verbum*," n. 25.

6. Regarding the prayer of Jesus, see "*Institutio generalis de Liturgia Horarum*," nn. 3-4.

7. Cf. "*Institutio generalis de Liturgia Horarum*," n. 9.

8. Pseudognosticism considered matter as something impure and degraded which enveloped the soul in an ignorance from which prayer had to free it, thereby raising it to true superior knowledge and so to a pure state. Of course not everyone was capable of this, only those who were truly spiritual; for simple believers, faith and observance of the commandments of Christ were sufficient.

9. The Messalians were already denounced by Saint Ephraim Syrus ("*Hymni contra Haereses*" 22, 4, ed. E. Beck, CSCO 169, 1957, p. 79) and later, among others, by Epiphanius of Salamina ("*Panarion*," also called "A*dversus Haereses*": PG 41, 156-1200; PG 42, 9-832), and Amphilochius, Bishop of Iconium ("Contra haereticos": G. Ficker, "Amphilochiana" I, Leipzig 1906, 21-77).

10. Cf., for example, St. John of the Cross. "*Subida del Monte Carmelo*," II, chap. 7. 11.

11. In the Middle Ages there existed extreme trends on the fringe of the Church. These were described not without irony, by one of the great Christian contemplatives, the Flemish Jan van Ruysbroek. He distinguished three types of deviations in the mystical life (*"Die gheestelike Brulocht"* 228. 12-230, 17: 230. 18-32. 22: 232. 23-236. 6) and made a general critique of these forms (236, 7-237, 29). Similar techniques were subsequently identified and dismissed by St. Teresa of Avila who perceptively observed that "the very care taken not to think about anything will arouse the mind to think a great deal," and that the separation of the mystery of Christ from Christian meditation is always a form of "betrayal" (see: St. Teresa of Jesus. Vida 12, 5 and 22, 1-5).

12. Pope John Paul II has pointed out to the whole Church the example and the doctrine of St. Teresa of Avila who in her life had to reject the temptation of certain methods which proposed a leaving aside of the humanity of Christ in favor of a vague self-immersion in the abyss of the divinity. In a homily given on November 1, 1982, he said that the call of Teresa of Jesus advocating a prayer completely centered on Christ "is valid, even in our day, against some methods of prayer which are not inspired by the Gospel and which in practice tend to set Christ aside in preference for a mental void which makes no sense in Christianity. Any method of prayer is valid insofar as it is inspired by Christ and leads to Christ who is the Way, the Truth and the Life (cf. Jn 14:6)." See: *"Homilia Abulae habita in honorem Sanctae Teresiae:"* AAS 75 (1983), 256-257.

13. See, for example. "The Cloud of Unknowing," a spiritual work by an anonymous English writer of the fourteenth century.

14. In Buddhist religious texts, the concept of "Nirvana" is understood as a state of quiet consisting in the extinction of every tangible reality insofar as it is transient, and as such delusive and sorrowful.

15. Meister Eckhart speaks of an immersion "in the indeterminate abyss of the divinity" which is a "darkness in which

the light of the Trinity never shines." Cf. "Sermo 'Ave Gratia Plena'" in fine (J. Quint, "Deutsche Predigten und Traktate" Hanser 1955, 261).

16. Cf. Pastoral Constitution "*Gaudium et spes*" n. 19, 1: "The dignity of man rests above all on the fact that he is called to communion with God. The invitation to converse with God is addressed to man as soon as he comes into being. For if man exists it is because God has created him through love, and through love continues to hold him in existence. He cannot live fully according to truth unless he freely acknowledges that love and entrusts himself to his creator."

17. As St. Thomas writes of the Eucharist: ". . . *proprius effectus huius sacramenti est conversio) hominis in Christum ut dicat cum Apostolo: Vivo ego iam non ego; vivit vero in me Christus*" (Gal 2:20)" (In IV Sent: d. 12, q. 2, a. 1).

18. Declaration "*Nostra aetate*" n. 2.

19. St. Ignatius of Loyola, "*Ejercicios espirituales* n. 23 et passim.

20. Cf. Col 3:5: Rom 6:11ff.: Gal 5:24.

21. St. Augustine. "*Enarrationes in Psalmos*" XLI, 8: PL 36. 469.

22. St. Augustine, "Confessions" 3. 6. 11: PL 32, 688. Cf. "*De vera Religione*" 39. 72: PL 34, 154.

23. The positive Christian sense of the "emptying" of creatures stands out in an exemplary way in St. Francis of Assisi. Precisely because he renounced creatures for love of God, he saw all things as being filled with his presence and resplendent in their dignity as God's creatures, and the secret hymn of their being is intoned by him in his "*Cantico delle Creature.*" Cf. C. Esser, "*Opuscula Sancti Patris Francisci Assisiensis*" Ed. Ad Claras Aquas, Grottaferrata (Roma) 1978, pp. 83-86. In the same way he writes in the "*Lettera a Tutti i Fedeli:*" "Let every creature in heaven and on

earth and in the sea and in the depth of the abyss (Rev 5: 13) give praise, glory and honor and blessing to God, for he is our life and our strength. He who alone is good (Lk 18: 19), who alone is the most high, who alone is omnipotent and admirable, glorious and holy, worthy of praise and blessed for infinite ages of ages. Amen" ("ibid Opuscula" 124). St. Bonaventure shows how in every creature Francis perceived the call of God and poured out his soul in the great hymn of thanksgiving and praise (cf. "Legenda S Francisci" chap. 9, n. 1, in "Opera Omnia" ed. Quaracchi 1898, Vol. VIII p 530).

24. See, for example, St. Justin, "*Apologia*" I 61, 12-13: PG 6 420- 421: Clement of Alexandria, "*Paedagogus*" I, 6, 25-31: PG 8, 281- 284; St. Basil of Caesarea, "*Homiliae diversae*" 13. 1: PG 31, 424- 425; St. Gregory Nazianzen, "*Orationes*" 40, 3, 1: PG 36, 361.

25. Dogmatic Constitution "*Dei Verbum*" n. 8.

26. The Eucharist, which the Dogmatic Constitution "*Lumen Gentium*" defines as "the source and summit of the Christian life" (LG 11), makes us "really share in the body of the Lord": in it "we are taken up into communion with him" (LG 7).

27. Cf. St. Teresa of Jesus, "Castillo Interior" IV 1, 2.

28. No one who prays, unless he receives a special grace, covets an overall vision of the revelations of God, such as St. Gregory recognized in St. Benedict. or that mystical impulse with which St. Francis of Assisi would contemplate God in all his creatures, or an equally global vision, such as that given to St. Ignatius at the River Cardoner and of which he said that for him it could have taken the place of Sacred Scripture. The "dark night" described by St. John of the Cross is part of his personal charism of prayer. Not every member of his order needs to experience it in the same way so as to reach that perfection of prayer to which God has called him.

29. The Christian's call to "mystical" experiences can include both what St. Thomas classified as a living experience of God via the gifts of the Holy Spirit. and the inimitable forms (and for that reason forms to which one ought not to aspire) of the granting of grace. Cf. St. Thomas Aquinas, "*Summa Theologiae*" Ia, IIae, 1 c, as well as a. 5, ad 1.

30. See, for example, the early writers, who speak of the postures taken up by Christians while at prayer: Tertullian, "*De Oratione*" XIV PL 1 1170, XVII: PL I 1174-1176: Origen, "*De Oratione*" XXXI 2: PG 11, 550-553, and of the meaning of such gestures; Barnabas, "*Epistula*" XII, 2-4: PG 2, 760-761: St. Justin, "*Dialogus*" 90, 4-5: PG 6, 689-692; St. Hippolytus of Rome, "*Commentarium in Dan*" III, 24: GCS I 168, 8-17; Origen, "*Homiliae in Ex*" XI 4: PG 12, 377-378. For the position of the body see also, Origen, "*De Oratione*" XXXI, 3: PG 11, 553-555.

31. Cf. St. Ignatius of Loyola, "*Ejercicios Espirituales*" n. 76.

32. Such as, for example, that of the Hesychast anchorites. Hesychia or external and internal quiet is regarded by the anchorites as a condition of prayer. In its oriental form it is characterized by solitude and techniques of recollection.

33. The practice of the "Jesus Prayer," which consists of repeating the formula, rich in biblical references, of invocation and supplication (e.g., "Lord Jesus Christ, Son of God, have mercy on me"), is adapted to the natural rhythm of breathing. In this regard, see St. Ignatius of Loyola, "*Ejercicios Espirituales*" n. 258.

34. Cf. 1 Thes 5: 17, also 2 Thes 3: 8-12. From these and other texts there arises the question of how to reconcile the duty to pray continually with that of working. See, among others, St. Augustine, "*Epistula*" 130, 20: PL 33, 501-502 and St. John Cassian, "*De Institutis Coenobiorum*" III, 1-3: SC 109, 92-93. Also, the "Demonstration of Prayer" by Aphraat, the first father of the Syriac Church, and in particular nn. 14-15, which deal with the so-called "works of Prayer" (cf. the edition of J. Parisot, "*Afraatis Sapientis Persae Demonstrationes*" IV PS 1, pp. 170-174).

35. Cf. St. Teresa of Jesus, "Castillo Interior" VII, 4, 6.

36. St. Augustine, *"Enarrationes in Psalmos"* CXLII 6: PL 37, 1849. Also see: St. Augustine, "Tract in Ioh." IV 9: PL 35, 1410: *"Quando autem nec ad hoc dignum se dicit, vere plenus Spiritu Sancto erat, qui sic servus Dominum agnovit, et ex servo amicus fieri meruit.*

Made in United States
Orlando, FL
17 November 2024

54000762R10163